The Granger Collection

The Companion Book to *Granger's Fiddle Tunes for Guitar*

By Bill Nicholson

Granger's Fiddle Tunes for Guitar, by Adam Granger,
distributed by Mel Bay Publications, Inc.,
contains the same 508 tunes
presented in guitar tablature.

First Edition, 2022

See List of Recordings after the Index.

Exclusive Distributor: Mel Bay Publications, Inc.
WWW.MELBAY.COM

☸ACKNOWLEDGEMENTS☸

Dedicated to Doc Watson, Norman Blake, Mike Seeger, Dan Crary, Clarence White, David Grisman and Tony Rice.

☸ ☸ ☸

☸ ☸ ☸

Unending gratitude to Adam Granger. His musical life is exemplified by the *Granger's Fiddle Tunes for Guitar* collection. We have worked on many shows, recordings, and publication projects throughout my life, and I am pleased and proud to be his friend and collaborator.

☸ ☸ ☸

My beautiful bride Peggy is the center for my life. Our life together started with a love for this music, and her tolerance has allowed me to chase vocational and avocational unicorns. She deserves credit for this work.

☸ ☸ ☸

The cover was designed, and advice and technical assistance offered, by Rick Korab, korabdesign.com.

☸ ☸ ☸

☸ CONTENTS OF FRONT SECTION ☸

[The tune index and audio track list are at the back of this book.]

❁ INTRODUCTION ❁

***The Granger Collection* is the result of years of collection and transcription of fiddle tunes, driven by an abiding passion for fiddle music coupled with a longstanding love of the music. *Granger's Fiddle Tunes for Guitar* was first published in 1979. This edition of transcribed musical notation uses the third edition of this publication, released in 2021.**

The Book You Are Holding - A Note from Bill Nicholson

The Granger Collection was a direct response to requests that the collection of tunes in *GFTFG* be made available in standard music notation. I was happy to oblige because I have long felt this collection is a wonderful and lively representation of traditional tunes and is worthwhile to all musicians, regardless of their chosen instrument (guitar, fiddle, mandolin, banjo, tinwhistle, saxophone, and so forth).

As a multi-instrumental hobbyist myself, I have used *GFTFG* since the first printing and done transcriptions of the tunes to notation, mandolin tablature, and banjo tablature to have a printed guide to a tune in a different format. I have followed Adam's tablature faithfully, and have rarely used other printed sources for guidance on some transcriptions.

The tunes were gathered by Adam, and he deserves full credit for this book. My transcriptions are a doff of my hat to his efforts.

I was asked by Adam to add some thought to this collection. I was gobsmacked as his notes to the source book, *Granger's Fiddle Tunes for Guitar*, describe my feelings about this music, and this book's driving force. Anything I might add feels almost superfluous.

If you have picked up this volume you may well have been exposed to the collection that was the source. My effort to transcribe Adam's entire book began with a discussion when work on the Third Edition of *GFTFG* was planned. Adam mentioned he had received requests from musicians who wanted the tunes in standard music notation, rather than (or in addition to) the guitar tablature.

I have many other fiddle tune books and use them regularly, but *GFTFG* is always on the top of the pile. The straight-forward presentation of this collection draws me to it not when playing not only guitar, but also mandolin, banjo, and other instruments. Musical notation seems an obvious next step for this collection. I want all musicians to have these tunes available.

While spending my days preparing these tunes, I often recalled old friends who had been drawn together by these melodies. I remembered where I learned the tune, the people from whom I learned the tune, and the jam sessions that brought the tune to life. Revisiting these tunes feels like finding my old dog, sitting up and making me laugh.

I hope you get years of enjoyment and enlightenment from this book. This collection of tunes has been a significant part of my musical life for many decades (See *The History of GFTFG*, p. viii.)

❁ The Granger Collection is written by a musician for all musicians. Enjoy it! ❁

The next 10 pages are packed with info which should answer any questions, starting with instructions for the musical notation style, then moving into identification of the elements of my fiddle tune presentation format, and ending with Adam's story of *Granger's Fiddle Tunes for Guitar.* (See Contents listings for what is where).

❁ ABOUT THESE TUNES ❁

One of the greatest assets of *The Granger Collection* is that it presents straight-ahead fiddle melodies with minimal ornamentation. For the most part, the tunes from *GFTFG* were so faithfully transcribed to guitar tablature that they are here returned to standard musical notation and are played, as a rule, just as they are on the fiddle, or other instrument. That said, the fiddle-guitar-fiddle journey has produced some interesting and unusual phrases.

No attempt is given to suggest fingerings: the sources of these tunes were mostly from fiddle music (but not exclusively), and melodies you're picking are tailored to the fiddle. My effort here is to present the music so anyone with the ability to read musical notation will be able to use this resource to create their own experience on their instument. Your experience with your instrument will determine the method of playing the tune.

❁ A note to fiddle and mandolin players: these tunes were transcribed from guitar tab. The guitar can range almost an octave lower than the violin or mandolin, so some alterations will be required to accomodate this. For most of the affected tunes, this means a slight re-working of the pickup notes, perhaps descending to the downbeat note instead of ascending to it. Special thanks to Mary DuShane and Tom Schaefer for reminding me of this fact. My playing of the transcriptions was done on the guitar; once I got out my mandolin it was obvious.

❁ Many Old-Time and Southern fiddle tunes employ long-bow techniques, rather than the multiple note approach that was the source of these transcriptions. Non-plectrum instruments can use their own experience to work on their method to play these tunes.

❁ Some of these tunes, like *Big John MacNeill's*, will need to be moved up one octave. I have left that as an exercise for the player.

❁ To see a list of the fiddlers from whose bows these tunes sprang, see **Sources**, p. vii.

❁ To make the musical notation more uniform, I have added directions to tunes that do not end with the last part. For example, the "A" part of *Ace of Spades (*the first tune in the book) is repeated to complete the tune. I have used the musical direction *Fine* and *D.C. al Fine* at the end of the first and third staves of the tune. This instructs the player to "go to the head of the piece, and play to the *Fine* (end) marker." This replaces the intructions in *GFTFG* directing players that "Tune Ends After First Part."

❁ And finally, for those who like to learn by ear, or who just want to hear what these tunes sound like, Mp3 recordings recorded by Adam for *GFTFG* are listed. These recordings only include the original key settings of the tunes; the additional key transpositions are not available in the recordings. The recordings are played through once: the rhythm track in the left channel, and the melody played in the right channel.

HOW TO USE *THE GRANGER COLLECTION*

Here is part one of a tune from this book, *Cricket on the Hearth*, with all of its parts identified, followed by detailed descriptions of these parts:

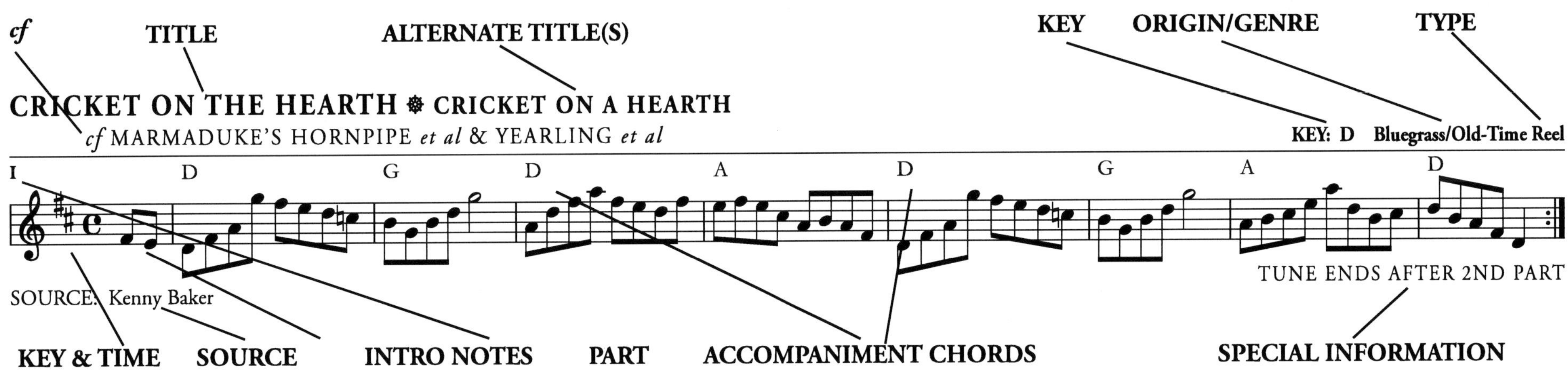

Title

Each tune is listed under the title by which Adam Granger learned it, with alternate titles, if any, following. The listed title is in a larger font size, but all titles should be considered equals, and all titles are listed in the index.

cf

Some tunes have a *cf* below the title(s). This is *confer*, a fancy word meaning, essentially, "see also." It directs you to other closely-related tunes in *TGC*.

Note that alternate titles attributed to a certain tune and *cf* cross-references suggesting relationships among certain tunes are open to debate. Deciding whether two tunes were identifiably separate or the same tune with different titles was a judgment call; the next person might well make different decisions. (Information about tune type and origin, on the following page, is offered with a similar disclaimer.)

Key

Following the title is the tune's key listing. Simple listings, such as "G," indicate a fiddle tune in the key of G. Omitted from this volume are the capoed Key and Chords from *GFTFG.* All tunes are presented in their common key, and tunes that are frequently played in multiple keys (depending on the player and region) are transcribed in those keys, as well. These additional settings are listing immediately following the original key setting.

Some tunes change keys (modulate). The key listing "G/D," for example, indicates a tune which modulates from one key to another (from G to D, in this instance). Modulations are usually to the five chord (the V), and generally call for the tune to resolve to its original key before ending. This usually requires that the tune end after its first part (see **Parts**, p. vii).

The key listing "C or D" indicates a tune which is known to be played either in C or in D. In cases where a tune is played in different keys which require different settings, as with *Hull's Victory* (pp. 61 & 62), which is played in both the keys of D and F, both settings are given.

Where a tune's key is an identifying part of its distinction from another tune of the same title, it is listed in the heading with the title (as with *Lark in the Morning—D* and *Lark in the Morning—Em*, pp. 74 & 75). The distinct tune in the alternate key is transcribed (and remains adjacent to the primary tune).

Where the same melody is played in different keys and under different titles, the keys are listed with their respective titles (as with *The Sailor's Hornpipe*—G or A, also played as *The College Hornpipe* in B♭, pp. 114 & 115).

Tune Origin/Genre

As with titles, there are a lot of opinions about lineages of fiddle tunes. Adam's opinions are offered in this book and they aren't very strongly held ones. They are based on the contexts in which he learned the tunes, and you wouldn't have to look far to find disagreement. The purpose of this little section is to provide, in one or two words, a gentle indicator of one place that a tune has been—the genre in which Adam learned it.

Here are the terms used to define tune types in *The Granger Collection*

Old-Time:

The largest and most wide-ranging term. Includes Appalachian and old-time tunes as well as old popular tunes, such as *The Year of Jubalo*, *Pop Goes the Weasel* and *I Don't Love Nobody*, and published 19th-century tunes such as those found in *Ryan's Mammoth Collection* and *Cole's One Thousand Fiddle Tunes.* Accompaniment varies, depending on the genre.

Southern:

Almost as variegated as old-time, southern tunes are often shuffle-based, and include square dance and hoedown repertoires as well as Missouri, Oklahoma, Arkansas and, especially, Appalachian tunes. Application of long-bowing techniques to smooth the tunes would be worth considering. Guitar accompaniment is alternate-bass with runs thrown in, Riley Puckett style.

Irish:

Also known as Celtic tunes. Irish music is a sun with many planets. One of those is the Galway/Kerry style, which is well-represented in this collection by the tunes of Kathleen Collins, Joe "Banjo" Burke and Johnny Cronin (see **Sources**, p. vii). This style is rather straight-ahead, with minimal ornamentation, and it lends itself beautifully to guitar adaptation, whereas, say, Sligo fiddling is more ornate, requiring the transcriber constantly to make decisions as to which ornamentation to leave in and which to take out. Not all tunes of Irish origin in *TGC* are listed as Irish; many have found their ways into other genres. Accompaniment is all over the map, in the good sense of that phrase. Rhythm guitar players like the great Daithe Sproule like to push the limits, with fantastic results.

Northern:

Another far-reaching group. Northern tunes tend more toward the melodic and less toward the shuffle, and include the New England, French-Canadian, Canadian, Metis, and Cape Breton genres. Most traditional contra-dance repertoire is Northern. Accompaniment is often punchy, and can have themed bass lines and jazzy passing chords. Piano is a common accompaniment instrument.

Bluegrass:

Includes tunes Adam learned in a bluegrass context, as well as tunes originally introduced as bluegrass tunes. Guitar accompaniment is alternate-bass with runs thrown in.

Texas:

Characterized by a slower-than-reel tempo and a smooth jazzy feel. This genre includes tunes originating in Texas, Oklahoma, Arkansas and Missouri that are played in a Texas style. Texas tunes are common repertoire in United States fiddle contests. Guitar accompaniment is often closed chord with themed bass lines and passing chords.

Scandinavian:

Comprised of Swedish and Finnish schottisches, polkas and walking tunes. Accompaniment varies, depending on tune type.

Tune Type

The Granger Collection lists the following types of fiddle tunes:

• **Reels, Breakdowns, Hoedowns, Polkas** and **Rags** are played up-tempo, ranging from "parlor tempo" (60 bpm), through jam tempo (70-110 bpm), past square dance/hoedown tempo (120 bpm) into bluegrass/hot picker territory (130 bpm and up). They have eight notes or rests per measure, and are counted "ONE-two-three-four TWO-two-three-four."

Depending on geographical, national and stylistic elements, these tunes are played with a variety of feels (an Irish polka, for example is smoother than a Scandinavian polka), but they are all in common time.

• **Hornpipes**, when played traditionally (as when accompanying a hornpipe dance), are slower than reels (60-100 bpm) and with a pronounced lope to their beat, but are in common time and are counted and picked the same as reels *et al.* Note that, in most genres in which they can be found, hornpipes are indistinguishable from reels in feel and tempo. If, for example, a tune is identified as being a bluegrass hornpipe, as in the case of *Durang's Hornpipe* or *Fisher's Hornpipe*, it has shed its hornpipe skin and has been reborn lopeless and faster.

• **Jigs** and **Slides** are 6/8 tunes, played up-tempo (88-152 bpm). They have six notes or rests per measure, comprised of two eighth-note triplets, and are counted "ONE-two-three TWO-two-three." Single jigs are based on quarter notes—*Pop Goes the Weasel*, (p. 101)—and double jigs are based on eighth notes—*Irish Washerwoman*, (p 64).

• **Slip-Jigs** are 9/8 tunes played up-tempo (88-152 bpm). They have nine notes per measure, comprised of three eighth-note triplets, and are counted "ONE-two-three-TWO-two-three-THREE-two-three."

A Note On Time Signatures: The tunes (not mentioned above) are marked as Common Time, which is a general way of saying 4/4 time. This is my choice. I could have used other time signatures, such as 2/4; by not presenting the tunes in that signature we were able to eliminate 16th notes. I feel this makes the scores appear less cluttered and easier to read. The exception to common time are unusual tunes, Like *Texas* (p. 130) which begins in 4/4 time, but has a measure with two spare beats, and changes to 6/4 time.

Intro Notes

It is common for fiddle tunes to have intro notes, almost always two eighth notes or the equivalent. Where this happens (as in approximately half of the tunes in this book), all parts of the tune have the same number of intro notes, and the last measures of each part have an equal number of notes missing from them. (You may have to read that sentence twice.) This keeps the tune "square," so that it doesn't end up containing extra beats. For example, *Cricket on the Hearth* (p 26) has a two-eighth-note intro for each of its parts, and two notes are missing from the last measure of each of its parts, so the parts knit together without dropping or adding beats. And, *The Hawk* (p. 57) has an eighth note and an eighth rest (or, a quarter note, depending on whether you let the note ring or not) as an intro for its first part, and two eighth notes for its second part. And again, the last measures of each part have only six notes in them instead of eight, to accommodate the intro notes.

Ending Notes

Some tunes, such as *Big John MacNeill's* (p. 9) and *Morning Dew* (p. 87), have a single note to the right of the last part's staff. This is an ending note, and is used to resolve the tune to its tonic (main) chord. *Morning Dew*, for example, is in Em, but its second part ends on a D chord. This is not a problem while repeating the tune, as it leads right back into the first part. When ending the tune, however, it is generally agreed that it's preferable to end on the tonic (except for cajun and zydeco music, but that's another book). Thus the presence of an ending note. Note that the accompaniment chord above the ending note also resolves to the root, or main, chord.

Accompaniment Chords

Accompaniment chords are given above the tablature staffs.

A measure of a standard reel would be accompanied, on guitar, by two "boom-chucks" (bass-note/chord pairs).

Perhaps nowhere in the world of fiddle tunes is there more room for disagreement than in a tune's chord progression. The overwhelming majority of fiddle tunes were composed long before chords were ever put to them. Different players—often within different genres—can give the same tune a wide range of treatments, chord-wise. There are, for example, many ways to play chords behind *Sally Goodin* (p. 115), ranging from an old-timey style of playing nothing but the root chord all the way through, to an elaborate jazz-chord themed-bass-line backup. Texas and Northern tunes in particular will often be accompanied by creative, punchy, jazzy, dynamic chording, and Irish musicians, especially, possess a proclivity toward innovative chordal accompaniment. Accompaniment of Southern tunes tends to be straight-ahead alternated bass, with bass runs often thrown in.

Parts

Parts of tunes are indicated above the staffs on the left side. In tunespeak, letters are usually used to define parts, *i.e.*, A Part and B Part, although they are often simply called the first part and the second part. I use Roman numerals in this book (*i.e.*, I and II), in order to avoid confusion with the accompaniment chords near them above the staff. Yet another way of describing parts—this one in old-time parlance—is Low Part and High Part, because the second part of a fiddle tune is usually, wait for it, higher.

Most fiddle tunes are "square:" two parts of eight-measures each, with each part being repeated (AABB, or I I II II, or Low Low High High), but tunes with as few as one and as many as five parts will be found in this book, and some parts will have no repeat instruction.

The standard notation left (beginning) or right (end) repeat instruction is used, and double vertical barlines demark parts.

Tunes that are crooked—those with extra beats within measures, or with odd numbers of measures—are so indicated, as with *Yellow Gal* (p. 143) and *Texas* (p. 130).

Special Information

Special information about parts is provided below the last staff on the right side of the tune.

This will usually be an instruction to end the tune after some part other than the last (usually the first: "END AFTER I"). Where this is the case, it is the prerogative of the picker to play that part once or twice, although it is more common to play the part only once.

Upon occasion, an instruction will appear to play the parts in some order other than sequential. Example: "PART ORDER: 1232" in *Fiddler's Hoedown* (p. 40).

Sometimes a part is played in one of a tune's incarnations, but not another. This will be noted. Example: "PART III IN BLUEGRASS VERSION ONLY" in *Fisher's Hornpipe* (pp. 42-43).

Source

This is the fiddler from whose playing I learned the tune. This might be directly from a recording, or from information supplied by another player from whom I learned the tune. The person cited might or might not be the author, and the version presented in *TGC* might be note-for-note from the source, or partially from the source, or only inspired by the source. Regardless, the source shown provides a great starting place for those wishing to research the tune (see **Introduction**).

For a list of fiddlers from whose playing many tunes in this book appear, and for other source references, see **Sources**, p. vii.

❁ ABOUT SOURCES ❁

Below are some of the musicians whose repertoires provided many of the tunes in *GFTFG & TGC* and whose names you will find affixed to tunes they provided. Variously, Adam Granger recorded contributions directly from the source, or bought recordings, or the player from whom he got a tune was able to cite a source (taking him one step further up the provenance ladder, as it were). In some cases, the cited source is the composer of the tune, but in most cases the tune was simply in their repertoire. Adam tried, always, to transcribe the source versions note-for-note.

Zeke Backus
Kenny Baker
Dick Barrett
Lucien Beauchemin
Louis Beaudoin
Byron Berline
Norman Blake
Boys of the Lough
Conrad Brierre
Enoch Cameron
John Campbell
Ken Campbell
Scot Campbell
Gus Cannon
Jean Carignon
David Carr
The Chieftains
Curly Ray Cline
Earl Collins
Donald Commo
Dan Crary
Rudy Darling
The Dillards
Bob Douglas
Wilson Douglas
Camile DuBois
Mary DuShane
Lyman Enloe
Winston Scotty Fitzgerald
Howdy Forrester
J P Fraley
Raymond Frechette
Joe Gagne
King Ganam
Frank George
Paul Gosselin
Bill Guest
Ben Guillemette
Lee Guthrie
The High Level Ranters
Reg Hill
Donna Hinds
Bill Hinkley
E J Hopkins
Willie Hopper
Santiago Jiminez
Herman Johnson
James Kelly
Peter Kennedy
Clark Kessinger
Rich Klatt
Joe LaBrosse
Ned Landry
Clarence Langen
Libby Larsen
Leroy Larsen
Frank Livingston
Joe MacLean
George Maille
Levi Masse
Sean McGuire
Pete McMahon
Roma McMillan
Don Messer
Kerry Mills
Henry Moore
Melody Morin
Dudley Murphy
Sonja Nordstrom
Dick Nunneley
Paddy O'Brien
Tim O'Brien
Joe Pancerzewski
Ray Park
Conrad Pelletier
Red Rector
The Red Clay Ramblers
Henry Reed
Dick Rees
Bill Reser
Joseph Robichaud
Eck Robertson
Joe Robertson
Don Roy
Buck Ryan
Llewellyn Sexsmith
Arthur Smith
Bill Spence
Daithe Sproule
Cyril Stinnett
George Stinson
Lowe Stokes
Gid Tanner
Tater Tate
Benny Thomason
Eleanor Townsend
Graham Townsend
Doc Watson
Delores White
Vern Williams
Bob Wills

A few players deserve special thanks for recording albums which proved particularly fruitful in Adam's search for tunes:

Kathleen Collins released *Traditional Music of Ireland* on Shanachie Records in 1976, and Johnny Cronin and Joe "Banjo" Burke, recorded an album, *Cronin and Burke*, on Shanachie Records in 1977. These musicians all three played in the relatively unornamented Galway/Kerry style. Dudley Laufman recorded an album of contra dance tunes, *Swinging on a Gate*, on Front Hall Records in 1974, and eastern Kentucky fiddler Buddy Thomas made field recordings in the early 70s.

The common thread among these musicians' recordings is that the recordings were relatively unornamented "declarative sentence" statements of tunes which translated beautifully to flatpick guitar. Adam couldn't resist being piggish in his plundering of the above-cited recordings, and the results—some thirty tunes—are peppered liberally throughout *GFTFG* and *TGC*.

And, in Adam's continuing gluttony, K-Tel International released an album in 1972 called *25 Old Tyme Fiddle Favorites*, from which he mined nine more tunes. At the time, K-Tel was a Canadian company and, coincidentally or not, most of the tunes on the album are Canadian. There were no musician credits listed, but he had always heard that Graham Townsend was one of the fiddlers. Research credits, as musicians, "The Fiddle Beaus," but there is no information anywhere about them. Other sources cite "various performers." We would love to know more!

Other Sources

There were precious few published fiddle tune collections in the mid-70s. Four of these were particularly helpful in compiling tunes for *Granger's Fiddle Tunes for Guitar*: *One Thousand Fiddle Tunes*, published by M M Cole (cited as "Cole's," which is what we and our musician friends call it); Miles Krassen's *O'Neill's Music of Ireland*, published by Oak Publications; *The Old-Time Fiddler's Repertoire*, by R P Christeson, published by the University of Missouri Press; and *The Fiddle Book*, by Adam's old friend Marion Thede, published by Oak Publications.

There is now unlimited access to fiddle music collections, so one has to be reminded of the importance and relative rarity of earlier collections such as these. Present day, two online databases were tremendously helpful in finding not tunes, but new alternate titles for the third edition: *The Traditional Tune Archive* and, for Irish music, *The Session*.

❁The History of *Granger's Fiddle Tunes for Guitar*❁

By Adam Granger

In the Beginning. . .

In 1974, I moved from my native state of Oklahoma to Minnesota. I had been playing guitar and banjo in Arkansas and Nashville, and had been on the road a lot, and was tired of travel, hot weather, flat terrain and anti-hippie sentiment. Since I had roots in Minnesota (my mother being from St Paul) and had always loved visiting there, the state was a logical relocation choice.

Shortly after my arrival, Garrison Keillor, who had started *A Prairie Home Companion* at about that time, decided that he wanted a regular house band, instead of the band being made up of whichever musicians happened to be on the show that week. Look up serendipity in the dictionary and you will find the story of how I came to his attention.

Joining the Band

I was working at the Guthrie Theater in Minneapolis in 1975. An in-house performance of mine there was recorded. My first wife, Sherry, was managing a deli where musician Jerry Rau would customarily come for a free cup of coffee and some conversation. One morning, Sherry was playing the tape of the Guthrie performance. Jerry, who was during that time doing the booking for the legendary Coffeehouse Extempore, in Minneapolis, heard the recording and started booking me at the Extemp as a solo act one Sunday each month. Local musicians heard me, and when Garrison started asking around as to who might work well on guitar and vocals, my name came up.

What followed was four years of weekly work and touring with the *Companion* as part of The Powdermilk Biscuit Band. It was a string band, and were responsible, in the role of house band, for instrumental "bumper" and background music as well as the requisite vocals. The instrumental music generally took the form of fiddle tunes, and I found myself learning new tunes at the rate of two or three a week, thanks to my bandmates.

These three players became very important to my musical life. In 1975, when I joined the band, I fancied myself as a pretty hot flatpicker. After all, hadn't I competed in the flatpick contest at the second Winfield Festival and tied for sixth? (For those who don't know, "tieing for sixth" means you lost: there were only five winners.) I knew the entire flatpick repertoire—*i.e.*, the same twenty fiddle tunes that every flatpicker knows—the tunes we had learned from Doc Watson, Norman Blake and Dan Crary recordings—and figured that was about it. How many more fiddle tunes could there be?

I Find Out

Enter the bandmates: Bob Douglas, Mary DuShane and Dick Rees. Serious tunesmiths all, who, along with *Home Companion* regular, multi-instrumentalist Bill Hinkley, turned me on to worlds I didn't know existed: Irish tunes, Cape Breton tunes, Canadian tunes, French-Canadian tunes, northern tunes, southern tunes, jigs, slip-jigs, hornpipes, schottisches and on and on. To learn these tunes, I would tab them out during the first of the two weekly rehearsals, learn them before the second rehearsal, and then play them on the show.

When, around 1978, the number of tunes in my notebook reached 250, I started entertaining thoughts of assembling them into a publishable book. I sensed a need for a large collection of flatpick tunes, along the lines of the *Cole's* and *O'Neill's* collections, but written in tablature instead of standard music notation.

I further realized that, because of the wide variety of fiddle tunes the Biscuit Band played, I had acquired a very interesting collection. I had proven, in front of thousands of people, that the tunes worked well on the guitar and yet, far from being the same-old same-old, there were tunes of all types from all over the place, especially reels, jigs and hornpipes from America, Canada and Ireland. I came to realize that flatpickers fished in a very small pond—that there should be more to flatpicking than *Red-Haired Boy* and *Whiskey before Breakfast.*

I had initially planned to collect a thousand tunes, but it soon became clear that five hundred was a more realistic number. I was already halfway to that goal, and began to collect and mine recordings and the above-mentioned books for more tunes. I would take a cassette recorder to fiddling friends' houses, or to wherever else there were fiddlers, and hit them up for tunes, and bought and borrowed whatever fiddle albums I could find.

Thus was I introduced to the wide world of fiddle music, where my world up to that point had been bluegrass, flatpicking, swing jazz, five-string banjo and contemporary country music.

A Book Is Born

The first edition of *Granger's Fiddle Tunes for Guitar* was published in 1980. It was rustic—a glorified quick-print publication. The printer, thinking the page numbers were intended only for his use in laying out the book, eliminated them, so each copy of the book had to be hand-numbered. Adam threw a series of "numbering parties:" events which separated my good friends from my so-so friends. Half a dozen or so volunteers would meet at the Homestead Pickin' Parlor, in Richfield, Minnesota, and I'd bring a few cartons of books, a few six-packs and pizza (Bill Nicholson was part of this cohort).

In that first edition, I presented the tunes in 4/4 time and used asterisks instead of dots to denote rests. And, the Granger scrawl was in full flower. It was funky in its appearance, but it was accurate and it was the first of its kind.

I began to get requests for the recordings of the tunes, so I recorded about two hundred of the tunes on three sixty-minute cassettes. These were as primitive as the book: they were recorded and dubbed on funky equipment, but they were functional and they sold well.

The Second Edition

By the time the first print run of a thousand copies of *GFTFG* was exhausted, in the early 90s, I had a partner. Paul Christianson, a retired pharmacist, was my guitar student. He came aboard initially as a backer of the second edition of *GFTFG* and stuck around to eventually become an equal partner. Since then, he has done the accounting, the shipping and receiving, the billing, the phone-answering, and has accompanied me to a number of festivals and trade shows. Like Bill Nicholson, he has become a good friend.

With Paul aboard, the second edition was soon ready to go. It was several steps up from the first edition: the tablature, while still handwritten, was more neatly laid-out, tunes were converted to 2/4 time, rests were changed from asterisks to dots, and the title blocks were typeset, thanks to Bill Nicholson. I added additional informational and instructional appendices and had a better printing job done on better paper. The second edition also had a better cover and, in response to requests, a water-resistant one: apparently, *GFTFG* was used by more than one picker as a beverage coaster.

One mistake we made with the second edition was that Paul and I believed the printer when he told us that his perfect binding (squared off spine, with pages glued in) would allow the book to lay open and that pages would not come loose. Neither was true, and, toward the end of that press run's life, I took to recommending to buyers that they take the book to their local quick-print place and have it spiral-bound. I didn't raise the price for decades, so it was easy to suggest that the buyer could use the five bucks they saved on the book price for this purpose. (*Granger's Fiddle Tunes for Guitar* started out at $30 in 1980, and stayed at that price until 2005.)

Naming Easytab

Although I had used my tab style since 1972, it wasn't until the second edition of *GFTFG* that I thought of naming it, whereupon I came up with the moniker "Easytab" and the goofy-but-true slogan (since abandoned), "Like regular tab—but easier!"

Granger Publications didn't do a copyright search on the name Easytab, and we assumed that we would run across it in a nonmusical context or two. This happened sooner than we expected, however. On the same day as we received the first printing of 3000 copies of the second edition of *GFTFG*, I walked into my pantry, picked up a box of prezels, opened it, and saw on the tab-into-slot box flap "Easytab." So far, we haven't heard from the pretzel company's attorneys, although we did hear from a guitar teacher in California who had used the name Easytab for his form of notation for almost as long as I had for mine. In a cordial phone call, we agreed to peacefully coexist.

Recording Madness

Drawing upon the success of the first tapes, I decided to record all 508 tunes in the book for the second edition of the tapes, and to do so on better equipment. Studio time for a project such as this would have broken me, so I did the best I could using consumer-level technology available at that time. I recorded the tunes onto a Tascam 424 cassette recorder through a Shure condenser microphone, playing my 1989 Santa Cruz Tony Rice model guitar.

I then mastered those onto DATs (digital audio tapes), which were then sent to the duplicator to create a five-cassette set of recordings. Starting about 1994, I began to get requests for the recordings in CD form. It was, of course, a great idea, but the then-$12,000 price tag to get the collection onto CD was prohibitive for as modest a company as ours, and we had to answer such requests with a wistful "some day."

To CD. . .and beyond!

"Some day" arrived in on December 31 1998, when my good friend, computer and audio expert and guitar and mandolin picker Bill Nicholson, came to a party bearing with him the gift of an out-of-print album of mine duplicated onto a CD. He had just gotten a good CD burner and was anxious to put it and the assorted software associated both with it and with digital audio production through their paces.

As mentioned, this was hardly Bill's first contact with *GFTFG*: He was at the numbering parties mentioned earlier, he can play most of the tunes in the book, he typeset the second edition titles, he helped me design the companion cassettes and he designed a lot of the early advertising. It was even his DAT that I borrowed to master the recordings. *But other than that. . .*

Despite all of his past experience with *GFTFG*, Bill may not have realized the enormousness of digitally mastering 508 separate WAV files, but he did the job, and, as always, he did it well. He finished the job the night before being placed in the Minnesota Home for the Musically Befuddled (his wife called the authorities when she couldn't get him to stop humming *Sheep and Hogs Walking through the Pasture* in his sleep). Ever the loyal friend, I visit him. Not as often as I should, but I do visit him.

We had the recordings burned onto CDs and duplicated, and the seven-CD set that resulted was very popular over the course of its lifespan. In 2021, however, it went the way of the cassette tapes that preceded it, and Granger Publications began to offer the recordings on a thumb drive.

The Third Edition (the source for the book you are holding)

There are a number of changes in the third edition of *Granger's Fiddle Tunes for Guitar*, the most dramatic and visible being an increase in the number of alternate titles from 1000 to 2500, thanks to the advent of online databases, and the typesetting of the tablature. I tried never to be an apologist for the handwritten tab in *GFTFG*: it was legible, it was functional and at any rate it was the only game in town at the time that I wrote the earlier editions of *GFTFG*. That said, I was delighted when the option to typeset my tablature came along.

Dan Miller, in the mid-90s, was just starting *Flatpicking Guitar Magazine* and had asked me to be a columnist. Happy to accommodate my Easytab, he came up with the basic idea for "typesetting" it, and Bill Nicholson and I refined it, creating an Easytab program. I used it—and further refined it—in my *Flatpicking Guitar Magazine* column for 20 years, and it's how this book was created.

In a nutshell: using a monospace (non-justified) type font, I fill a tab staff with invisible zeros—sixty-four across and six down. Then, using the arrow keys, I place the cursor where a note is desired, delete the invisible zero, and type in the number.

The process is painstaking; every note and symbol is hand-placed. And, a comparison of the tunes on any given page will reveal that each tune is different with regard to spacing, to suit the needs of the tune and the design of the page. For example, if a tune has a string of numbers along its top line—the high E string—the accompaniment chords are placed a bit higher above the staff than I otherwise would have placed them.

The accompanying texts—including the section you're reading right now—have also been expanded and improved, reflecting what I've learned since the 70s, and have been moved to the front of the book, instead of being appendicized at the back.

And, finally, I have re-inserted my source citations for the tunes, which I had excised from the second edition. I had been worried that readers would think of those names as being the composers of the tunes, which is generally not the case, but I decided that they are too important not to be included.

The End

That's the story of *Granger's Fiddle Tunes for Guitar*. It may be much more than you need or want to know, but there are those among us (such as musicologist Patrick Sky, who exhaustively researched the Ryan's collection) who are curious about odysseys and oddities such as this history. Maybe one day some budding young PhD candidate will come across this collection and its story.

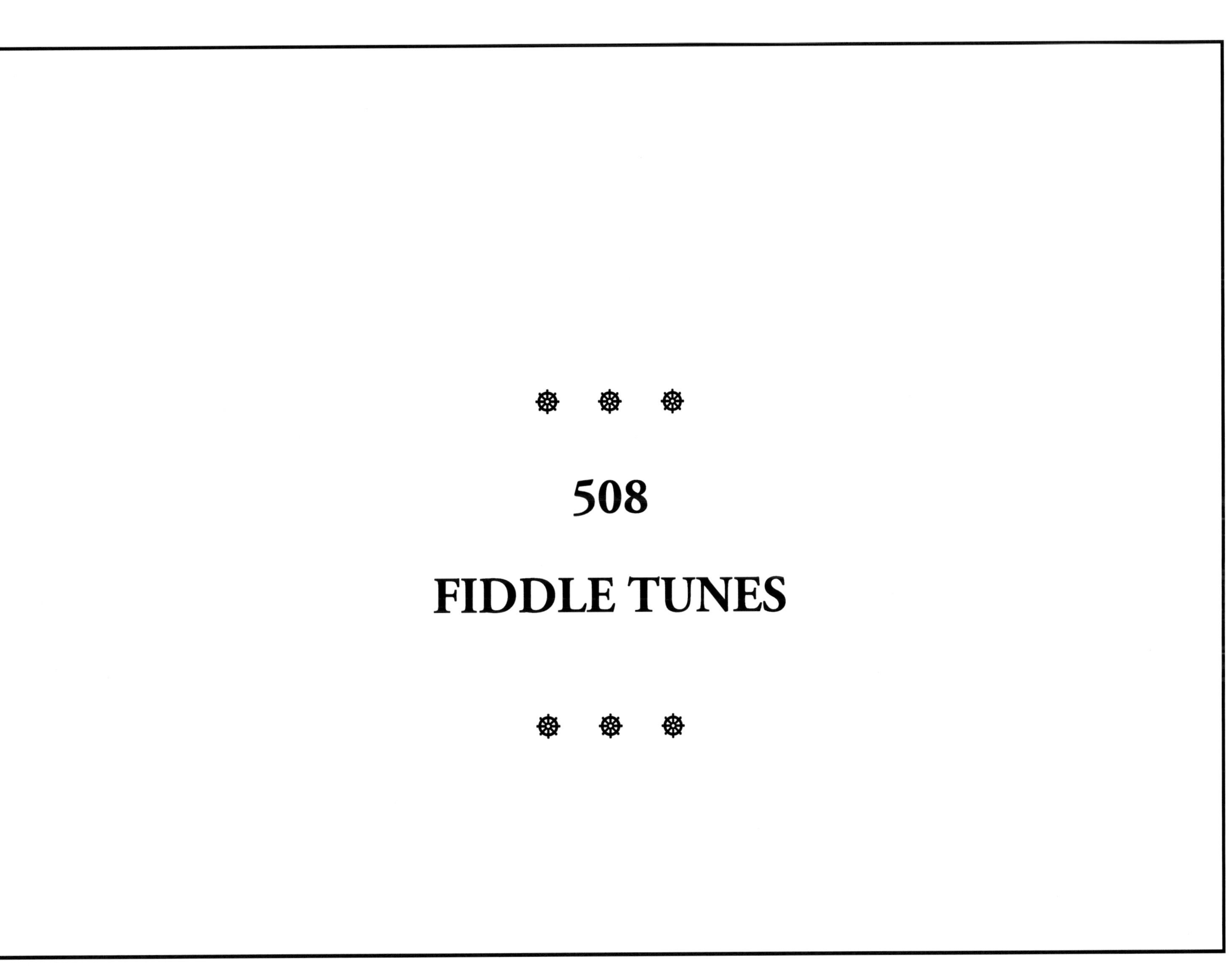

508

FIDDLE TUNES

ACE OF SPADES ❁ BILLY WILSON
KEY: A Texas
I
A D A E A E A D A E A
Fine
II
A D E A E A D E A
III
D.C. al Fine
E B E B E B E
SOURCE: Benny Thomason

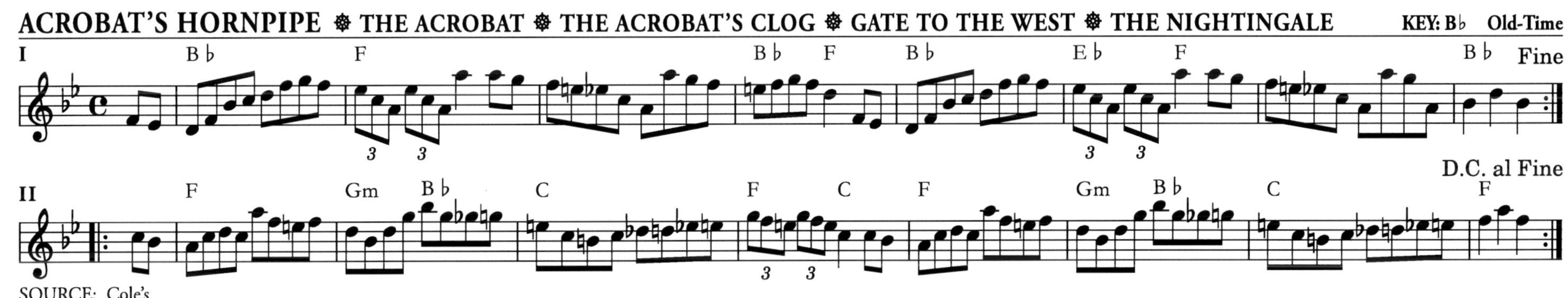
ACROBAT'S HORNPIPE ❁ THE ACROBAT ❁ THE ACROBAT'S CLOG ❁ GATE TO THE WEST ❁ THE NIGHTINGALE
KEY: B♭ Old-Time
I
B♭ F B♭ F B♭ E♭ F B♭
Fine
3 3 3 3
II
D.C. al Fine
F Gm B♭ C F C F Gm B♭ C F
3 3
SOURCE: Cole's

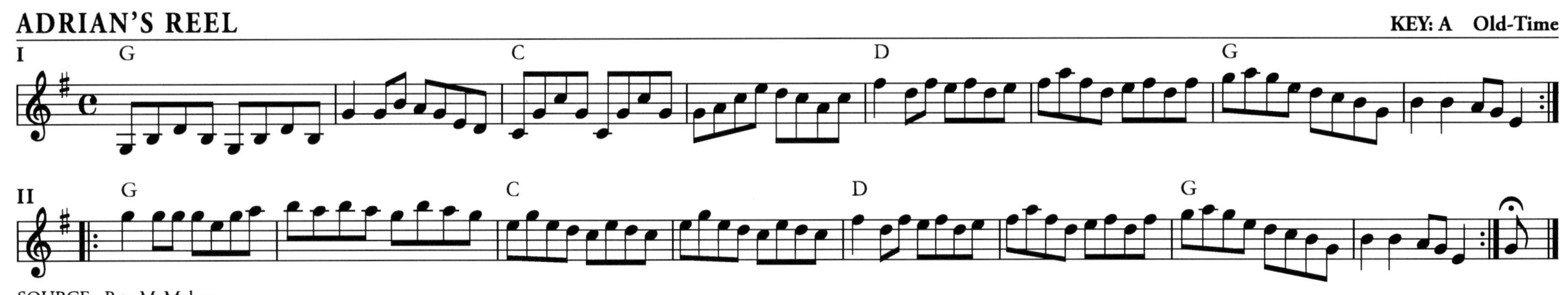
ADRIAN'S REEL
KEY: A Old-Time
I
G C D G
II
G C D G
SOURCE: Pete McMahon

ALFIE'S HORNPIPE ❁ ALFY'S HORNPIPE ❁ ALLEN'S REEL ❁ ALLAN'S REEL

KEY: A Northern

SOURCE: Joe Pancerzewski

AMATEUR HORNPIPE

KEY: A Old-Time

ANDERSON'S REEL ❁ DON'T BE FOOLISH ❁ FLOWERS OF REDHILL ❁ FLOWERS OF RED HILL ❁ THE FLOWERS OF THE RED MILL ❁ THE HOD CARRIER ❁ JILLY NEARY'S FAVOURITE ❁ MAIDS OF FAIR HILL ❁ MAIDS OF PALESTINE ❁ MIKE ANDERSON'S ❁ THE WILD IRISHMAN

KEY: F Irish

ANDERSON'S REEL ❁ DON'T BE FOOLISH ❁ FLOWERS OF REDHILL ❁ FLOWERS OF RED HILL ❁ THE FLOWERS OF THE RED MILL ❁ THE HOD CARRIER ❁ JILLY NEARY'S FAVOURITE ❁ MAIDS OF FAIR HILL ❁ MAIDS OF PALESTINE ❁ MIKE ANDERSON'S ❁ THE WILD IRISHMAN

KEY: G   Irish

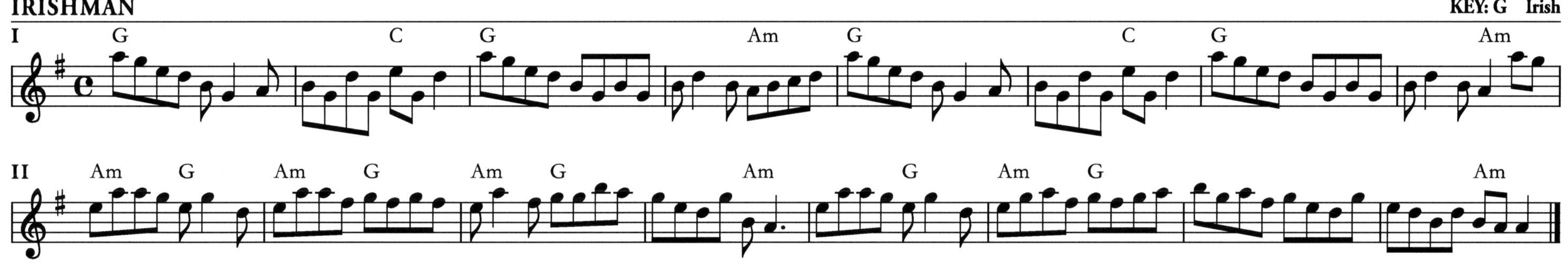

ANGELINE THE BAKER ❁ ANGELINE ❁ ROCKY ROAD ❁ COON DOG ❁ GEORGIA ROW ❁ WALK UP GEORGIA

KEY: D   Southern

ANNE-MARIE REEL ❁ ANNE MARIE'S REEL

KEY: A   Northern

SOURCE: Ned Landry/25 Fiddle Favorites

ARIEL HORNPIPE ❁ BALL AND PIN ❁ M^c^CUSKER'S DELIGHT

cf BALL AND CHAIN HORNPIPE

KEY: A **Old-Time**

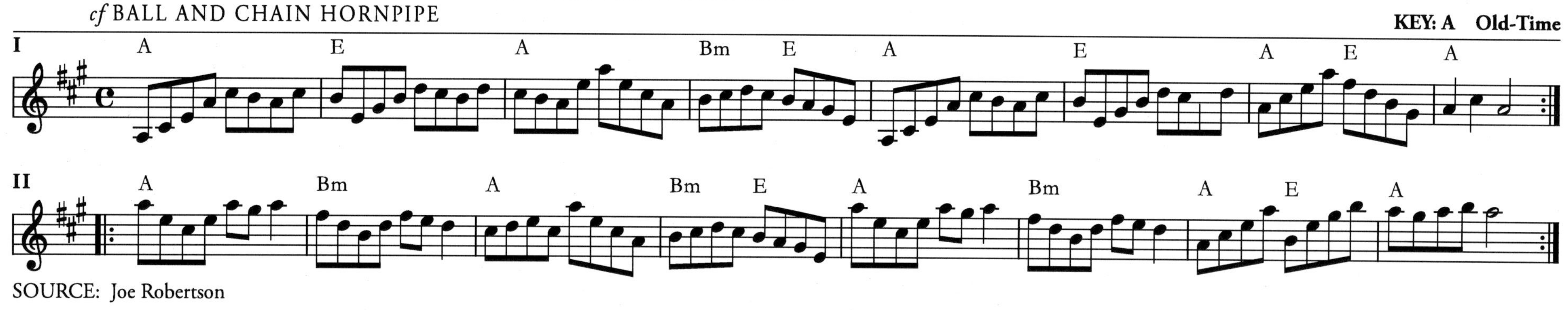

SOURCE: Joe Robertson

ARKANSAS TRAVELER ❁ REEL ARKANSAS ❁ REEL DES VOYAGEURS

KEY: D **Southern**

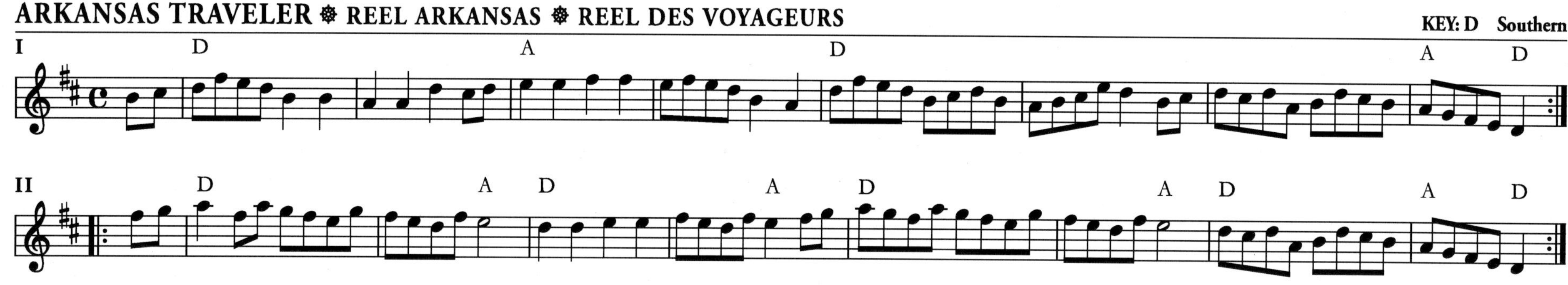

AS I WENT OUT UPON THE ICE ❁ THE GIN COTTAGE POLKA ❁ JOHNNY O'LEARY'S ❁ AS I WENT ON THE ICE ❁ AS I WENT OUT ON THE ICE ❁ AS I WENT UPON THE ICE ❁ DAVE PIGGOTT'S ❁ O'LEARY'S FAVOURITE ❁ OUT ON THE ICE

KEY: Am **Irish Polka**

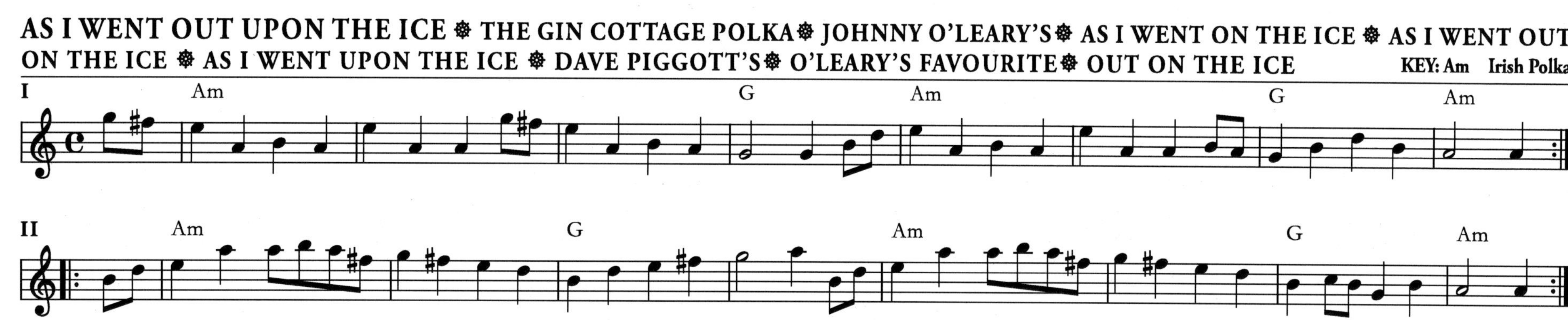

BACHELOR JIG ❁ BACHELOR'S JIG

KEY: A Northern

SOURCE: Joe McLean

BALL AND CHAIN HORNPIPE ❁ BALL AND PIN HORNPIPE ❁ BALL AND PIN

cf ARIEL HORNPIPE *et al*

KEY: A Bluegrass/Old-Time

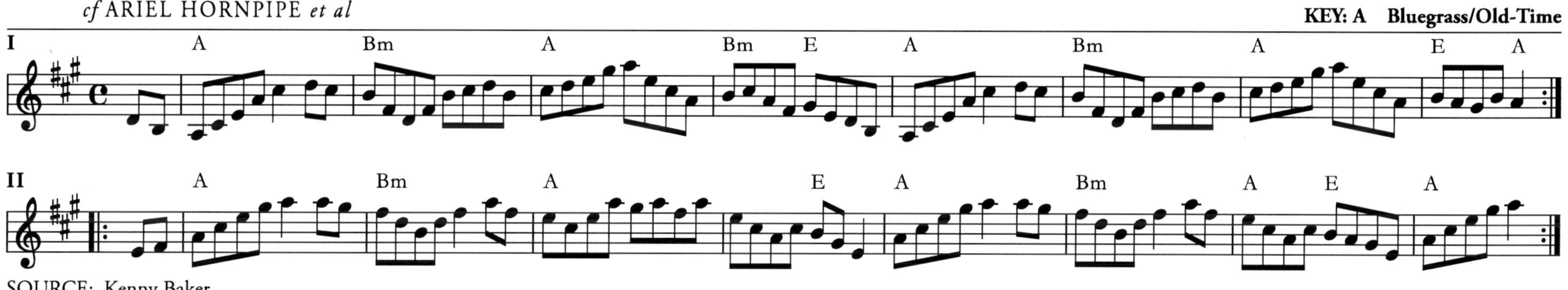

SOURCE: Kenny Baker

BALLY DESMOND

KEY: Am Irish Polka

SOURCE: Johnny Cronin and Joe Burke

BANISH MISFORTUNE ❁ THE BAG OF MEAL ❁ HUMORS OF MULLINAFAUNA ❁ NANCY HINES ❁ 'ROUND THE CART HOUSE ❁GEORGE WHELAN'S JIG ❁ LITTLE BAG OF MEAL ❁ NANCY HYNES ❁PARISH GIRL ❁THE SHADY GROVES ❁ SHADY GROVES OF PIEDMONT ❁ COME TO THE BRIDAL ❁BANISHED MISFORTUNE ❁ THE HORSE UNDER THE STAIRS ❁ MAMMY'S HORSE IS DYING ❁ THE MANGLED BADGER ❁ STOAT THAT ATE ME SANDALS ❁ THE WHORE AMONGST THE NETTLES ROARING

KEY: D Irish Jig

THE BANJO OLD TIME POLKA ❁ GARY'S POLKA

KEY: G Old-Time

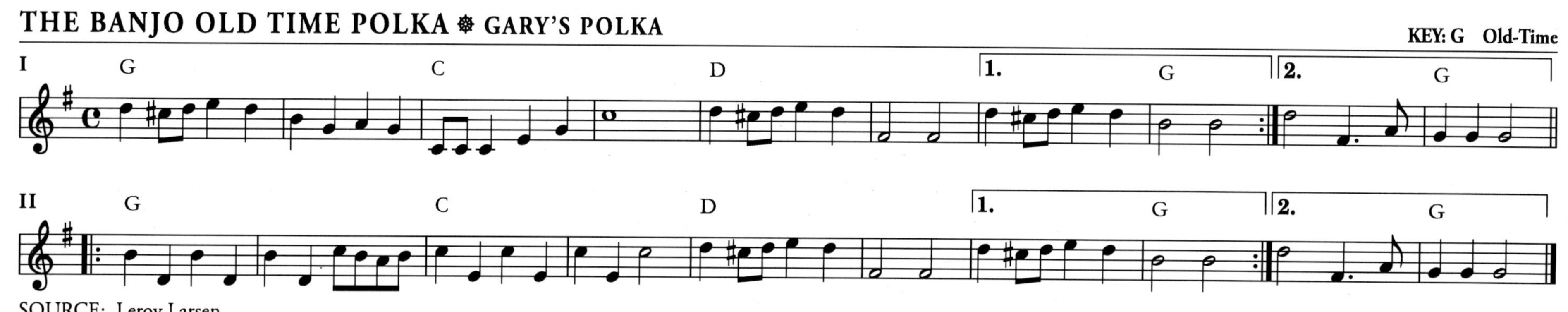

SOURCE: Leroy Larsen

BANJO TRAMP

KEY: D Old-Time

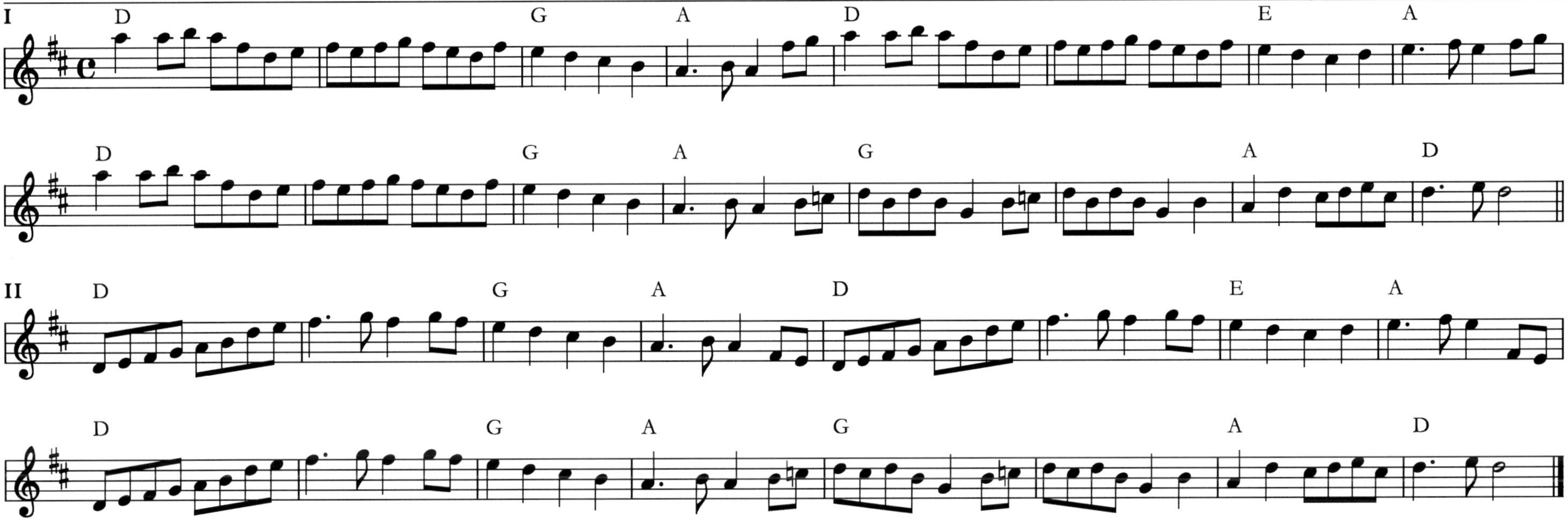

I
D G A D E A
D G A G A D
II
D G A D E A
D G A G A D

BANTRY BAY ☸ THE GARDEN WHERE THE PRATIES GROW ☸ THE LITTLE STACK OF WHEAT ☸ THE LITTLE STACKS OF WHEAT ☸ THE STACK O' WHEAT ☸ THE STACK OF WHEAT ☸ THE UNION ☸ JAMES McKENNEY'S HORNPIPE

KEY: G Irish Hornpipe

I
G Am E Am C Em Am D G C D G
II
G Em G D G C G C D G

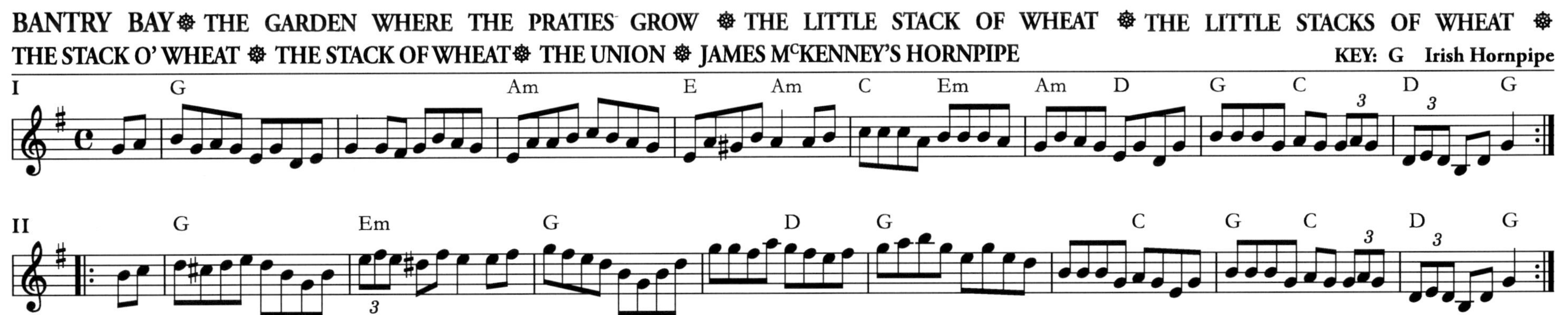

BARLOW KNIFE ❁ CABIN CREEK ❁ BLUE GOOSE

KEY: G Southern

THIRD PART IS UNCOMMON

THE BARMAID ❁ CLONMELL LASSIES ❁ GREEN MOUNTAIN ❁ JUDY'S REEL ❁ KISS THE MAID BEHIND THE BARN ❁ KISS THE MAID BEHIND THE BARREL ❁ THE MAID BEHIND THE BAR ❁ INDY'S FAVORITE ❁ HAYMAKER REEL ❁ LITTLE JUDY ❁ THE HAYMAKER ❁ LITTLE JUDY'S ❁ NEW YORK

KEY: D Irish

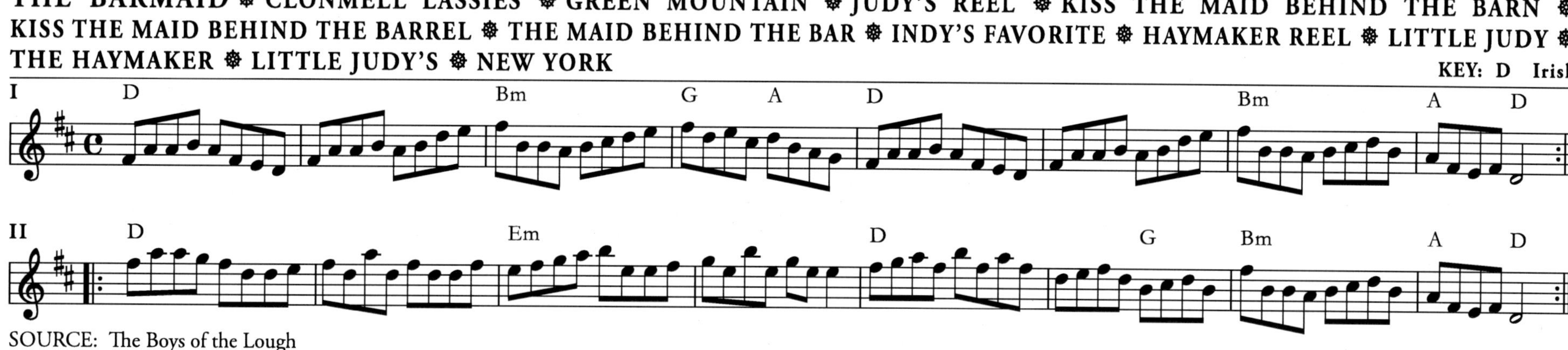

SOURCE: The Boys of the Lough

LA BASTRINGUE ❁ LA BASTRAINE ❁ LA BASTRANGE

KEY: D Northern

THE BATTERING RAM ❁ THE QUEEN OF THE RUSHES

KEY: G Irish Jig

BAY OF FUNDY ❁ FUNDY BAY

KEY: D Northern

BEE'S WING ❁ BEESWING HORNPIPE

KEY: B♭ Irish Hornpipe

I

II

BEET PIE ❁ TUNESMITH'S CRAMP ❁ XENIA REEL

KEY: D Old-Time

BELFAST ❁ SWEEP'S ❁ THE SWEEP'S HORNPIPE ❁ LANCASHIRE CLOG ❁ MILLICENT'S HORNPIPE ❁ GREAT EASTERN HORNPIPE ❁ THE GREAT WESTERN HORNPIPE ❁ MILLICEN'S FAVOURITE ❁ MILLICENT'S FAVOURITE ❁ ROYAL BELFAST ❁ THE GREAT WESTERN CLOG ❁ GREAT WESTERN ❁ GREAT WESTERN LANCASHIRE CLOG ❁ SAILOR'S DELIGHT

KEY: D Irish Hornpipe

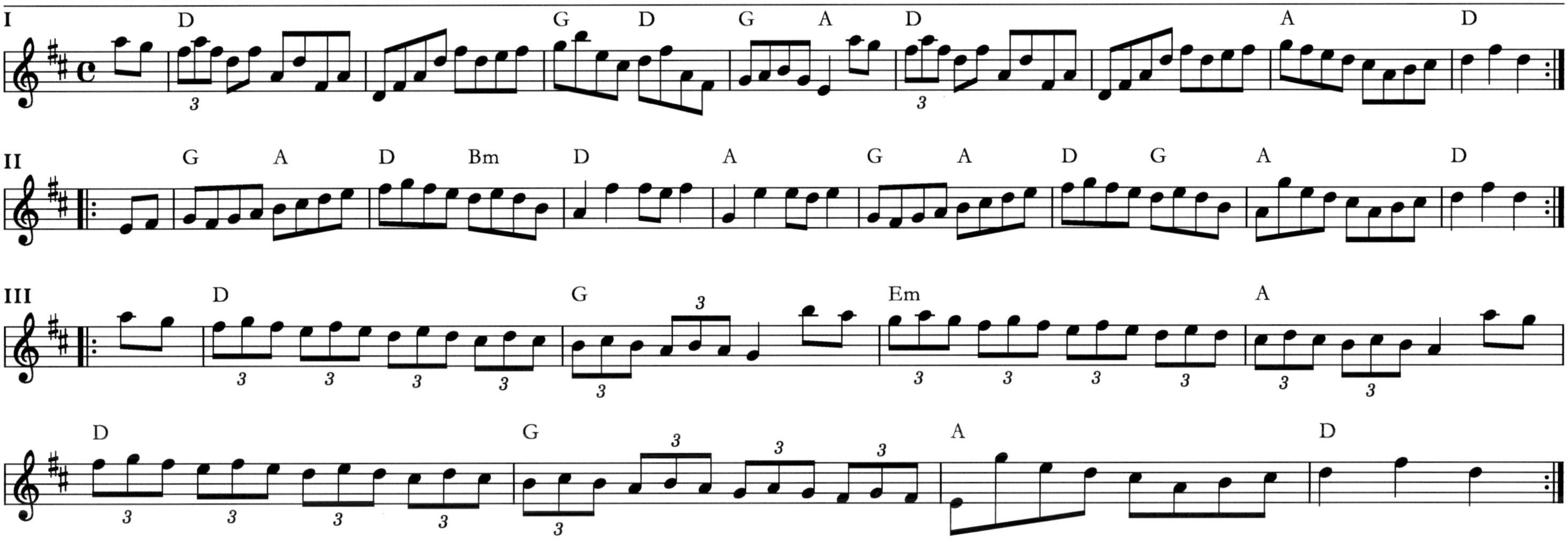

I
D G D G A D A D
II
G A D Bm D A G A D G A D
III
D G Em A
D G A D

BELFAST JIG ❁ BELFAST HAM

KEY: D Northern

I
D A D G D G D G D A D
II
D G Em A D A D G Em A D

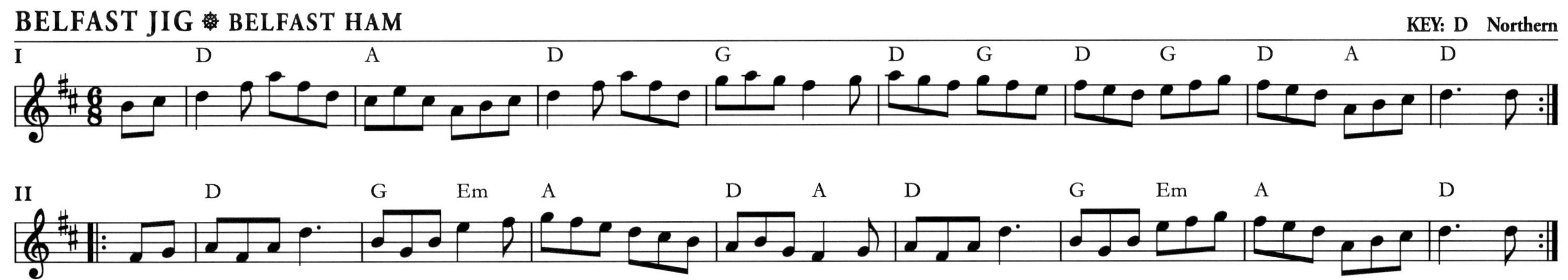

SOURCE: Bill Guest

BELLE OF LEXINGTON ❁ BELLES OF LEXINGTON ❁ BELL'S ELECTION ❁ BELLE'S ELECTION

cf HAULING HOME *et al*

KEY: D Old-Time

BESSIE BROWN

KEY: D Northern Jig

BIG INDIAN HORNPIPE

KEY: A Bluegrass

SOURCE: Buddy Thomas

BIG JOHN MACNEILL'S ❁ BIG JOHN McNEAL ❁ JOHN McNEIL'S REEL ❁ LORD RAMSAY'S REEL

KEY: A Northern

BILL CHEATHAM ❁ BILL CHEATUM ❁ CHEATUM ❁ BILL CHEATEM ❁ CHEAT 'EM

KEY: A Bluegrass/Old-Time

BILLY IN THE LOW GROUND ❁ BILLY IN THE LOW LAND ❁ THE KERRYMAN'S DAUGHTER ❁ BEAUS OF ALBANY ❁ BRAES OF AUCHTERTYRE ❁ FIDDLER'S DRUNK AND THE FUN'S ALL OVER ❁ JINNY IN THE LOWLANDS ❁ KERRY FULTON'S SCHOTTISHE ❁ RED CHURCH ❁ BILLIE IN THE LOWGROUND

KEY: C Bluegrass/Old-Time

Billy Wilson's Clog, Cincinnati Hornpipe, Fred Wilson's Clog ***and*** **Harvest Home** ***may be found under any of the titles below, as members of*** **"The Billy Wilson's Clog Family"**

Brown's ❁ The California Schottische ❁ Cincinnati ❁The Cincinnati Cliffs ❁The Cliff ❁ The Cliffe ❁ The Fisherman's Favorite ❁ Fisherman's Favourite ❁ Fred Wilson's ❁ Fred Wilson's Clog ❁ Higgens ❁ Higgens' ❁ The Ruby Lip ❁ The Ruby ❁ Wilson's Clog ❁ O'Higgins Hornpipe ❁ Brown's Hornpipe ❁ Cliff Hornpipe ❁ Cork Hornpipe ❁ The Dundee Hornpipe ❁ Granny Will Your Dog Bite ❁ Kildare Fancy ❁ Higgin's Hornpipe ❁ Lady of the Lake ❁ Snyder's Jig ❁ Standard Hornpipe ❁ Zig-Zag Hornpipe ❁ Zig-Zag Clog ❁ Reel des Recoites ❁ Wooden Shoe Clog

BILLY WILSON'S CLOG

cf CINCINNATI HORNPIPE, FRED WILSON'S CLOG & HARVEST HOME

KEY: D Northern

I

D G D A D E A D G D A D

II

A D G D A D

BITTER CREEK ❁ BITTER CREEK BREAKDOWN

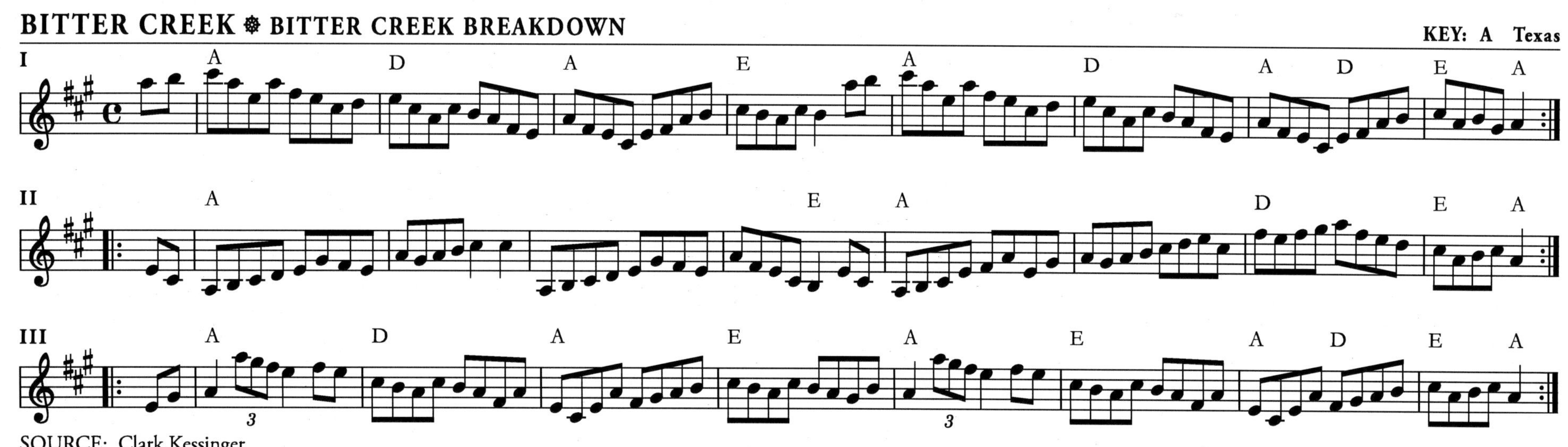

SOURCE: Clark Kessinger

BLACKBERRY BLOSSOM

KEY: G Bluegrass/Old-Time

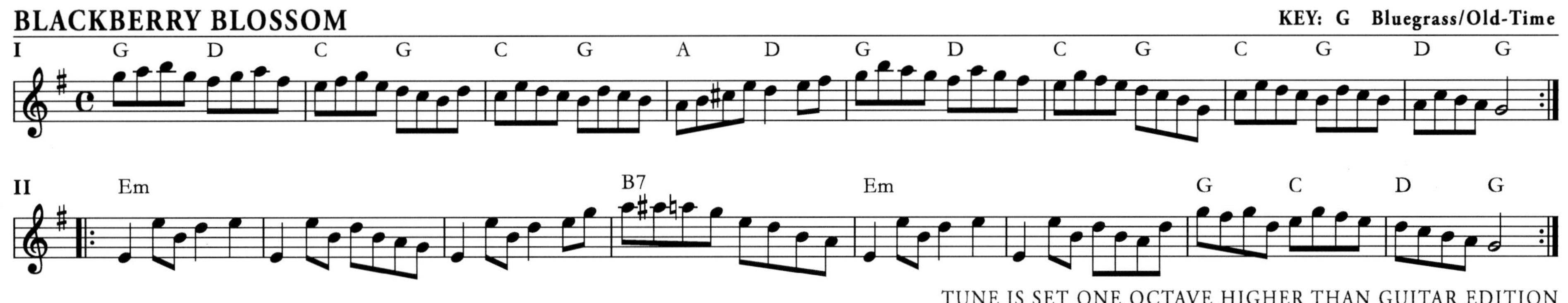

TUNE IS SET ONE OCTAVE HIGHER THAN GUITAR EDITION

BLACKBERRY BLOSSOM

KEY: A Bluegrass/Old-Time

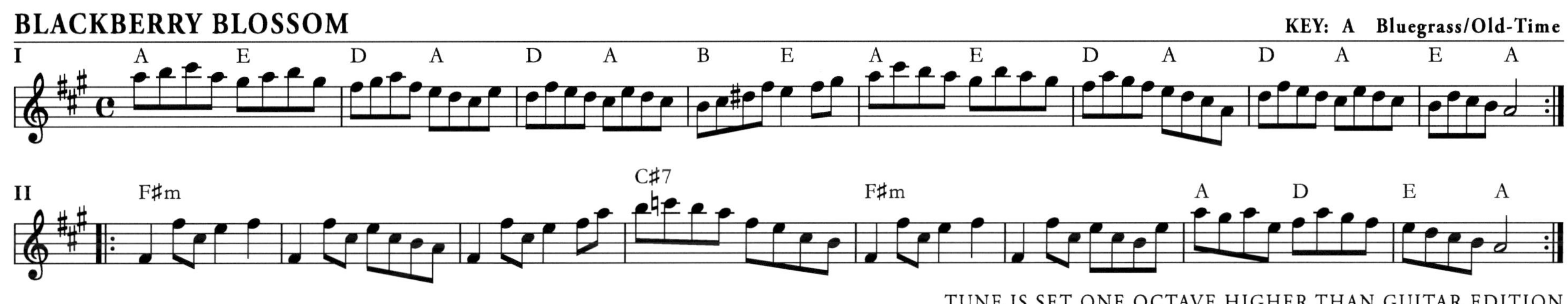

TUNE IS SET ONE OCTAVE HIGHER THAN GUITAR EDITION

BLACKBERRY RAG

KEY: C Bluegrass/Texas

BLACK CAT IN THE BRIAR PATCH ☸ BLACK CAT IN THE BRIARPATCH
KEY: G Old-Time/Southern
Fine
D.C. al Fine
BLACK MOUNTAIN RAG ☸ BLACK MOUNTAIN BLUES
KEY: A Bluegrass
gliss.
THE BLACK NAG ☸ THE BLACK NAGG ☸ THE GALLOPING NAG
KEY: Am Old-Time Jig
SOURCE: Bill Spence

THE BLACKTHORN STICK ❁ THE BOYS OF BOCK HILL ❁ CLEAR THE ROAD ❁ THE INCH OF GARTH ❁ THE IRISHMAN'S BLACKTHORN STICK ❁ THE JOLLY CLAMDIGGERS ❁ THE OLD BLACKTHORN ❁ THE RISING OF THE SUN ❁ THE RISING SUN ❁ COUNTESS OF LOUDON ❁ THE COUNTESS OF LOUDON'S REEL ❁ JACK McGUIRE ❁ THE JOLLY CLAREMAN ❁ RISING OF THE SUN ❁ THE OLD BLACK THORN ❁ RAFFERTY'S ❁ STRONE JOHNNY

KEY: D Irish

SOURCE: Johnny Cronin and Joe Burke

THE BLARNEY PILGRIM ❁ JACKSON'S RAMBLES ❁ THE PARISH GIRL ❁ KILLOUGHERY ❁ KILLOUGHERY JIG No 1

KEY: G Irish Jig

BLUE EAGLE HORNPIPE

KEY: D Texas

BLUE GOOSE

KEY: G Old-Time

SOURCE: Buddy Thomas

BLUE MOUNTAIN HORNPIPE

KEY: A Northern

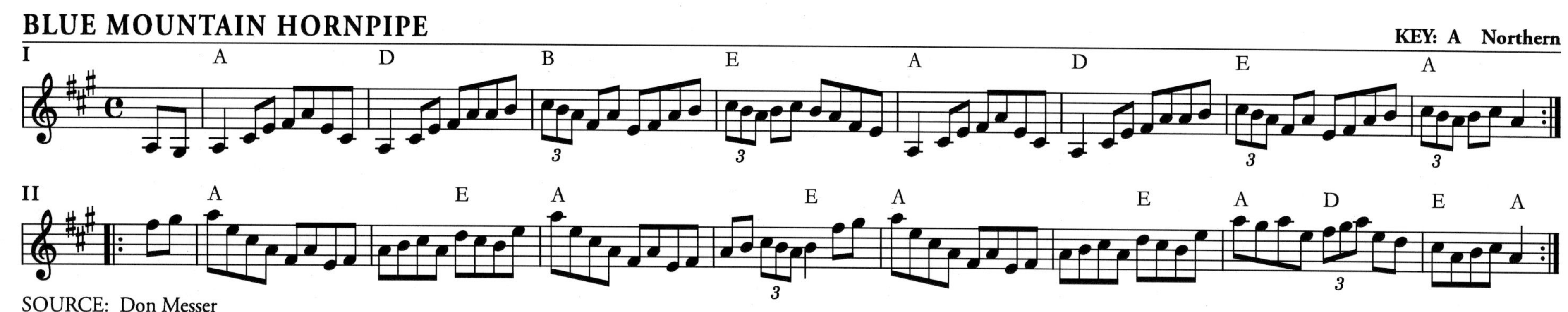

SOURCE: Don Messer

BLUE MULE ❁ BUFFALO NICKEL ❁ CHINKY PIN ❁ DARLING CHILD ❁ FOURTH OF JULY ❁ I'M OVER TOO YOUNG TO MARRY ❁ I'M OVER TOO YOUNG TO MARRY YET ❁ I'M OVER YOUNG TO MARRY YET ❁ LEAD OUT ❁ LOVE SOMEBODY ❁ MIDNIGHT SERENADE ❁ MY LOVE IS BUT A LASSIE-O ❁ MY LOVE IS BUT A LASSIE YET ❁ OLD LADY TUCKER ❁ SHOOT THE TURKEY BUZZARD ❁ SWEET SIXTEEN ❁ TEN NIGHTS IN A BARROOM ❁ TOO YOUNG TO MARRY ❁ CROOKED STOVEPIPE ❁ THE FARMER HAD A DOG ❁ GREY-EYED CAT ❁ HAIR IN THE BUTTER ❁ I'M MY MOMMA'S DARLING ❁ RICHMOND BLUES ❁ TRIPPING ON THE MOUNTAIN ❁ YELLOW-EYED CAT

KEY: D Old-Time

BOBBY SHAFTO ❁ BOBBY SHAFTOE

KEY: D Old-Time

SOURCE: Dudley Laufman

BONAPARTE'S RETREAT ❁ BONAPARTE ❁ BONEYPARTE'S RETREAT ❁ BONEY'S DEFEAT ❁ BONYPARTE'S RETREAT

KEY: D Old-Time

BONNIE DUNDEE ❁ BONNY DUNDEE

KEY: G Northern Jig

I G D G D G

II G D G D G C G D G

SOURCE: Reg Hill

BOSTON BOY ❁ KATYDID ❁ TAKE ME BACK TO GEORGIA ❁ RATTLESNAKE BIT THE BABY ❁ LADIES IN THE BALLROOM

KEY: C Old-Time

BOSTON BOYS

KEY: C Old-Time

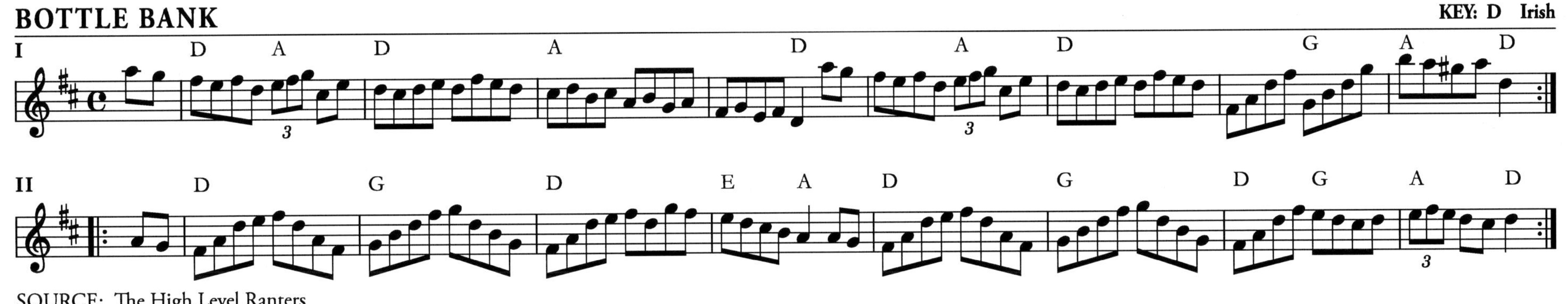
BOTTLE BANK
KEY: D Irish
I
D A D A D A D G A D
3
3
II
D G D E A D G D G A D
3
SOURCE: The High Level Ranters

THE BOYS OF BLUE HILL ✵ BEAUX OF OAKHILL ✵ THE BOYS FROM BLUE HILL ✵ THE BLOKES OF BLUEHILL ✵ THE BOYS OF THE BLUE HILL ✵ THE BLOKES OF BLUE HILL
KEY: D Irish Hornpipe
I
D G A D A D G D G A D A D
3
3
II
D Em A D A D G D G A D D
3

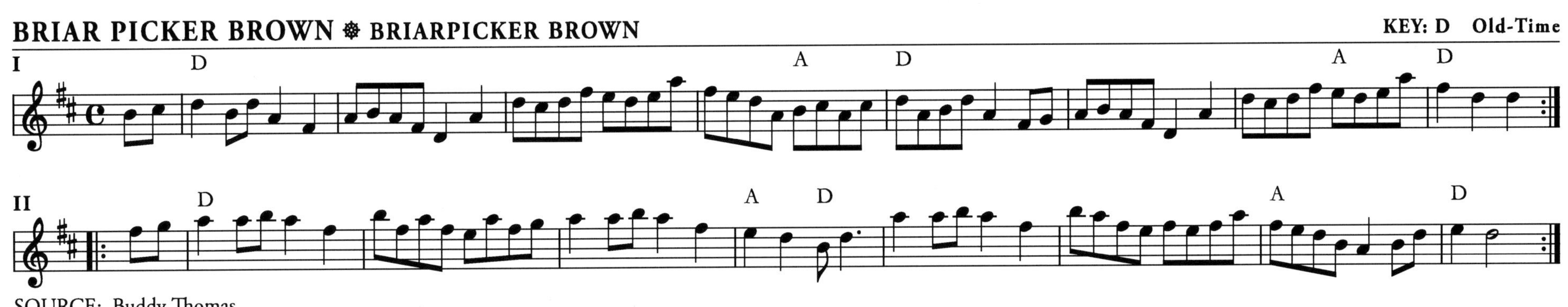
BRIAR PICKER BROWN ✵ BRIARPICKER BROWN
KEY: D Old-Time
I
D A D A D
II
D A D A D
SOURCE: Buddy Thomas

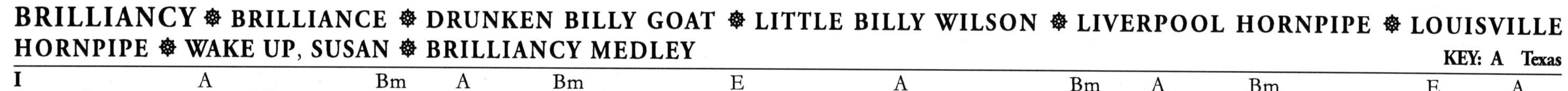

BRILLIANCY ❁ BRILLIANCE ❁ DRUNKEN BILLY GOAT ❁ LITTLE BILLY WILSON ❁ LIVERPOOL HORNPIPE ❁ LOUISVILLE HORNPIPE ❁ WAKE UP, SUSAN ❁ BRILLIANCY MEDLEY

SOURCE: Howdy Forrester

BROWN BUTTON SHOES

SOURCE: Buddy Thomas

BRUSHY RUN

SOURCE: Wilson Douglas

BUFFALO GALS ❁ AIN'T YA COMIN' OUT TONIGHT ❁ ALABAMA GALS ❁ ALABAMA GALS WON'T YOU COME OUT TONIGHT ❁ ANGELINA ❁ BUFFALO GALS AT NOME ❁ BUFFALO GIRL ❁ BUFFALO GIRLS ❁ HAGANTOWN GIRLS ❁ JOHNSTOWN GALS ❁ LOUISIANA GIRLS ❁ LUBLY FAN ❁ MIDNIGHT SERENADE ❁ OLD JOHNNIE WALKER ❁ RED-COAT GAL ❁ ROUNDTOWN GIRLS ❁ ROUNDTOWN GIRL WON'T YOU COME OUT TONIGHT ❁ WON'T YOU WALK OUT TONIGHT ❁ MAXWELL GIRL

KEY: G Bluegrass/Old-Time

I G D G D G

II G D G C G D G

SOURCE: Bill Reser

BULL AT THE WAGON

KEY: A Old-Time

SOURCE: Earl Collins

THE BUNRATTY BOYS ☸ JOHN KELLY'S SLIDE ☸ NELLY MAHONY'S ☸ NELLY MAHONY'S SLIDE ☸ KNOCKNAGREE ☸ NELLY MAHONEY'S

KEY: D Irish Slide

BURNT POTATO JIG ☸ LITTLE BURNT POTATO ☸ FRANK'S TWO-STEP

KEY: C Northern Jig

SOURCE: 25 Fiddle Favorites

BUTTERFLY SLIP-JIG ☸ THE BUTTERFLY

KEY: Em Irish

BYRNE'S FAVORITE HORNPIPE ❁ ALEXANDER'S HORNPIPE ❁ BALLYMANUS FAIR ❁ BYRNE'S FAVORITE ❁ THE JOLLY BUTCHERS ❁ KELLY'S HORNPIPE ❁ THE SANDLARK

KEY: D Irish

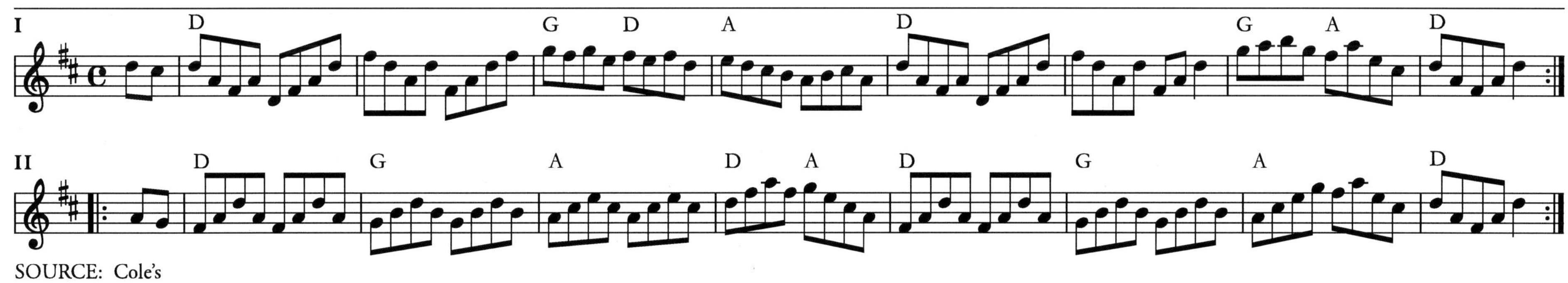

SOURCE: Cole's

BYRNE'S HORNPIPE ❁ BURN'S HORNPIPE ❁ TOMMY HILL'S FAVORITE ❁ BYRON'S ❁ BRYANT'S FAVORITE HORNPIPE ❁ THE BYRNE ❁ BYRNES'

KEY: D Irish

I
D G A D G A D G A D A D

II
A D G D G A D G A D A D

CAMPBELL'S FAREWELL TO RED GAP ✵ CAMPBELL'S FAREWELL TO REDCASTLE ✵ CAMPBELL'S FAREWELL TO RED CASTLE ✵ CAMPBELL'S FAREWELL TO REDCASTLE MARCH ✵ FAREWELL TO THE RED CASTLE OF CAMPBELL ✵ SHORT CUT TO THE PUB

cf SETH'S REEL *et al*

KEY: D Scottish

I

D C D C D

II

D C D C D

D C D C D

III

D D C D

CARMODY'S JIG ✵ MORRISON'S JIG ✵ LYON'S FAVOURITE ✵ MAURICE CARMODY'S FAVOURITE ✵ THE STICK ACROSS THE HOB ✵ HUMORS OF DINGLE ✵ PADDY STACK'S FANCY JIG

KEY: Em Irish

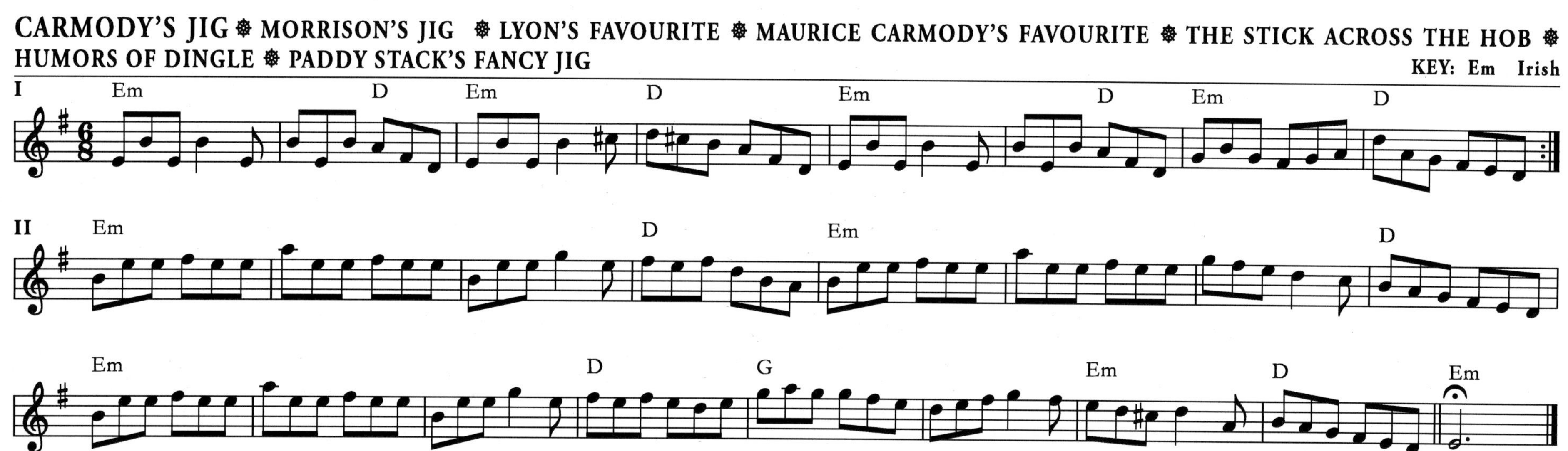

CARPENTER'S REEL ❁ WALKER STREET ❁ THE TRAVELLER ❁ REEL DES OUVRIERS ❁ REEL DE SAINT-MALOT

cf WALKER'S STREET REEL *et al*

KEY: G Northern

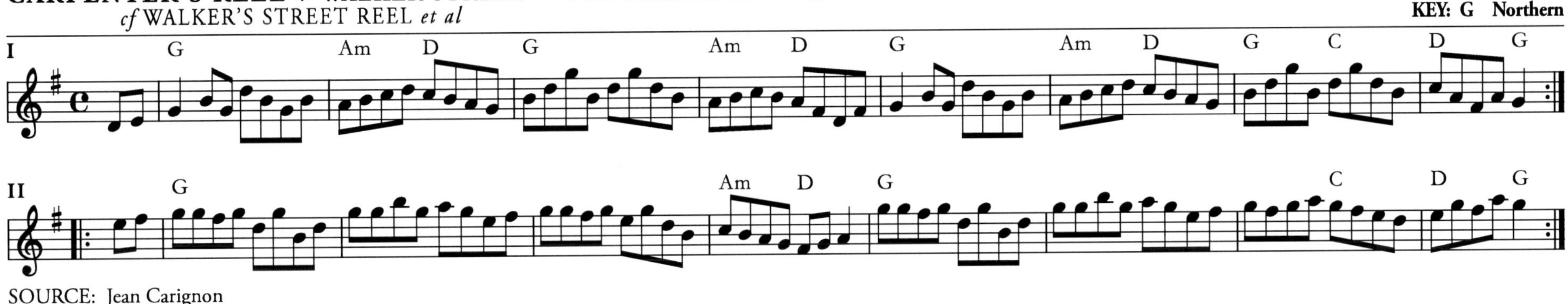

SOURCE: Jean Carignon

CARRICK JIG

KEY: C Old-Time

SOURCE: Lucien Beauchemin

THE CAT RAMBLES TO THE CHILD'S SAUCE PAN ❁ CAT'S RAMBLES TO THE CHILD'S SAUCEPAN ❁ CULLEN SLIDE ❁ THE GLOUNTANE SLIDE ❁ MARY WILLIE'S ❁ MICK MAHONY'S ❁ GLEANNTAN ❁ MARY WILLY'S ❁ MICK DUGGAN'S

KEY: D Irish Slide

SOURCE: Johnny Cronin and Joe Burke

CATTLE IN THE CANE ❁ CATTLE IN THE CORN

KEY: Am/A Southern

CHARMING MOLLY BRANNIGAN ❁ CHARMING MOLLY BRALLAGHAN ❁ JUDY BRANAGAN ❁ JUDY BRANNAGAN ❁ MOLLIE BRANAGAN ❁ PRETTY MOLLY BRALLAGHAN ❁ PRETTY JUDY BRALLAGHAN ❁ CHARMING JUDY BRALLAHAN

cf THE GREEN FIELDS OF AMERICA *et al* & OLD MOTHER FLANAGAN *et al*

KEY: G Old-Time

THE CHATEAUGUAY REEL ❁ BULL RUN PICNIC ❁ CHATEAU GAI ❁ THE CHATAGEE ❁ CHATEAU-GAIE ❁ REEL DE CHATEAUGUAY ❁ REEL DE LA CASERNE

KEY: G Northern

SOURCE: Reg Hill

CHEAT MOUNTAIN
KEY: D Southern
I
II
SOURCE: David Putnam

CHEROKEE SHUFFLE
cf LOST INDIAN et al
KEY: G Bluegrass
I
II

CHEROKEE SHUFFLE
cf LOST INDIAN et al
KEY: A Bluegrass
I
II

CHILDGROVE ❁ CHILD GROVE

KEY: Dm/F Old-Time

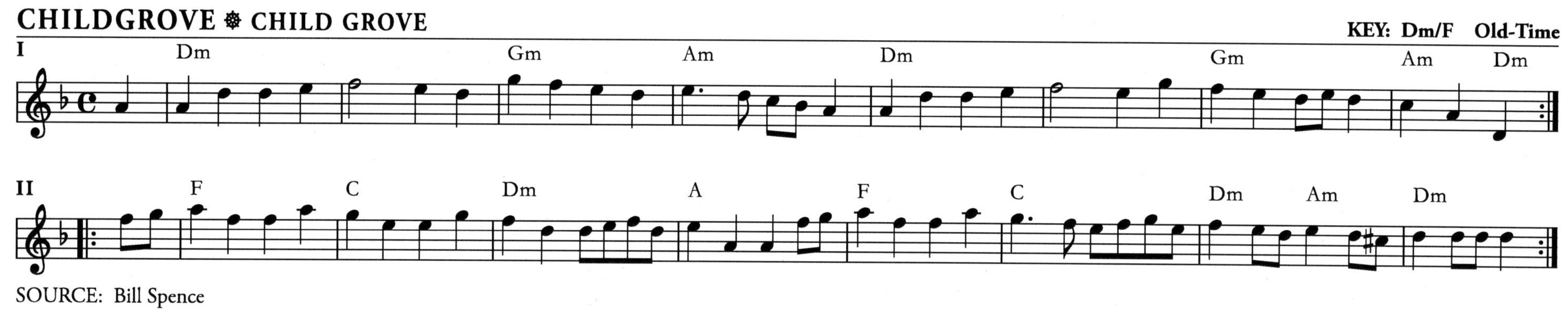

SOURCE: Bill Spence

CHIPPEWA BREAKFAST

KEY: G Bluegrass

SOURCE: Tater Tate

CINCINNATI HORNPIPE

cf BILLY WILSON'S CLOG *et al*, FRED WILSON'S CLOG & HARVEST HOME

KEY: D Old-Time

CINDY ❁ GET ALONG HOME, MISS CINDY

KEY: D Southern

CITACO ❁ DOWN TO THE WILDWOOD TO SHOOT THE BUFFALO ❁ CITIGO ❁ CITICO

KEY: G Southern

SOURCE: Lowe Stokes

COCK OF THE NORTH ❁ THE COCK O' THE NORTH ❁ AUNTIE MARY ❁ JOAN'S PLACKET ❁ JOAN'S PLACKET IS TOM ❁ JUMPING JOHN ❁ AUNTIE MARY HAD A CANARY ❁ CHASE ME CHARLIE

KEY: A Northern Jig

SOURCE: Reg Hill

PARTS ARE SOMETIMES REVERSED

COLD FROSTY MORNING ❅ FROSTY MORNING ❅ COLD FROSTY MORN

KEY: A/Am Old-Time

SOURCE: Henry Reed

COLEMAN'S CROSS ❅ GRIFFIN FROM THE BRIDGE

KEY: G Irish

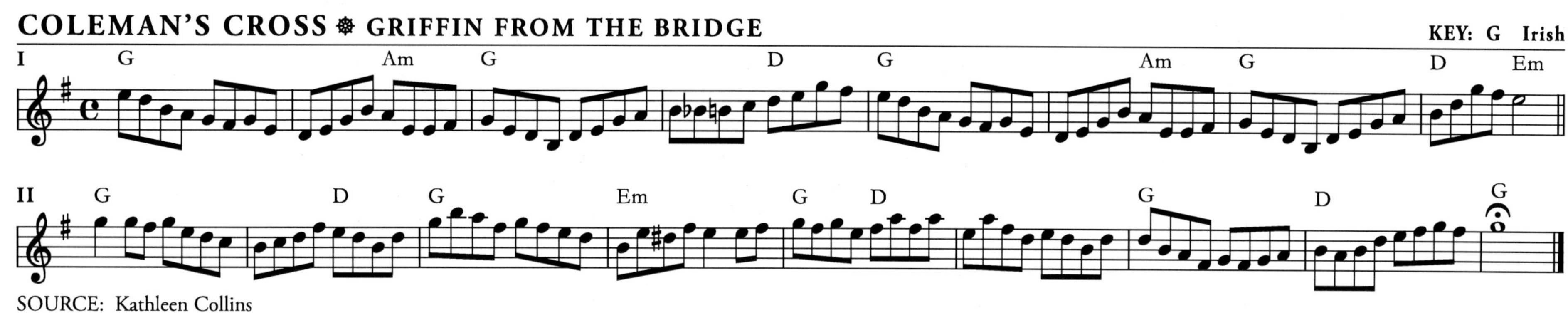

SOURCE: Kathleen Collins

COLERAINE ❅ COLAIRNE ❅ THE COLERANE ❅ COLRAINE ❅ CORELAINE ❅ KITTY OF COLERAINE

KEY: Am Irish Jig

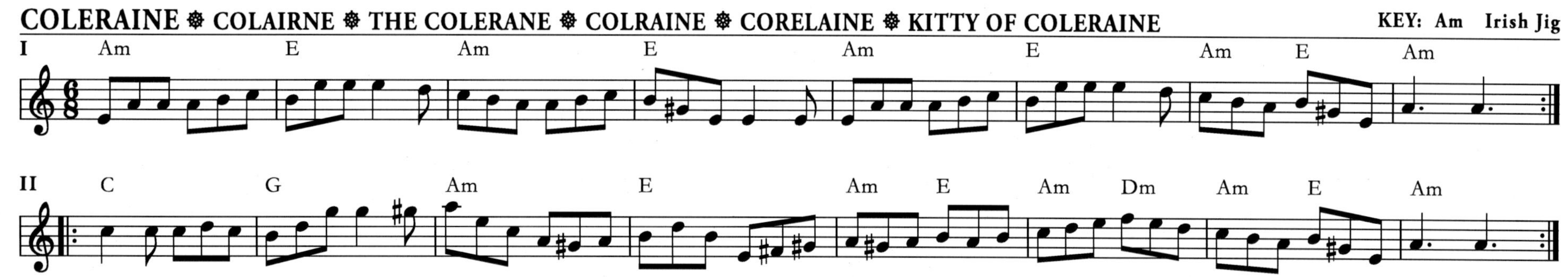

COLONIAL BREAKDOWN

KEY: G/D Bluegrass

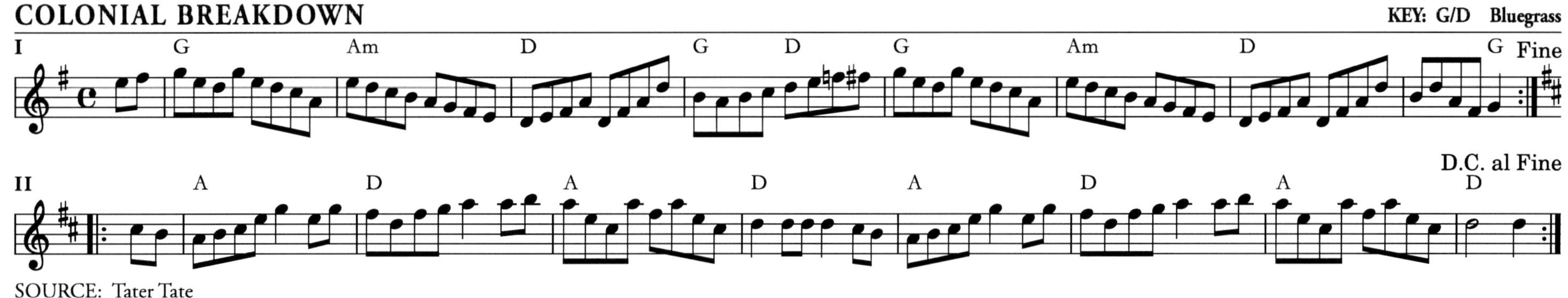

SOURCE: Tater Tate

COLORED ARISTOCRACY

KEY: G Old-Time

COMING DOWN FROM DENVER ☸ HERE AND THERE ☸ COWBOY'S ☸ THE HALFWAY HOUSE ☸ KING OF ALL REELS ☸ TURNPIKE ☸ COMING DOWN TO DENVER

cf LARDNER'S REEL *et al*

KEY: A Bluegrass/Old-Time

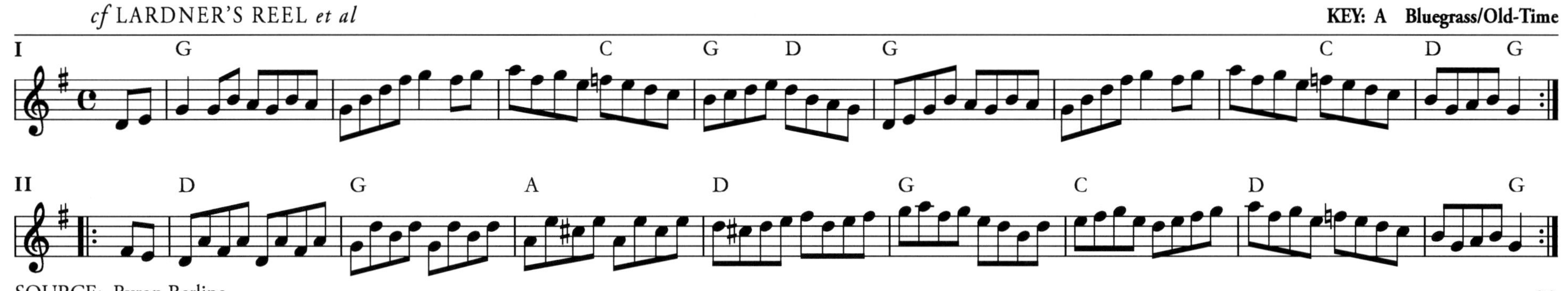

SOURCE: Byron Berline

CONSTITUTION HORNPIPE ☸ FLAT BOAT ☸ LONE APPENDICITIS

KEY: F Old-Time

SOURCE: Cole's

THE CORNER HOUSE ☸ THE CORNERHOUSE ☸ PADDY KELLY'S

KEY: Am Irish

CORNEY'S COMING ☸ TOM FITZMAURICE'S REEL ☸ CORNEY IS COMING ☸ THE BARRACK STREET BOYS ☸ THE BRIDE TO BED ☸ BRIDES TO BED ☸ BRIDES AWAY ☸ BRITISH NAGGON ☸ CHEESE IT ☸ CRAWFORD'S REEL ☸ I SAW HER ☸ KELLY'S REEL ☸ KNIT THE POCKY ☸ MERRY BITS OF TIMBER ☸ MISS WILSON ☸ MY LOVE IS IN THE HOUSE ☸ PACKIE DUIGNAN'S ☸ SHANNON BREEZE ☸ SIX MILE BRIDGE ☸ THE SPINNING WHEEL ☸ MY LOVE IS IN AMERICA

KEY: D Irish

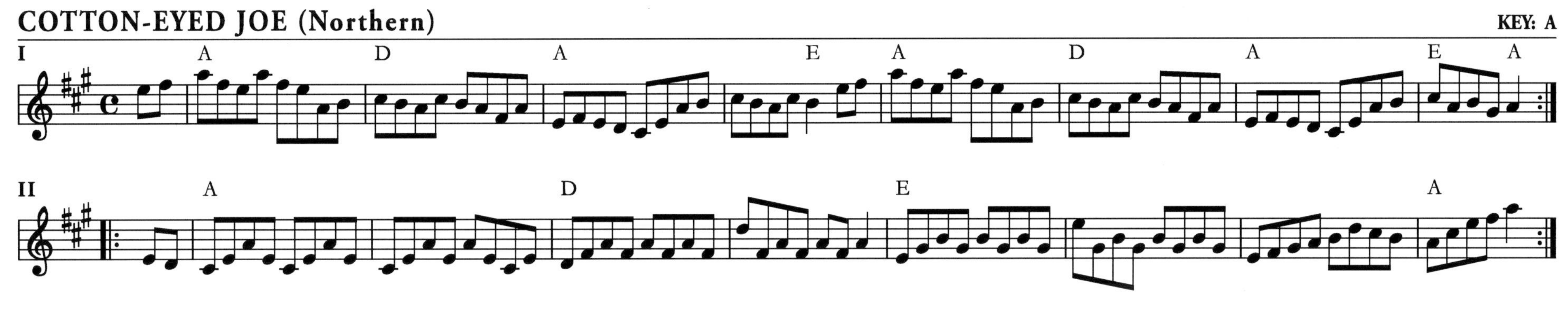
COTTON-EYED JOE (Northern)
KEY: A
I A D A E A D A E A
II A D E A

COTTON-EYED JOE (Southern) ❁ DUSTY MILLER
KEY: A
I A E A
II A E A

COTTON PATCH RAG

KEY: C Texas

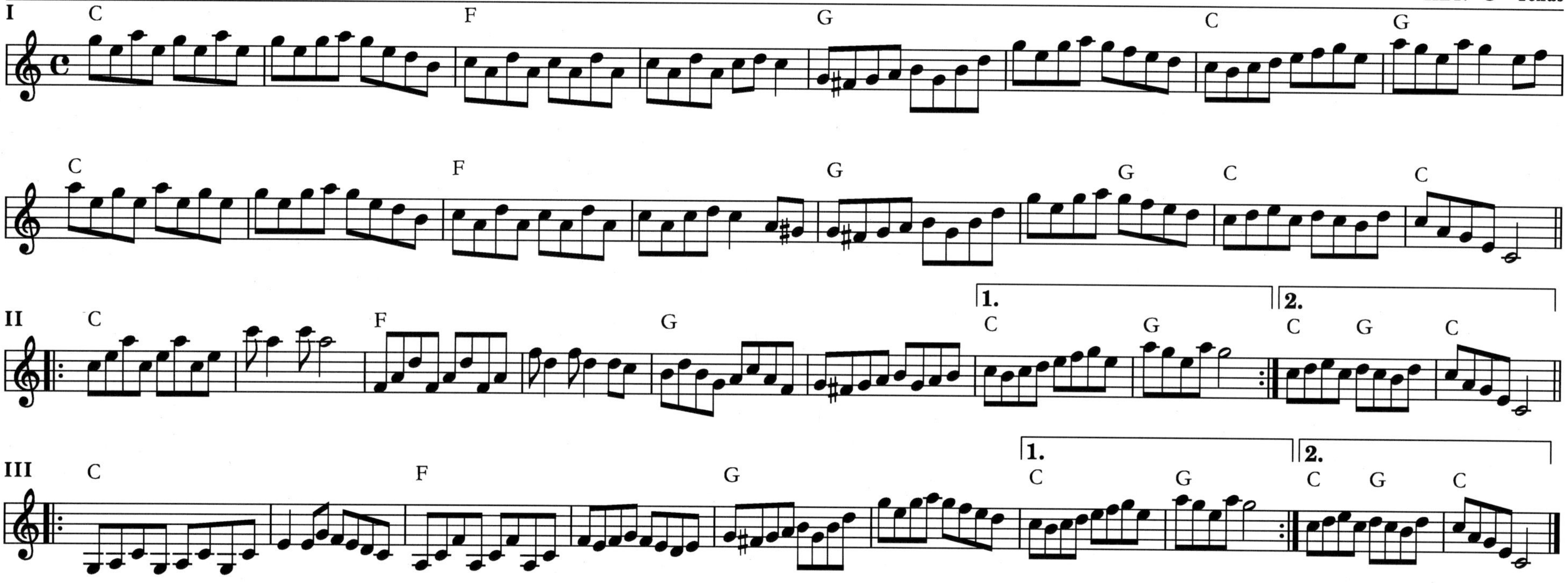

I C F G C G
C F G G C C
II C F G 1. C G 2. C G C
III C F G 1. C G 2. C G C

COWBOY'S DREAM

KEY: D Old-Time

I D A D A D A D G A D
II D A D A D A D G A D

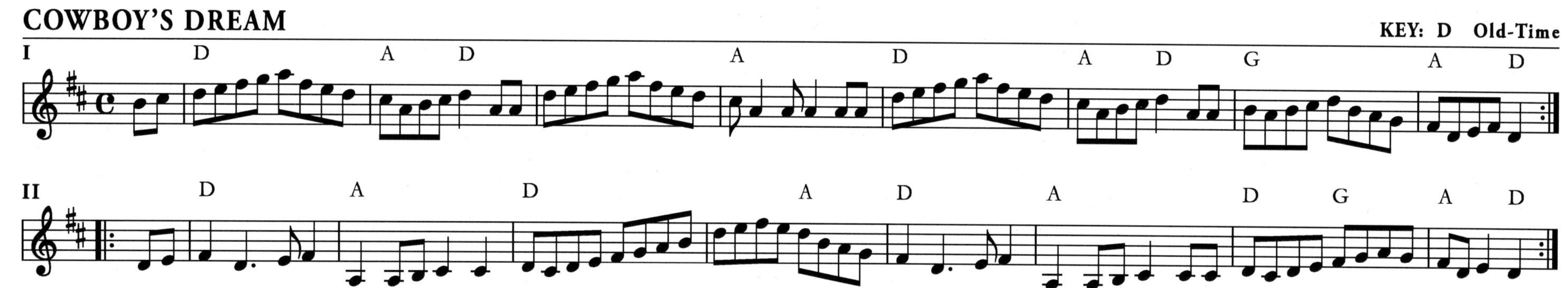

COWBOY'S JIG

KEY: G Old-Time Jig

COWBOY'S REEL

KEY: A Old-Time

SOURCE: Roma McMillan

CRICKET ON THE HEARTH ❁ CRICKET ON A HEARTH

cf MARMADUKE'S HORNPIPE *et al* & YEARLING *et al*

KEY: D Bluegrass/Old-Time

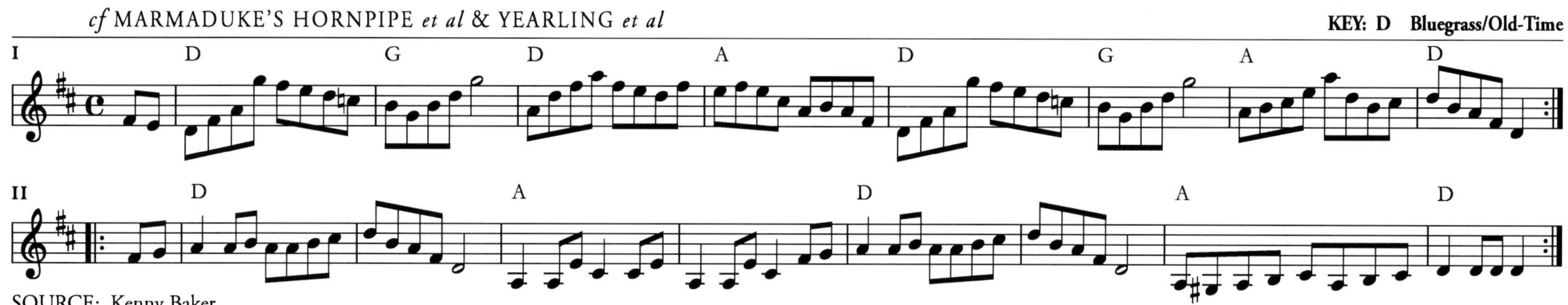

SOURCE: Kenny Baker

CRIPPLE CREEK ❁ GOIN' UP CRIPPLE CREEK ❁ LITTLE IDA RED ❁ GOING DOWN CRIPPLE CREEK ❁ GOING UP BRUSHY FORK ❁ GOING DOWN BRUSHY FORK ❁ GOING UP SHOOTING CREEK ❁ GOING DOWN SHOOTING CREEK ❁ RED CREEK ❁ SHOOTING CREEK

KEY: A Southern

THE CROOKED STOVE PIPE

KEY: G Northern

THE CUCKOO'S NEST ❁ COO-COO'S NEST ❁ CUCKOO HORNPIPE ❁ THE COO-COO'S ❁ THE CUCKOO'S NEST REEL

KEY: D Old-Time

SOURCE: Cole's

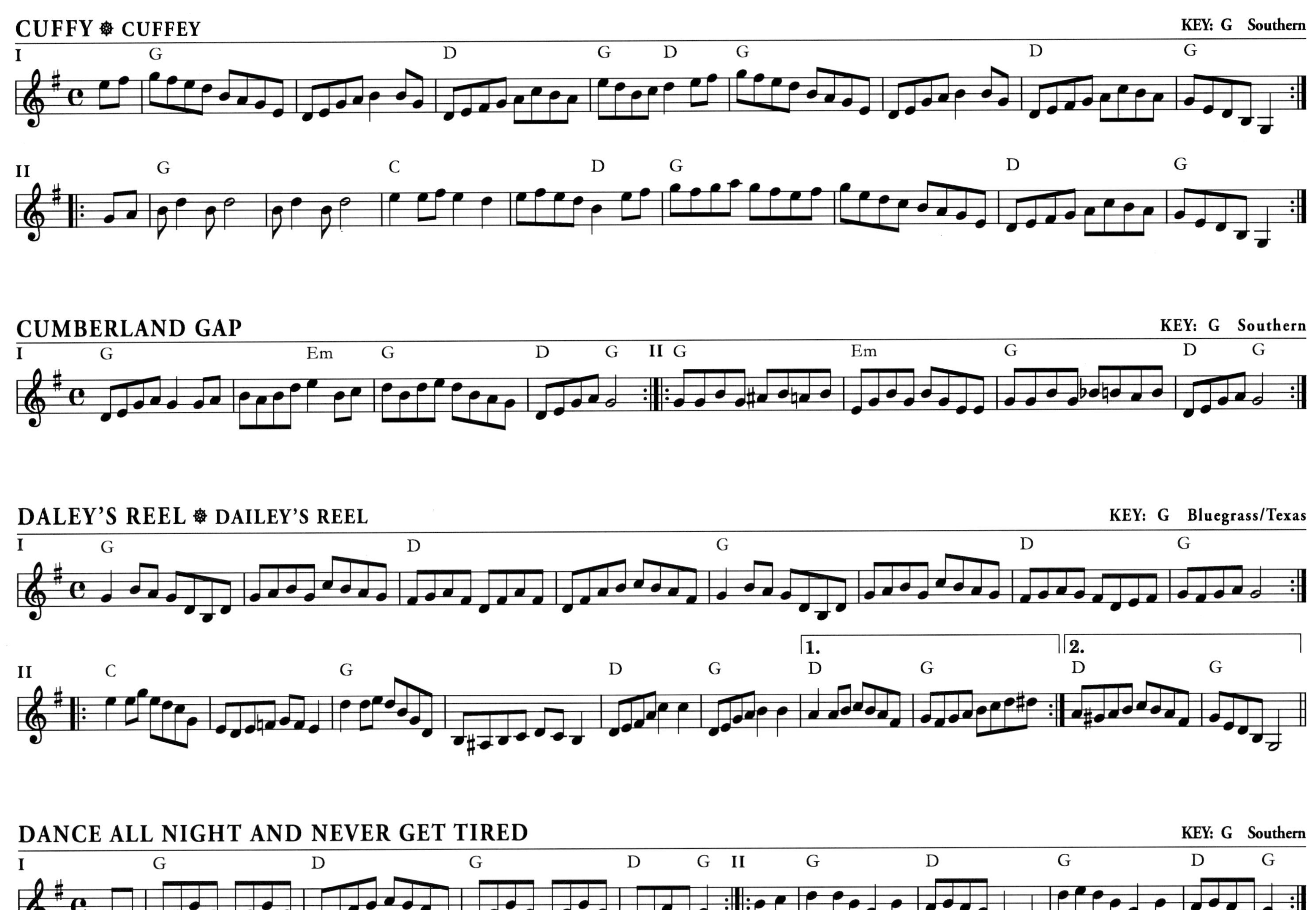
CUFFY ❁ CUFFEY
KEY: G Southern
CUMBERLAND GAP
KEY: G Southern
DALEY'S REEL ❁ DAILEY'S REEL
KEY: G Bluegrass/Texas
DANCE ALL NIGHT AND NEVER GET TIRED
KEY: G Southern

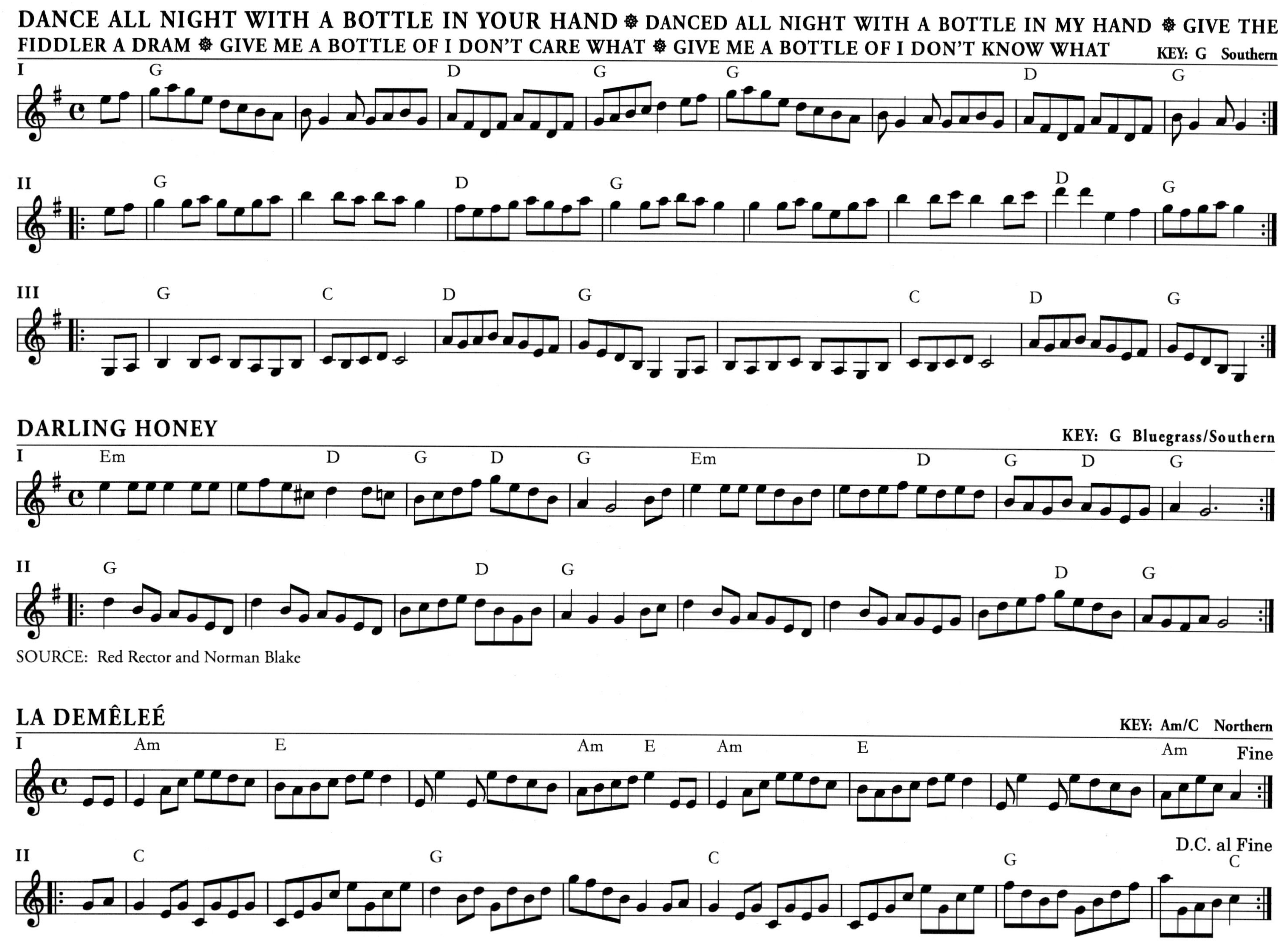
DANCE ALL NIGHT WITH A BOTTLE IN YOUR HAND ❁ DANCED ALL NIGHT WITH A BOTTLE IN MY HAND ❁ GIVE THE FIDDLER A DRAM ❁ GIVE ME A BOTTLE OF I DON'T CARE WHAT ❁ GIVE ME A BOTTLE OF I DON'T KNOW WHAT
KEY: G Southern
DARLING HONEY
KEY: G Bluegrass/Southern
SOURCE: Red Rector and Norman Blake
LA DEMÊLEÉ
KEY: Am/C Northern
Fine
D.C. al Fine

DENIS MURPHY'S POLKA ☸ SWEENEY'S POLKA ☸ CASEY'S POLKA ☸ THE BOSTON ☸ CHARLIE O'LEARY'S FAVOURITE ☸ THE CONNEMARA ☸ FLAHERTY'S FAVOURITE ☸ SWEENY'S ☸ SWEENY'S TJUM TJUM ☸ TEEHAN'S

KEY: D Irish

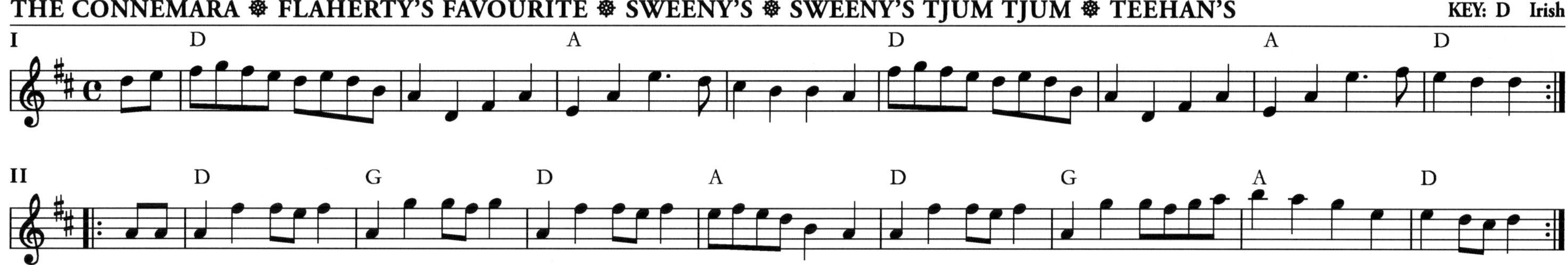

DEVIL'S DREAM ☸ DEVIL AMONG THE TAILORS ☸ SATAN'S NIGHTMARE ☸ DIEL'S DREAM ☸ DEIL AMONG THE TAILORS ☸ DEVIL AMONG THE TAYLORS ☸ LA RÉVE DU DIABLE ☸ REEL DU DIABLE

KEY: A Irish/Old-Time

THE DINGLE REGATTA ☸ DENIS MURPHY'S SLIDE ☸ TOM BILLY'S FAVOURITE ☸ GARÇON VOLAGE ☸ SLATTERY'S GROVE

KEY: G Irish Slide

SOURCE: Johnny Cronin and Joe Burke

DIVING SIX

KEY: G Northern Jig

DOG IN THE RYE STRAW

cf RYE STRAW *et al*

KEY: D Southern

SOURCE: Howdy Forrester

DOHENY'S FAVORITE

KEY: D Old-Time

SOURCE: Frank George

DOHERTY'S REEL ❁ JOHNNY DOHERTY'S REEL ❁ MOT MALLOY ❁ MOT MOLLOY ❁ WISE MAID ❁ ALL AROUND THE WORLD ❁ COOLEY'S REEL ❁ THE CONNEMARA RAKE ❁ GREHAN'S ❁ JOHN DOHERTY'S REEL ❁ JOLLY BEGGAR ❁ THE KNOTTED CHORD ❁ MATT MOLLOY'S ❁ THE MISTRESS ❁ TINKER DOHERTY'S

KEY: D Irish

SOURCE: Johnny Cronin and Joe Burke

DONE GONE ❁ ALL I'VE GOT'S DONE GONE

KEY: G Old-Time/Bluegrass

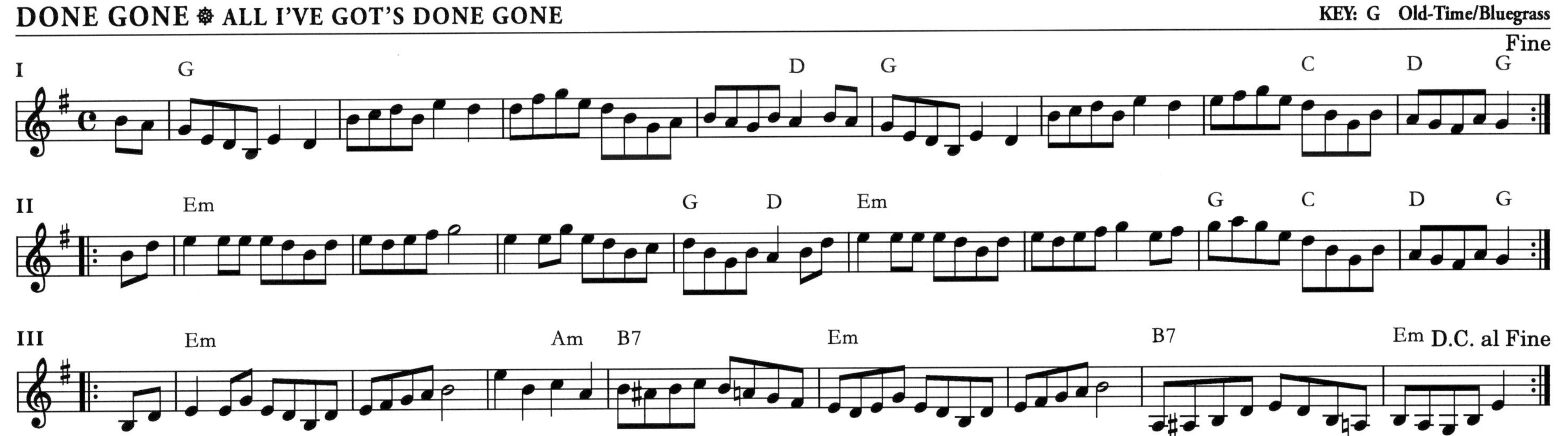

DONGAL JIG ☸ THE DONEGAL JIG

KEY: G Northern Jig

SOURCE: Don Messer

DON TREMAINE'S REEL

KEY: D Northern

DOWD'S REEL ☸ DOWD'S FAVORITE ☸ BRAES OF BUSHBIE ☸ O'DOWD'S REEL ☸ O'DOWD'S FAVORITE

KEY: Gm/B♭ Irish

SOURCE: Kathleen Collins

DRAG HER 'ROUND THE ROAD ❁ THE PULLET ❁ THE PULLET AND THE COCK ❁ ANDY McGANN'S No 42 BUNRATTY ❁ BUNRATTY REEL ❁ THE SHORES OF LOCH GRANEY ❁ SHORES OF LOUGH GRANEY ❁ 42 BUNRATTY ❁ ANDY McGANN'S ❁ ANDY McGANN'S No 42 ❁ BONRADY ❁ BURKE'S ❁ DRAG HER ACROSS THE ROAD ❁ DRAG HER ALONG THE ROAD ❁ DRAG HER AROUND THE ROAD ❁ DRAG HER CROSS THE ROAD ❁ DRAG HER UP THE ROAD ❁ DRAGGIN ACROSS THE ROAD ❁ THE KISS IN THE FURZE No 2 ❁ THE KISS IN THE GORSE No 2 ❁ THE KISS IN THE WHIN No 2 ❁ THE PIPER ON HORSEBACK ❁ PULLET AND COCK ❁ THE SHORES OF LOUGHGRANEY ❁ THROW IT ACROSS THE ROAD

KEY: Gm/B♭ Irish

SOURCE: Johnny Cronin and Joe Burke

DROPS OF SPRING WATER ❁ THE CLOUT ❁ COCK IN THE HEATH ❁ DROPS OF SPRINGWATER ❁ THE HUMORS OF CALEDON ❁ HUMORS OF WESTMEATH ❁ THE RAKES OF WESTMEATH ❁ A BLAST OF WIND ❁ A KISS IN THE FURZ ❁ THE HUMOURS OF CALEDON

KEY: D Irish Slip-Jig

DRUNKEN BILLY GOAT ❁ BRILLIANCY ❁ ROCKY MOUNTAIN GOAT ❁ MUD FENCE

KEY: A Texas

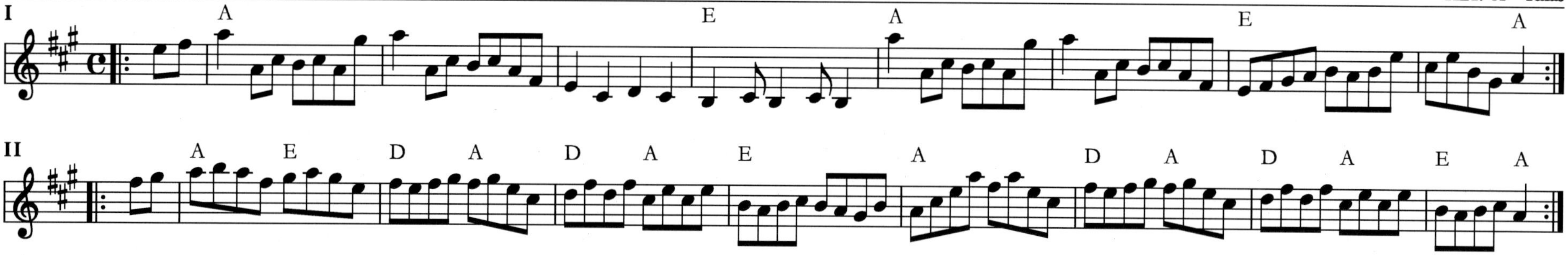
I
A E A E A
II
A E D A D A E A D A D A E A

DRY AND DUSTY ❁ THE CHARGE OF BONAPARTE ❁ BONAPARTE'S CHARGE ❁ PINEY RIDGE

KEY: E Bluegrass/Old-Time

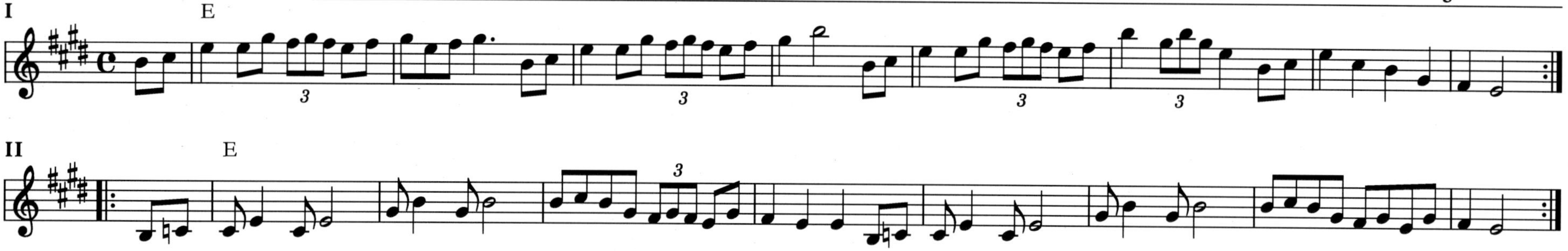
I
E
3 3 3 3
II
E
3

SOURCE: Kenny Baker/Collins Brothers

DRY CREEK REEL

KEY: D Southern

I
D A D A D
II
D G A D A D G A D

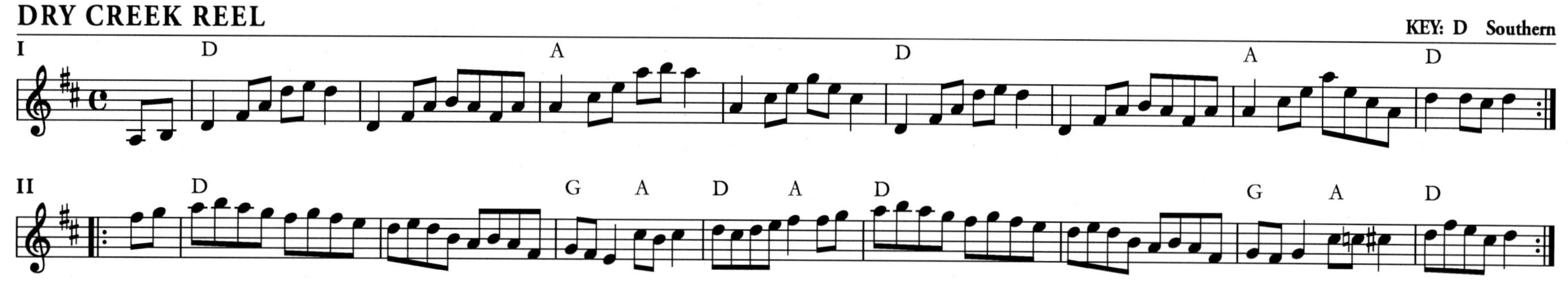

DUBUQUE ❁ BOB WALKER ❁ DUCK RIVER ❁ FIDDLING PHIL ❁ FIVE MILES FROM TOWN ❁ GENERAL LEE ❁ GOING DOWN TO MAYSVILLE ❁ HELL ON THE NINE MILE ❁ HELL UP COAL HOLLER ❁ LIGHTHOUSE ❁ MA FERGUSON ❁ MABEL ❁ MUDDY ROAD TO KANSAS ❁ PHIDDLIN' PHIL ❁ SALLY IN THE GREEN CORN ❁ TEXAS TRAVELER ❁ TROUBLE ON THE NINE MILE ❁ VILLAGE HORNPIPE

KEY: D Southern

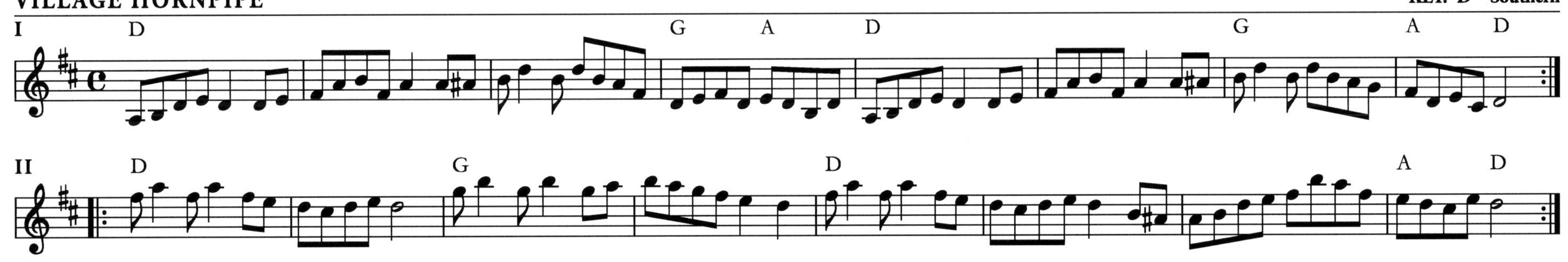

DUCKS ON THE MILL POND ❁ DEAF WOMAN'S COURTSHIP

KEY: D Old-Time

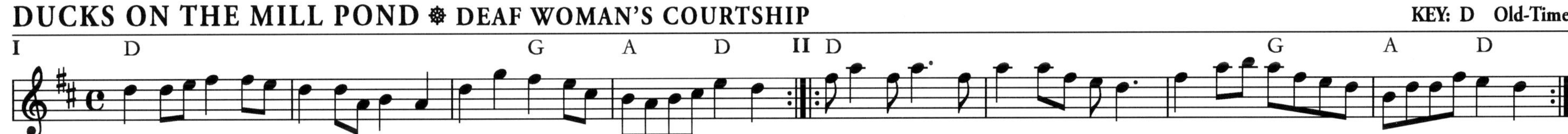

DUCKS ON THE POND ❁ LADY OF THE LAKE

KEY: A Old-Time

PARTS ARE SOMETIMES REVERSED

DURANG'S HORNPIPE (Bluegrass) ❁ WOBBLE GEARS ❁ LITTLE HORNPIPE

cf DURANG'S HORNPIPE (Irish)

KEY: D

I D G D A D G A D

II D G D G D A D G A D

III D F♯m G D G D A D G A D

SOURCE: Alan Munde/Byron Berline

DURANG'S HORNPIPE (Irish)

cf DURANG'S HORNPIPE (Bluegrass)

KEY: D

I D G D A D G A D

II D G D Em A E A D A D

DURHAM'S REEL ❁ DURHAM'S BULL

KEY: G Southern

I G C D G Fine

II G C A D D.C. al Fine

DUSTY BOB JIG ❁ DUSTY BOB'S JIG

KEY: G Northern

SOURCE: Dudley Laufman

DUSTY MILLER (Bluegrass)

KEY: G

SOURCE: Dan Crary

DUSTY MILLER (Bluegrass)

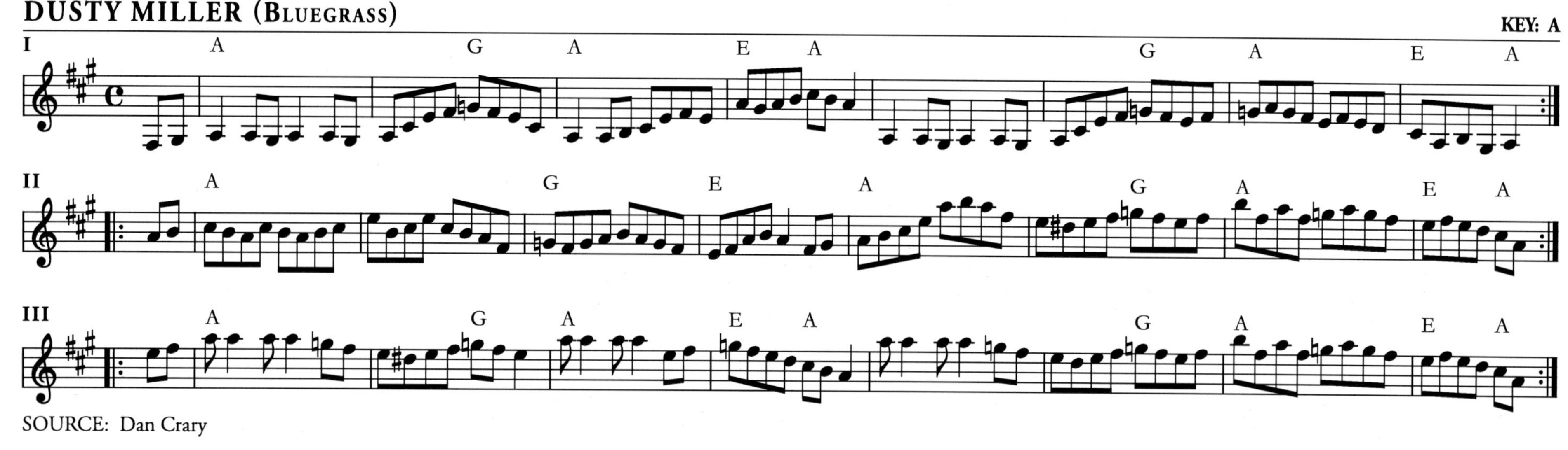

DUSTY MILLER (Irish)

EBENEEZER ❁ WEST VIRGINIA FAREWELL ❁ WEST VIRGINIA HIGHWAY ❁ EBENEZER

EDDIE KELLY'S ❁ EDDY KELLY'S
KEY: Dm Irish
I Am Dm B♭ Dm Am C Dm C Am Dm
II Dm Am Dm C Dm Am C Dm
SOURCE: Kathleen Collins
THE EIGHTH OF JANUARY—C ❁ JACKSON'S VICTORY
Southern
I C F G C II C G C
THE EIGHTH OF JANUARY—D ❁ JACKSON'S VICTORY
Southern
I D G A D II D A D
THE EIGHTH OF JANUARY—G
Southern
I G C D G II G D G
THE EIGHTH OF JANUARY—A
Southern
I A D E A II A E A

ELFIN JIG

KEY: D Northern

ELLEN O'GRADY ☸ KITTY O'HEA ☸ THE BARN DOOR ☸ SORRY THE DAY I WAS MARRIED

KEY: A Irish Slip-Jig

FAHY'S ☸ PADDY FAHY'S REEL

KEY: Dm Irish

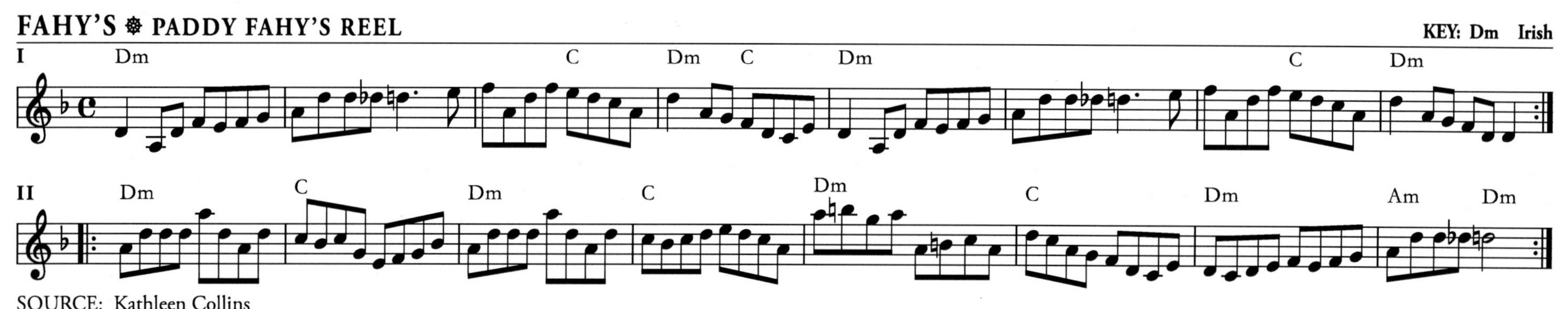

SOURCE: Kathleen Collins

FAIR MAIDEN ❁ THE RIVAL

KEY: G Irish Hornpipe

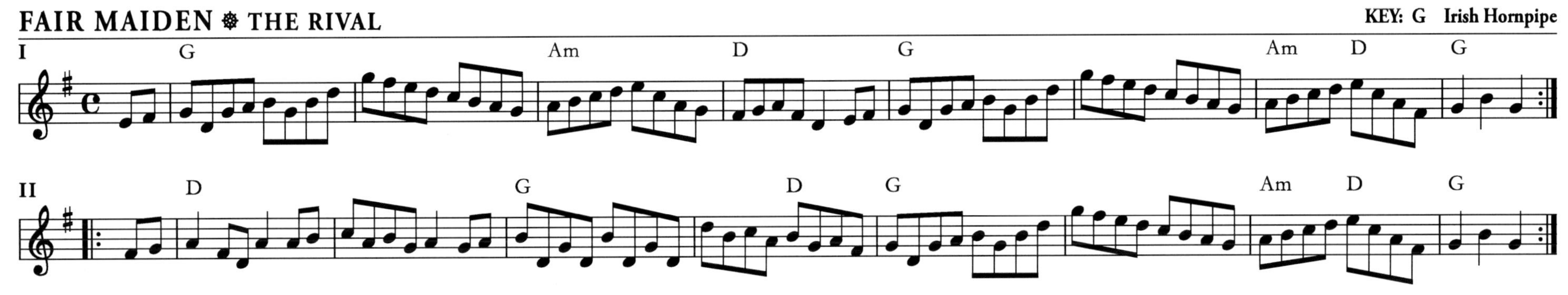

FAREWELL TO IRELAND

KEY: D Irish

SOURCE: Johnny Cronin and Joe Burke

FAREWELL TO OLD DECANCY ❁ FAREWELL TO AULD DECENCY ❁ FAREWELL TO OULD DECENCY ❁ FOR THE SAKE OF OLD DECENCY

KEY: G Irish

THE FARMER'S JAMBOREE ❁ DAISY'S JIG

KEY: A Northern Jig

SOURCE: King Ganam

FATHER KELLY'S

KEY: D Irish Jig

SOURCE: Kathleen Collins

FATHER O'FLYNN ❁ AT THE TOP OF CORK ROAD ❁ AT THE TOP OF THE CORK ROAD ❁ FR O'FLYNN ❁ ON THE TOP OF CORK ROAD ❁ THE ROLLICKING IRISHMAN ❁ TEN PENNY BIT ❁ THE TOP OF CORK ROAD ❁ TOP OF THE CORK ROAD ❁ THE YORKSHIRE LASSES

KEY: D Northern/Irish Jig

SOURCE: Reg Hill

FAT MEAT AND DUMPLINGS ❁ KNOCKING AT THE DOOR

KEY: C Northern

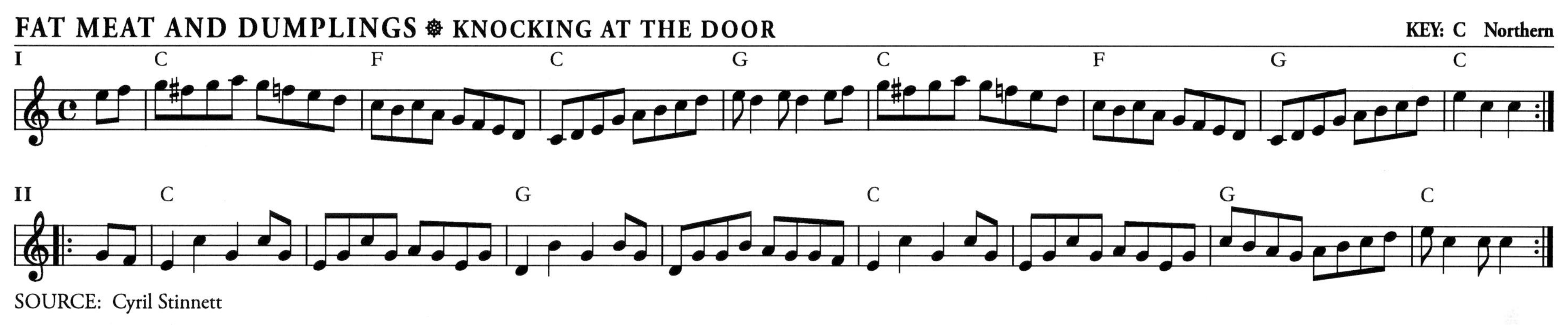

SOURCE: Cyril Stinnett

FIDDLEHEAD REEL ❁ FIDDLE HEAD REEL

KEY: D Old-Time

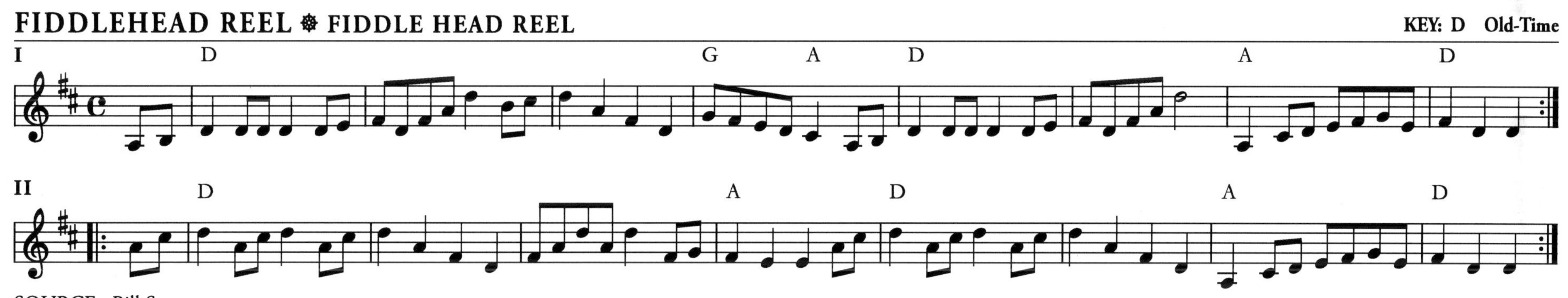

SOURCE: Bill Spence

FIDDLER'S DRAM ❁ GIVE THE FIDDLER A DRAM ❁ FIDDLER A DRAM

KEY: D Old-Time

FIDDLER'S DREAM ✽ FIDDLER'S TROUBLE

cf SANDY ROAD

SOURCE: Arthur Smith/Herman Johnson

FIDDLER'S HOEDOWN

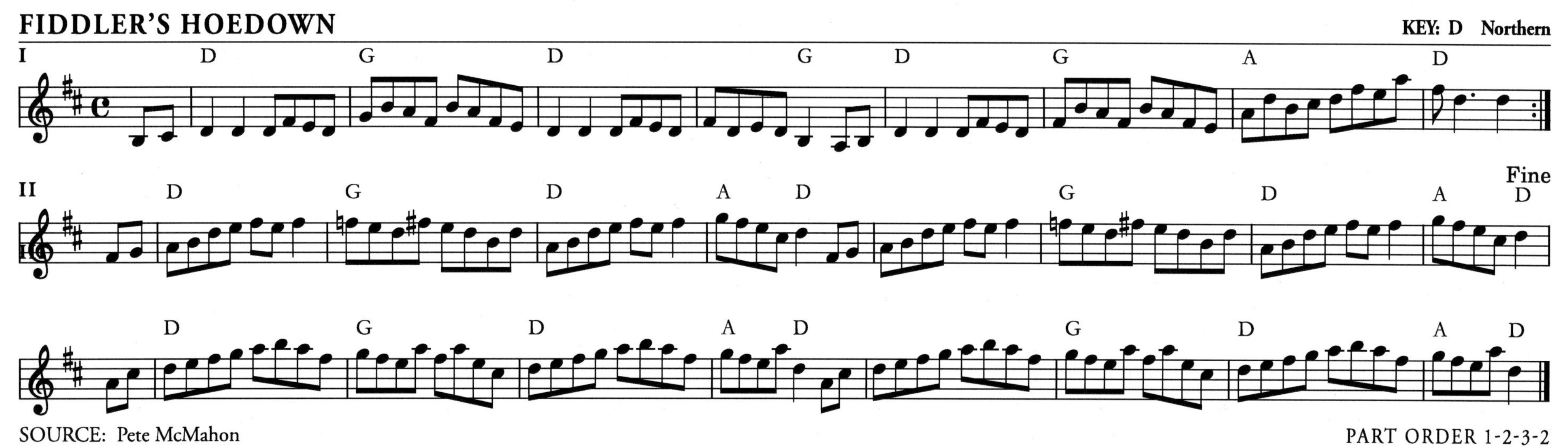

SOURCE: Pete McMahon

PART ORDER 1-2-3-2

FINNISH POLKA ❁ SAKKIJARVEN POLKA
KEY: Cm Scandinavian
I Cm G 3 Cm 3 G 3 Cm
II Cm G 3 Cm 3 G 3 3 Cm
III Cm G Cm
Cm C7 Fm Cm G Cm
IV Cm Fm G Cm Fm G Cm
FINNISH SCHOTTISCHE
KEY: Dm Scandinavian
I Dm Gm Dm A Dm Gm Dm A Dm
II D7 Gm C F Dm Gm Dm A Dm
III Gm Dm A Dm Gm Dm A Dm

FIREMAN'S REEL ❁ BUTTERMILK AND CIDER ❁ GOING TO CALIFORNIA ❁ OLD TOWSER ❁ WHISKEY YOU'RE THE DEVIL ❁ WHISKEY IN THE JAR ❁ BELLE OF THE KITCHEN ❁ THE SILVER CLUSTER ❁ YOU BET ❁ MISS JOHNSON'S HORNPIPE ❁ GYPSY HORNPIPE ❁ POSSUM UP A GUM STUMP COONIE IN THE HOLLOW ❁ LEXINGTON ❁ POSSUM UP A GUM STUMP ❁ FREEMAN'S REEL

cf OFF TO CALIFORNIA *et al*

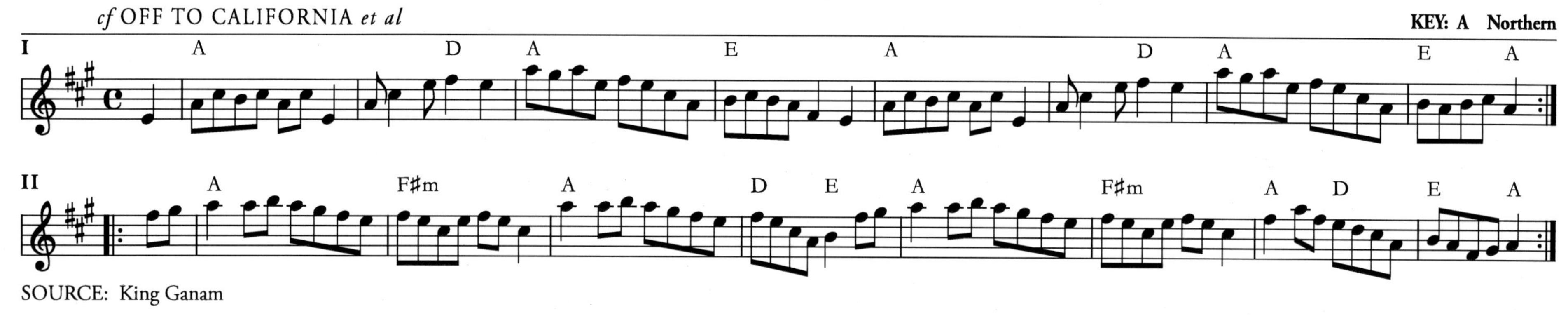

SOURCE: King Ganam

FIRE ON THE MOUNTAIN

THE FIRST OF MAY ❁ MAYDAY HORNPIPE ❁ LADY HARRINGTON'S REEL ❁ THE COLCANNON ❁ THE FOUR PROVINCES FLING Nº 1 ❁ THE FOUR PROVINCES HIGHLAND FLING ❁ THE SKILLET POT

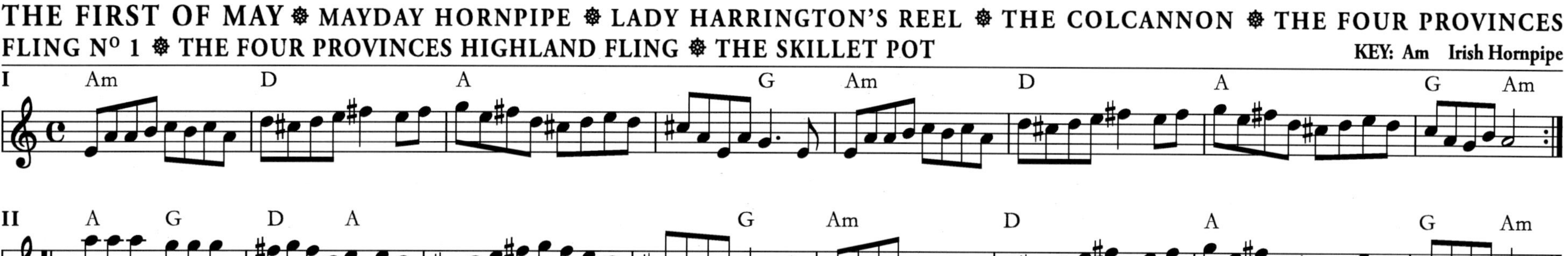

SOURCE: Cole's

THE FIRST SIGN OF LIGHT ❁ THE FIRST LIGHT OF DAY ❁ THE FIRST SIGN OF DAY ❁ FROM GALWAY TO DUBLIN ❁ FROM GALWAY TO DUBLIN TOWN ❁ NAPOLEON CROSSING THE RHINE

KEY: Em **Irish Hornpipe**

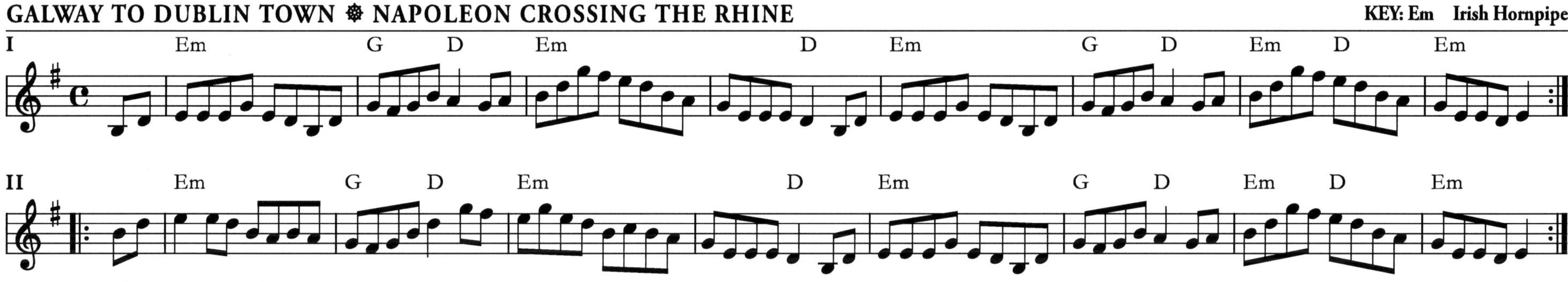

SOURCE: Johnny Cronin and Joe Burke

Fisher's Hornpipe *is played, under various titles, in the keys Of C, D, F and G.*
The G setting, **The Blacksmith's Hornpipe,** *is not provided in this book*

FISHER'S HORNPIPE—C ❁ THE BLACKSMITH'S HORNPIPE ❁ DURANG'S HORNPIPE ❁ FISCHER'S HORNPIPE ❁ FISHERMAN'S HORNPIPE ❁ LORD HOWE'S HORNPIPE ❁ SAILOR'S HORNPIPE ❁ WIGS ON THE GREEN ❁ BLANCHARD'S HORNPIPE ❁ CHINA ORANGE HORNPIPE ❁ EGG HORNPIPE ❁ THE FISHER'S ❁ FISHERMAN'S LILT ❁ THE FIRST OF MAY ❁ KELLY'S HORNPIPE ❁ O'DWYER'S HORNPIPE ❁ PECKHOVER WALK HORNPIPE ❁ REEL BOIVIN ❁ WEST'S HORNPIPE ❁ THE FISHER ❁ THE THRESHER

Old-Time/Bluegrass

THIRD PART IS IN BLUEGRASS VERSION ONLY

FISHER'S HORNPIPE—D ❁ SEE ALTERNATE TITLES ABOVE

Old-Time/Bluegrass

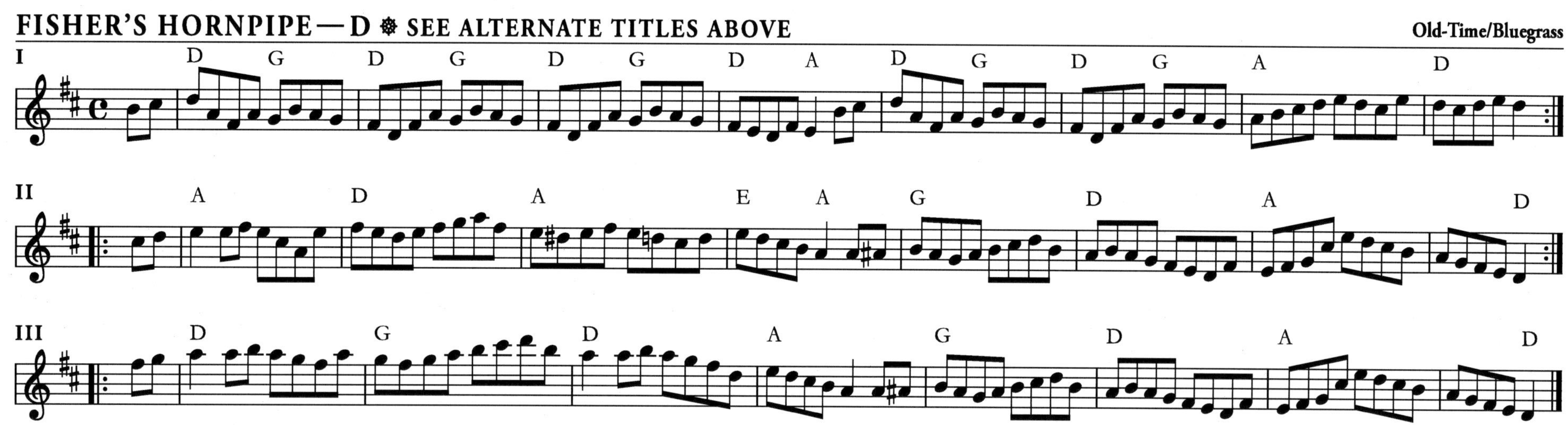

THIRD PART IS IN BLUEGRASS VERSION ONLY

FISHER'S HORNPIPE—F ❁ SEE ALTERNATE TITLES ABOVE

Old-Time

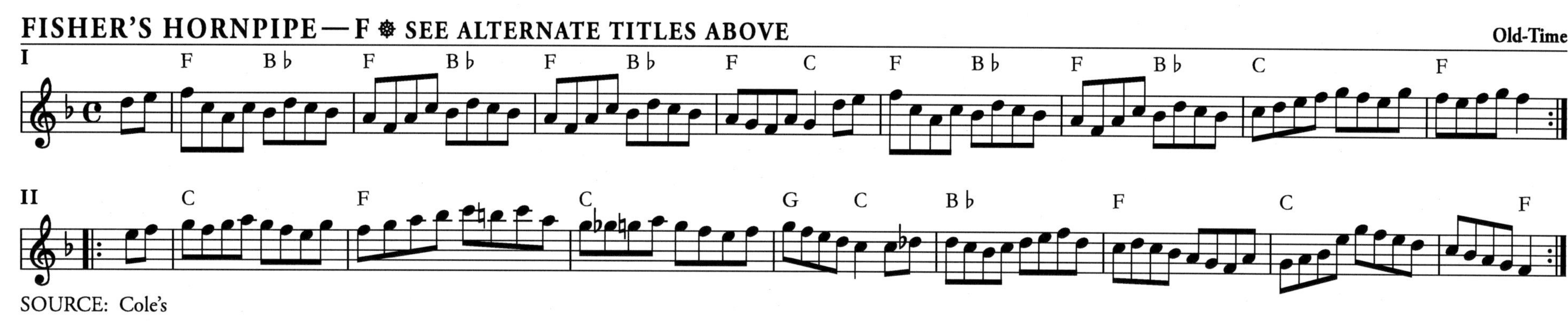

SOURCE: Cole's

FISHER'S HORNPIPE—G ❁ SEE ALTERNATE TITLES ABOVE

Old-Time

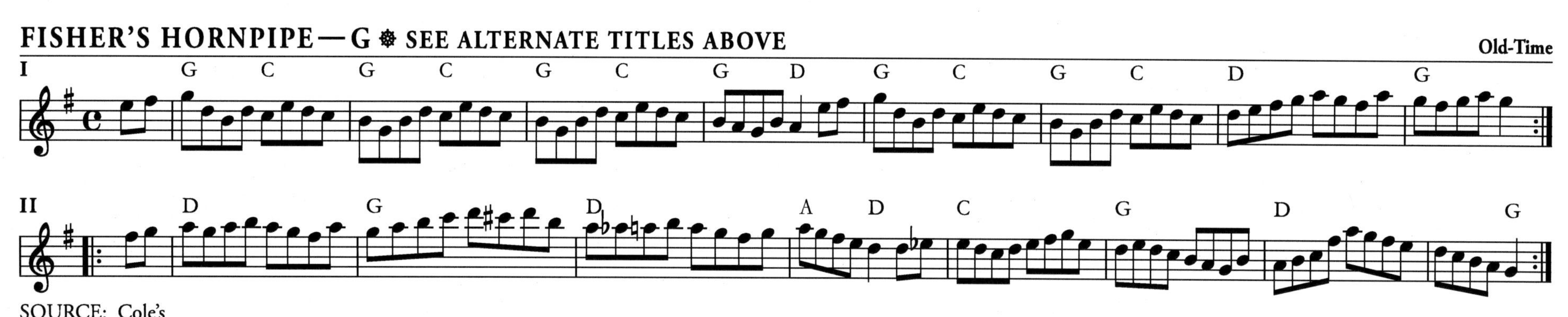

SOURCE: Cole's

FLIES IN THE BUTTERMILK ☸ SHOO FLY SHOO

KEY: G/D Texas

SOURCE: Bill Reser

FLOP-EARED MULE ☸ THE LONG-EARED MULE ☸ WHOA MULE ☸ ASHEVILLE ☸ BIGEARED MULE ☸ THE BLUEBELL POLKA ☸ COLLEGE SCHOTTISCHE ☸ COMIN' OVER THE MOUNTAIN ☸ D–A QUADRILLE ☸ D AND A SCHOTTISHE ☸ GRAPEVINE TWIST ☸ HELL AMONGST THE SLAVISH ☸ HELL OVER THE MOUNTAIN ☸ KARO ☸ LOP-EARED MULE ☸ MIKE AND CHARLIE ☸ MONKEY IN THE BARBERSHOP ☸ PEACH TREE LIMB ☸ RANGER'S HORNPIPE ☸ WILD GEESE

KEY: G/D Old-Time

FLOP-EARED MULE ☸ SEE ALTERNATE TITLES ABOVE

KEY: D/A Old-Time

THE FLOWERS OF EDINBURGH ❁ LA RONFLEUSE DE MME GOBEIL ❁ THE SNORING OF MRS GOBEIL ❁ BESIDE A RATH ❁ EARL OF HOPETOWN'S REEL ❁ FLOWERS OF DONNYBROOK ❁ MY LOVE'S BONNY WHEN SHE SMILES ON ME ❁ MY LOVE WAS ONCE A BONNIE LAD ❁ OLD VIRGINIA REEL ❁ CUSH LASSO ❁ COIS LEASA ❁ REEL DU PERE NOEL ❁ THE FLOURS OF EDINBURGH ❁ KNUCKLE DOWN ❁ TO THE BATTLE MEN OF ERIN ❁ THE WEOBLEY HANKIE DANCE ❁ THE WEOBLEY HANKY DANCE

KEY: G Scottish/Northern

THE FLOWING TIDE—G (Irish Hornpipe) ❁ PICNIC REEL—A (Northern Reel) ❁ HIGGIN'S BEST ❁ SEVENTH REGIMENT ❁ ANNE SHEEHY'S ❁ BIRMINGHAM ❁ BUNCH OF FERNS ❁ BURKE'S HORNPIPE ❁ THE SHYAN

KEY: G

I
G C G C D G C G C D G

II
G C G C D G C G C D G

KEY: A

THE FLY BY NIGHT HORNPIPE ☸ THE FLY IN THE NIGHT HORNPIPE ☸ ARTHUR'S SEAT ☸ ARTHUR'S SET ☸ FLY BY NIGHT #2 ☸ THE FLY BY NIGHT ☸ LOUIS QUINN'S ☸ THE LOW LEVEL

KEY: A Irish

I
A
E
A
D
E
A
II
A
E
A
D
E
A

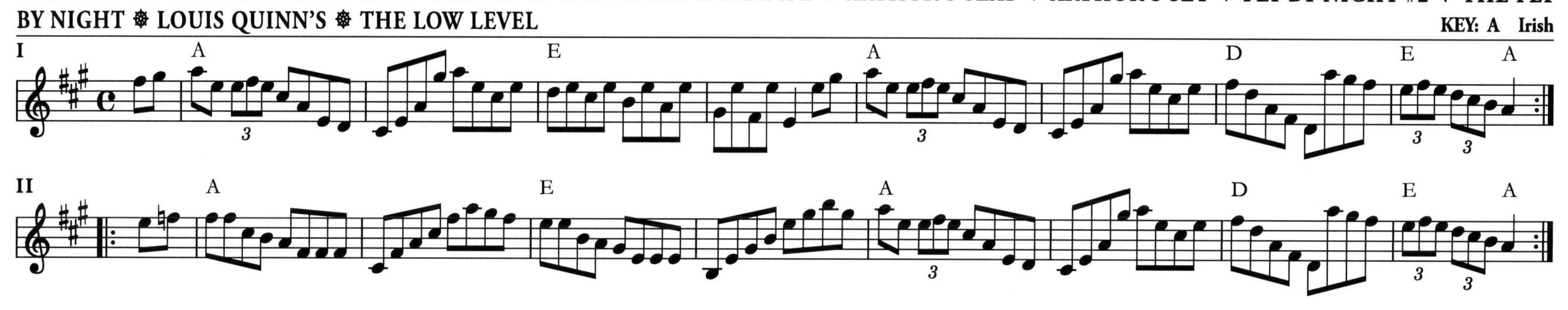

FLYING CLOUD ☸ FLYING CLOUD COTILLION ☸ FLYING CLOUDS

KEY: G/D Old-Time

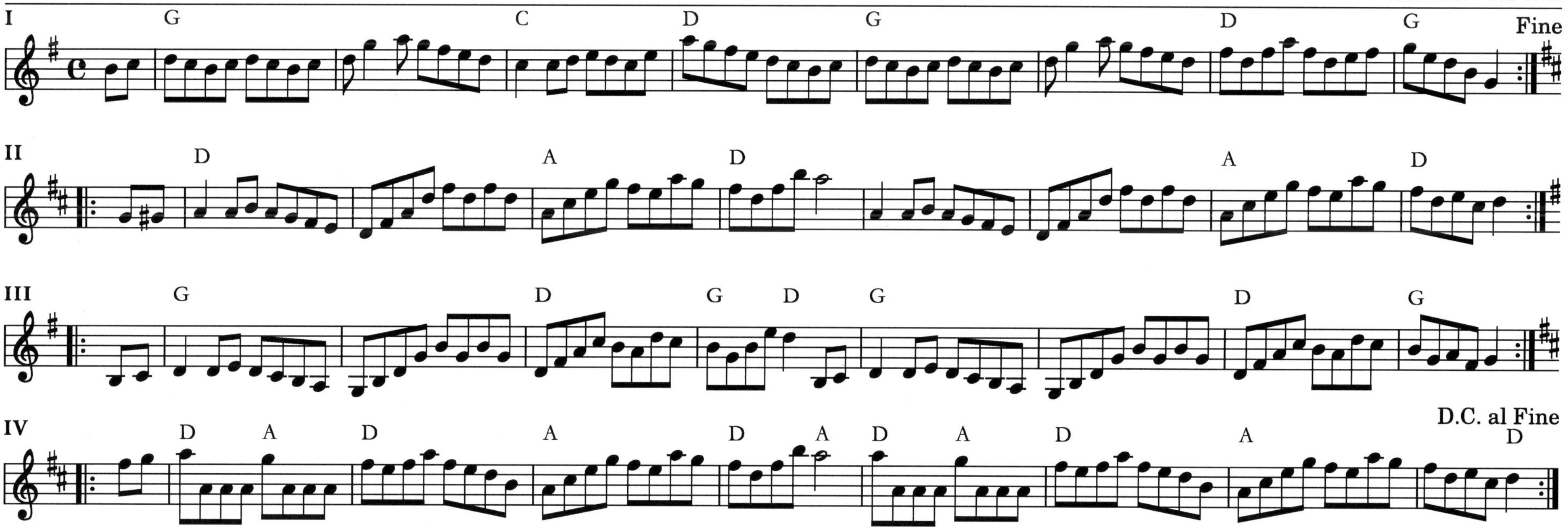

I
G
C
D
G
D
G
Fine
II
D
A
D
A
D
III
G
D
G D
G
D
G
IV
D A
D
A
D A
D A
D
A
D.C. al Fine
D

FORESTER'S HORNPIPE ❁ GREENFIELDS ❁ IKE FORRESTER'S REEL

KEY: D Northern

SOURCE: Joe Robertson/Cole's

FORKED DEER ❁ FORKED BUCK ❁ FORKY DEER ❁ BRAGG'S RETREAT ❁ DEER WALK ❁ FORKED-HORN DEER ❁ FORKED DEER HORNPIPE ❁ FORKED DEER RIVER ❁ HOUNDS IN THE HORN ❁ LONG-HORNED DEER ❁ OLD PORK BOSOM ❁ VAN BUREN

KEY: D Southern

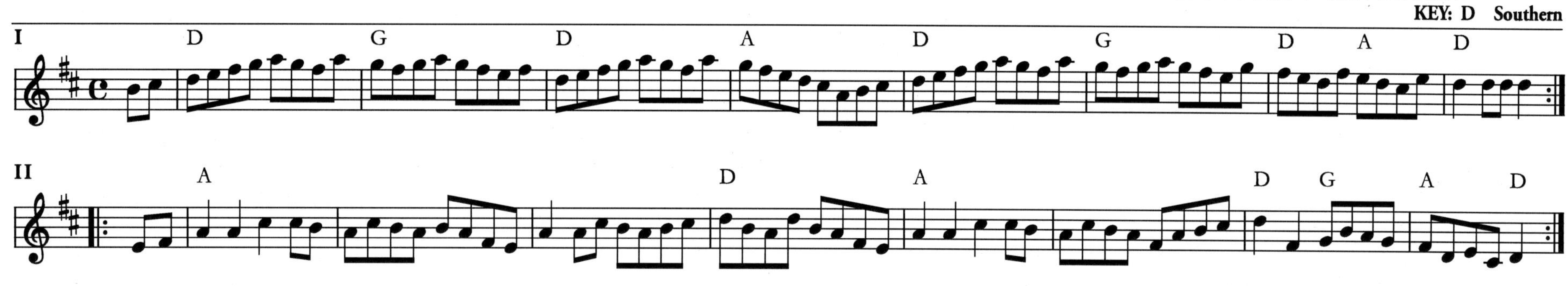

FORT SMITH ❁ ON THE BANKS OF THE CANE ❁ RABBIT IN THE GRASS ❁ OLD FORT SMITH

KEY: G Texas

FORTUNE ❁ ONCE I HAD A FORTUNE

KEY: D Old-Time

FOX-HUNTER'S SLIP-JIG—D ❁ THE FOXHUNT ❁ THE FOX HUNTER'S

Irish

SOURCE: Reg Hill

THE FOX-HUNTER'S SLIP-JIG—G ❁ THE HUMOURS OF DERRYCROSANE—A ❁ HUMORS OF DERRYKISSANE ❁ THE FOXHUNTER'S JIG ❁ HUMORS OF DERRYKROSANE

KEY: G Irish

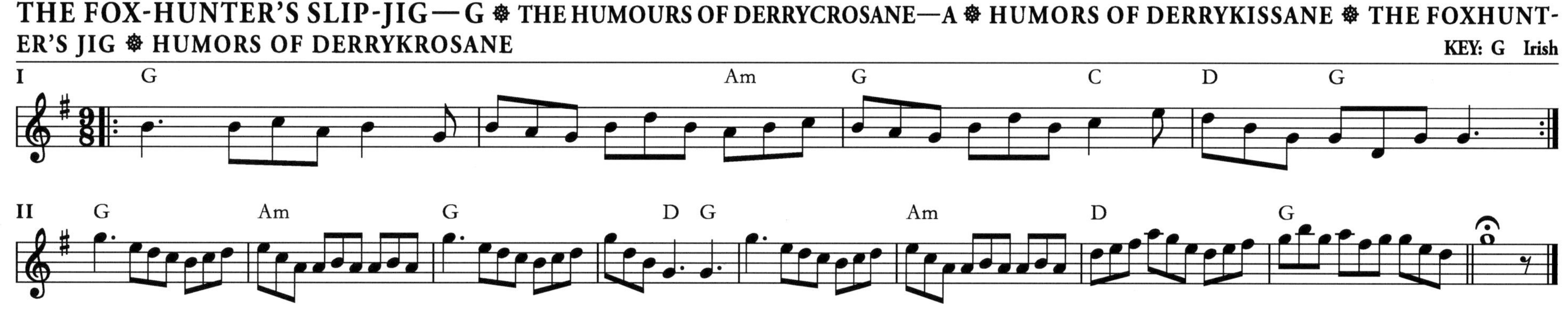

SOURCE: Joseph Robichaud

FRED WILSON'S CLOG
cf BILLY WILSON'S CLOG et al, CINCINNATI HORNPIPE & HARVEST HOME
KEY: F Northern
SOURCE: Cole's
FRENCH MARY ❁ THE BANKS OF THE TOBIQUE ❁ THE MOUTH OF THE TOBIQUE
KEY: G Northern
SOURCE: Clarence Langen
FULL-RIGGED SHIP ❁ DA FULL RIGGED SHIP ❁ NEW RIGGED SHIP
KEY: A/D Scottish Jig
SOURCE: The Boys of the Lough
SEQUENCE IS SOMETIMES II, III, I

GALWAY HORNPIPE ❁ THE BALDHEADED BACHELOR ❁ DAN LOWRY'S ❁ McDERMOTT'S HORNPIPE ❁ McDERMOT'S No 2 ❁ McDANAUGH'S CLOG ❁ McDONOUGH'S CLOG
KEY: D Irish
GARY OWEN ❁ GARRYOWEN ❁ THE FIELDTOWN ❁ GARYOWEN ❁ WALK OF THE TWOPENNY POSTMAN
KEY: G Old-Time Jig
GASPÉ REEL ❁ APEX REEL ❁ REEL DE GASPÉ
KEY: D Northern
THIRD PART IS OPTIONAL. IF IT IS PLAYED, TUNE ENDS AFTER FIRST PART

GEESE IN THE BOG ❁ THE HOUSEMAID ❁ SADDLE THE PONY ❁ JACKSON'S WALK TO LIMERICK ❁ THE PIPER'S FROLIC ❁ THE CORAVAT JIG ❁ TWICE TRICKED ❁ THE MOUNTAIN LARK ❁ JACKSON'S COOLA

cf LARK IN THE MORNING(D) *et al* & LARK'S MARCH *et al*

KEY: D   Irish Jig

GEORGIA

KEY: D Bluegrass/Old-Time

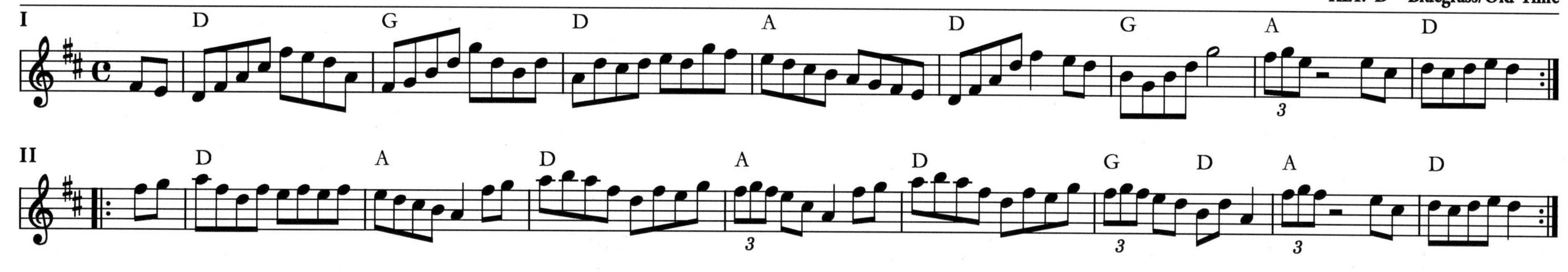

GEORGIA ROW ☸ COON DOG ☸ WALKING DOWN THE GEORGIA ROAD ☸ WALKING UP GEORGIA ROW

KEY: G Old-Time

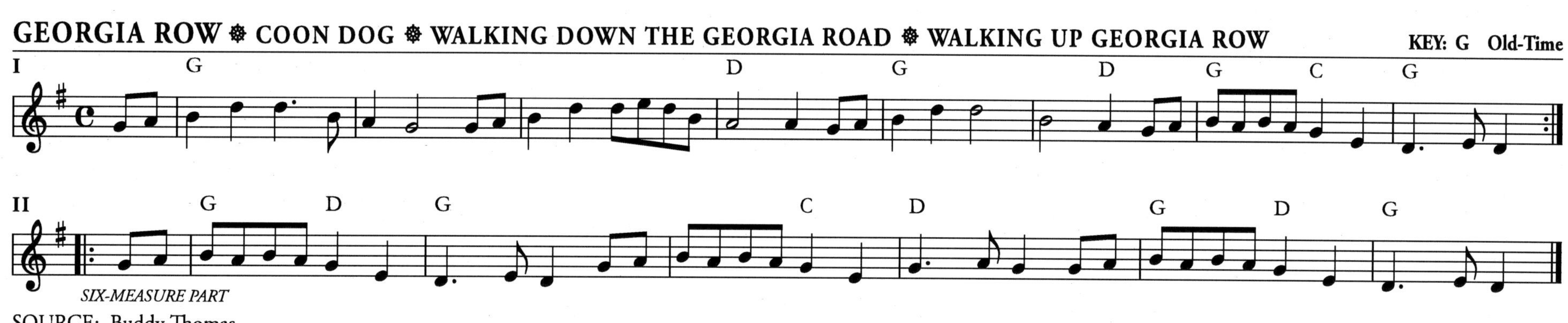

SOURCE: Buddy Thomas

KEY: A Old-Time

SOURCE: Buddy Thomas

THE GIRL I LEFT BEHIND ME ☸ BRIGHTON CAMP ☸ THE GAL I LEFT BEHIND ME ☸ AS SLOW OUR SHIP ☸ JOHNNY GOODWIN ☸ PRETTY LITTLE GIRL ☸ THE PRETTY LITTLE GIRL I LEFT BEHIND ME ☸ THE RAMBLING LABORER ☸ THE WANDERING HARVEST LABORER ☸ THE BRIDE IN CAMP ☸ BUY ME A BANANA ☸ THE GIRL THAT I LEFT BEHIND ME MARCH ☸ MAMMA WILL YOU BUY ME A BANANA ☸ THE SHIRT I LEFT BEHIND ME ☸ THE SPALPEEN FANACH

cf WAXIES DARGLE

GLOBE HORNPIPE

GLOBETROTTER'S JIG

SOURCE: Joe Pancerzewski

GOIN' DOWN TO CAIRO ❁ BLACK THEM BOOTS ❁ CAIRO ❁ GOODBYE LIZA JANE

THE GOLDEN EAGLE HORNPIPE ❁ GOLDEN EAGLE

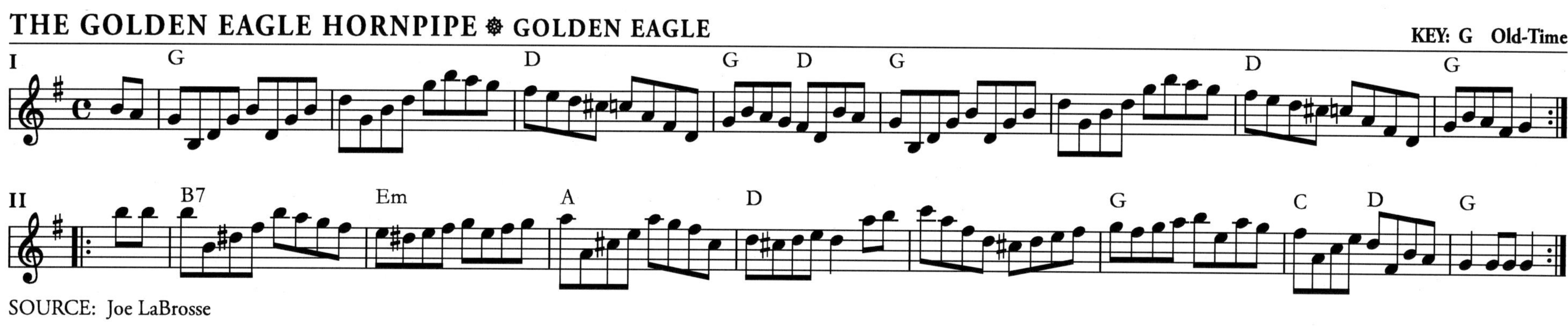

SOURCE: Joe LaBrosse

THE GOLDEN KEYBOARD ❁ GREEN'S REEL ❁ JOE COOLEY'S REEL ❁ McGANN'S ❁ MULHAIRE'S REEL ❁ REYNOLD'S REEL ❁ THE GOLDEN HEADBOARD

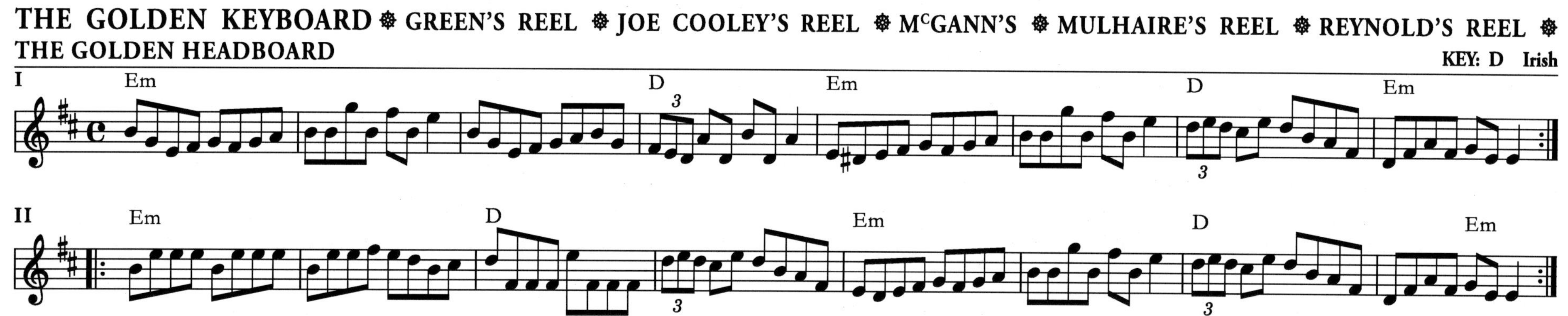

GOLDEN WEDDING HORNPIPE ✵ GOLDEN WEDDING

KEY: D Old-Time

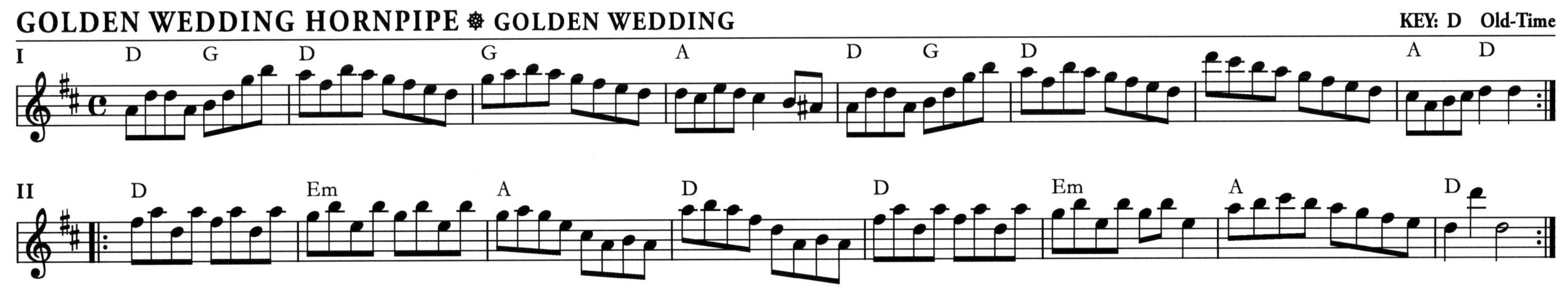

THE GOLDEN WEDDING REEL ✵ FARMER'S REEL ✵ RICHIBUCTO REEL

KEY: G Old-Time

THE GOLD RING
KEY: Am/G Irish Jig
I
Am G Am D Am C D Am G
II
Am G Am D Am C D Am G
III
G D G D G
IV
G D G D G D G D G D G
V
G D G D G
SOURCE: The Boys of the Lough
GOOD ALE SLIP-JIG
KEY: C Irish
I
C G C G C G F G C G C G C G F G C
II
C F C G C G C G C G F G C
III
C F C G C F E Am C F C G C F E Am C
SOURCE: Libby Larsen

GOOD FOR THE TONGUE ❅ GOOD ON THE TONGUE ❅ BLUESKIN'S HORNPIPE ❅ CLOG DOUBLE ❅ JENKINS' HORNPIPE ❅ WASHINGTON HORNPIPE

KEY: G Irish

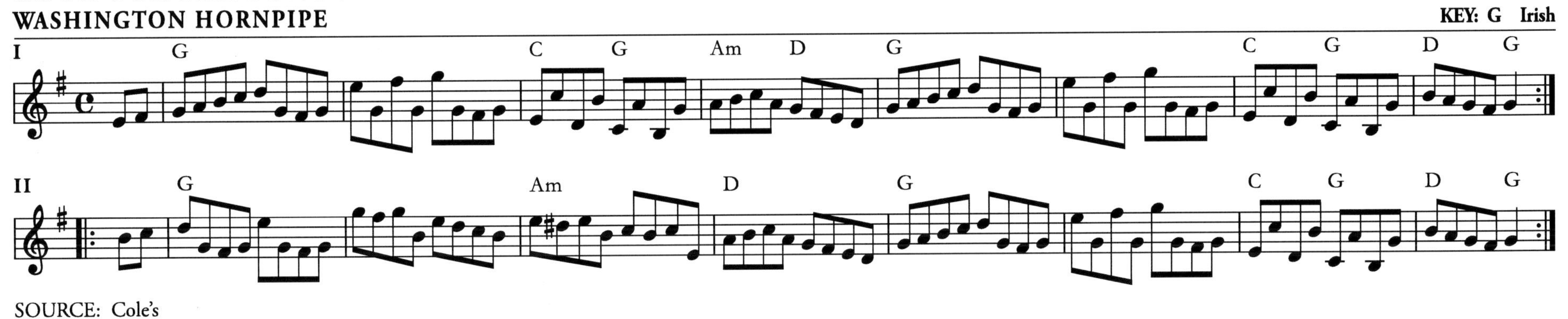

SOURCE: Cole's

GOOSEFEATHERS

KEY: G/D Old-Time Jig

SOURCE: Melody Morin

THE GRAEMSEY JIG

KEY: D Scottish

GRANDFATHER'S REEL

KEY: C/G Northern

SOURCE: Winston Scotty Fitzgerald

GRANT LAMB'S BREAKDOWN

KEY: C Northern

SOURCE: Buddy Thomas

THE GREEN BANKS OF ROSSBEIGH ❁ THE GREEN FIELDS OF ROSSBEIGH ❁ THE KERRY REEL ❁ THE WITCH OF THE GLEN ❁ THE GREEN BANKS OF ROS BEIGH ❁ THE GREENFIELDS OF ROSSBAE ❁ THE KERRY LASSES ❁ THE KERRY RING ❁ THE KERRY ❁ THE KERRYMAN ❁ TOM CLARK'S FANCY ❁ TOM CLARKE'S

KEY: Em Irish

THE GREEN FIELDS OF AMERICA ❁ GREENFIELDS OF AMERICA ❁ GREENFIELDS OF VIRGINIA ❁ GREENFIELDS OF CANADA ❁ MISS WEDDERBURN'S REEL ❁ COSSEY'S JIG ❁ JIMMY O'BRIEN'S JIG

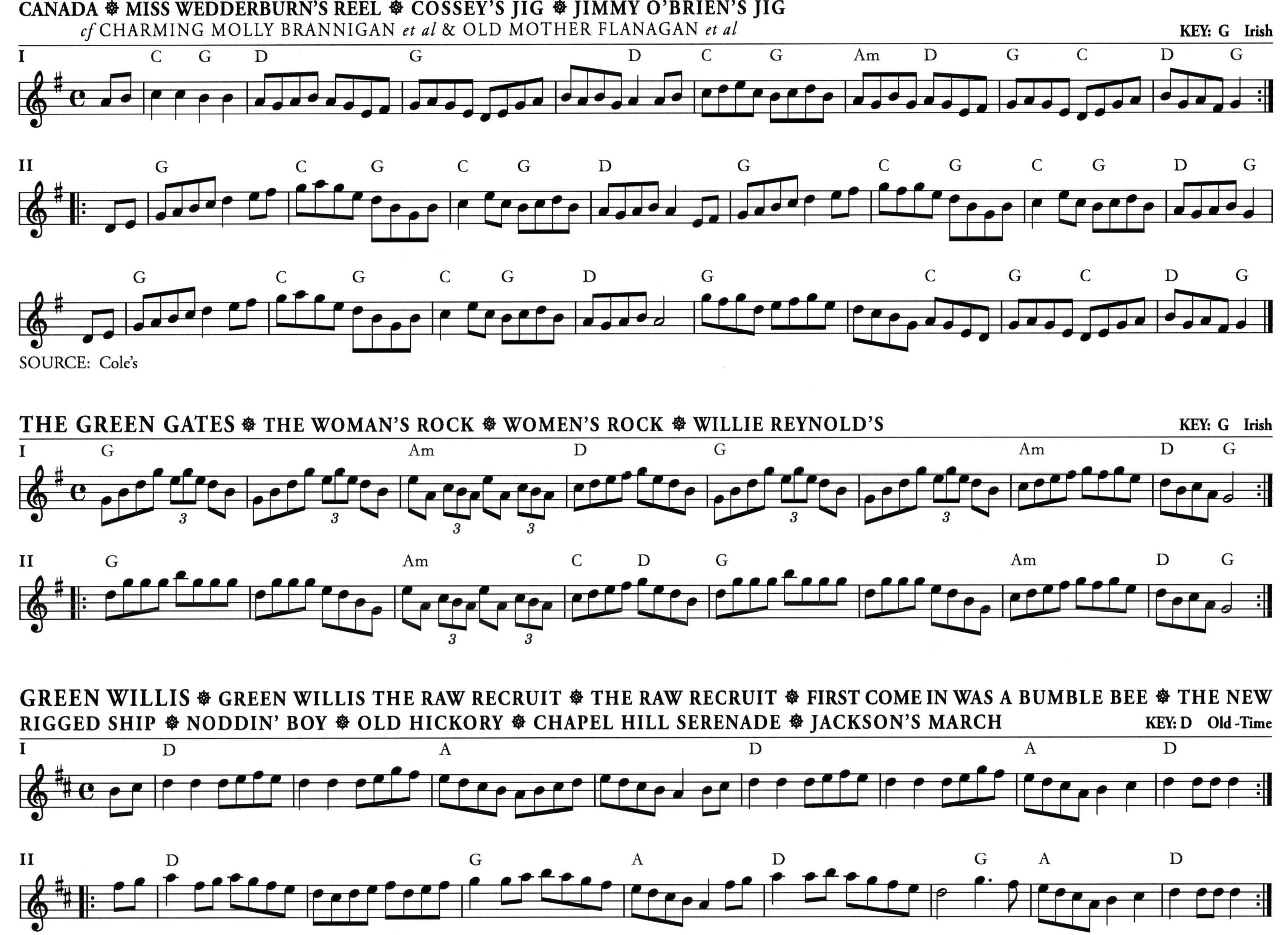

GREY EAGLE ❁ GRAY EAGLE ❁ THE GREY EAGLE HORNPIPE

KEY: A   Bluegrass/Texas

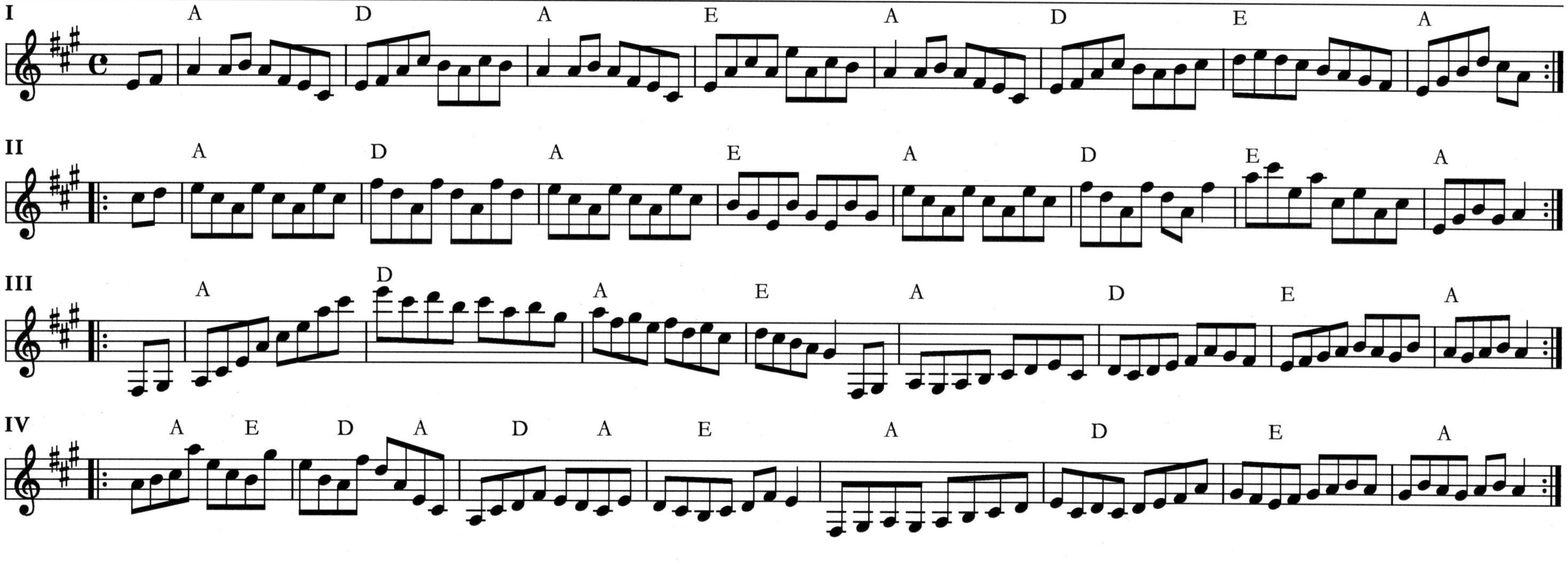

I
A D A E A D E A
II
A D A E A D E A
III
A D A E A D E A
IV
A E D A D A E A D E A

GRIFFIN HORNPIPE ❁ THE GRIFFIN ❁ GRIFFIN'S HORNPIPE

KEY: D   Northern

I
D A D A D A D A D
II
A G D A D A D A D

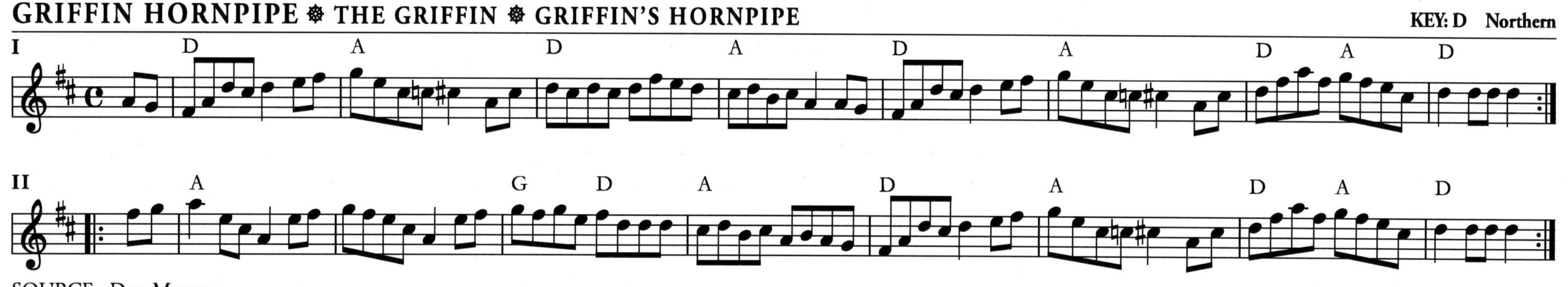

SOURCE: Don Messer

THE GROVE

KEY: C Old-Time

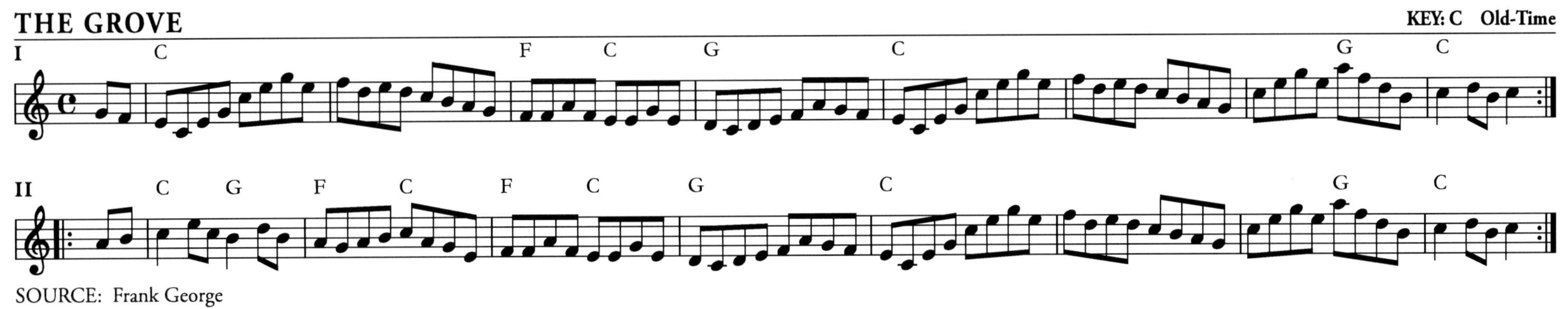

SOURCE: Frank George

GROWLING OLD MAN AND CACKLING OLD WOMAN ❁ GROWLING OLD MAN AND OLD WOMAN ❁ GROWLING OLD MAN, GROWLING OLD WOMAN ❁ GRUMBLING OLD MAN AND GROWLING OLD WOMAN ❁ THE OLD MAN AND THE OLD WOMAN ❁ GROWLING OLD MAN AND WOMAN ❁ LA MARMOTTEUSE ❁ LA CHICANEUSE ❁ THE DISPUTANT ❁ LA DISPUTEUSE ❁ REEL DE LA MI-CAREME ❁ LE BONHOMME ET LA BONNE FEMME ❁ LE VIELLARD ET LA VIELLE DAME

KEY: A/Am Northern

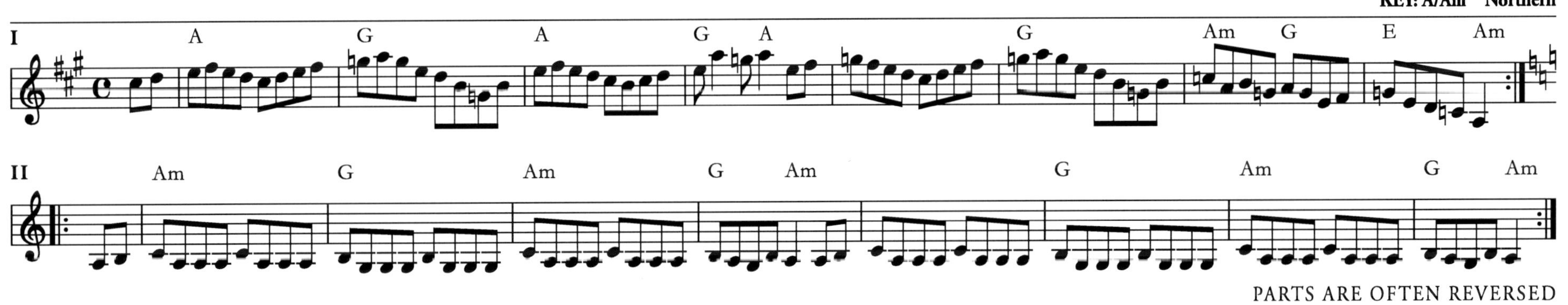

PARTS ARE OFTEN REVERSED

HAMILTON COUNTY ❁ GEORGIA SHUFFLE

KEY: G Bluegrass/Old-Time

HARVEST HOME

cf BILLY WILSON'S CLOG *et al*, CINCINNATI HORNPIPE & FRED WILSON'S CLOG

KEY: D **Irish/Old-Time**

HASTE TO THE WEDDING ❁ COME HASTE TO THE WEDDING ❁ JOHNNY, OH JOHNNY ❁ O! HASTE TO THE WEDDING ❁ PERRY'S VICTORY ❁ RURAL FELICITY ❁ SICILIAN CIRCLE ❁ FOOTPRINTS ❁ GRANNY PLAYS THE FIDDLE ❁ LET BRAINSPINNING SWAINS ❁ THE LONG EIGHT ❁ SMALL PIN CUSHION ❁ CAPE BRETON'S ❁ FAST TRIP TO RENO ❁ GIGUE DES PETITS MOUTONS ❁ HASTE TO THE SOU'WEST ❁ HASTE TO THE WEST ❁ HASTE YE TAE THE WEDDING ❁ HASTEN TO THE WEDDING ❁ MARY, CUT YOUR TOENAILS YOU'RE TEARING ALL THE SHEETS ❁ QUICK TRIP TO RENO ❁ THUROT

KEY: D **Irish/Old-Time Jig**

HAULING HOME ❁ KITTY'S WEDDING ❁ SMITH'S DELIGHT ❁ MRS SMITH'S REEL ❁ THE GOLDEN WEDDING ❁ THE IDEAL ❁ KITTY'S GERMAN ❁ OLD SMITH'S ❁ SHIPS IN FULL SAIL ❁ SMITH'S ❁ SMITH'S REEL

cf BELLE OF LEXINGTON *et al*

KEY: D **Irish Hornpipe**

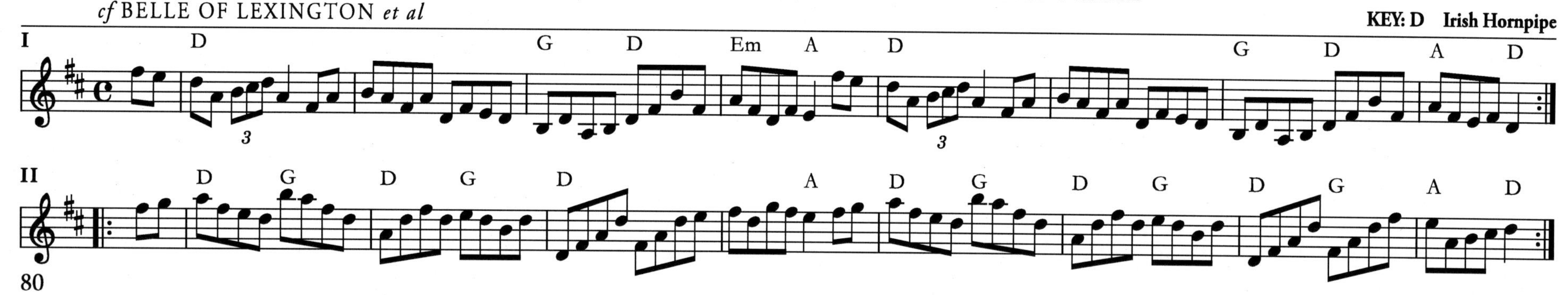

THE HAWK ❁ THE HAWK HORNPIPE ❁ BELLS OF ST LOUIS

SOURCE: The High Level Ranters

THE HAWK ❁ THE HAWK HORNPIPE ❁ BELLS OF ST LOUIS

SOURCE: The High Level Ranters

THE HEADLIGHT REEL

KEY: D Northern

SOURCE: Cole's/Reg Hill

HELL BROKE LOOSE IN GEORGIA ❅ POSSUM UP A GUM STUMP ❅ THERE'S NO HELL IN GEORGIA ❅ HELL BOUND FOR ALABAMA ❅ BEEN TO THE EAST BEEN TO THE WEST ❅ GREAT BIG YAM POTATOES ❅ STREAK OF LEAN STREAK OF FAT ❅ HELLBOUND FOR ALABAMA

KEY: C Southern

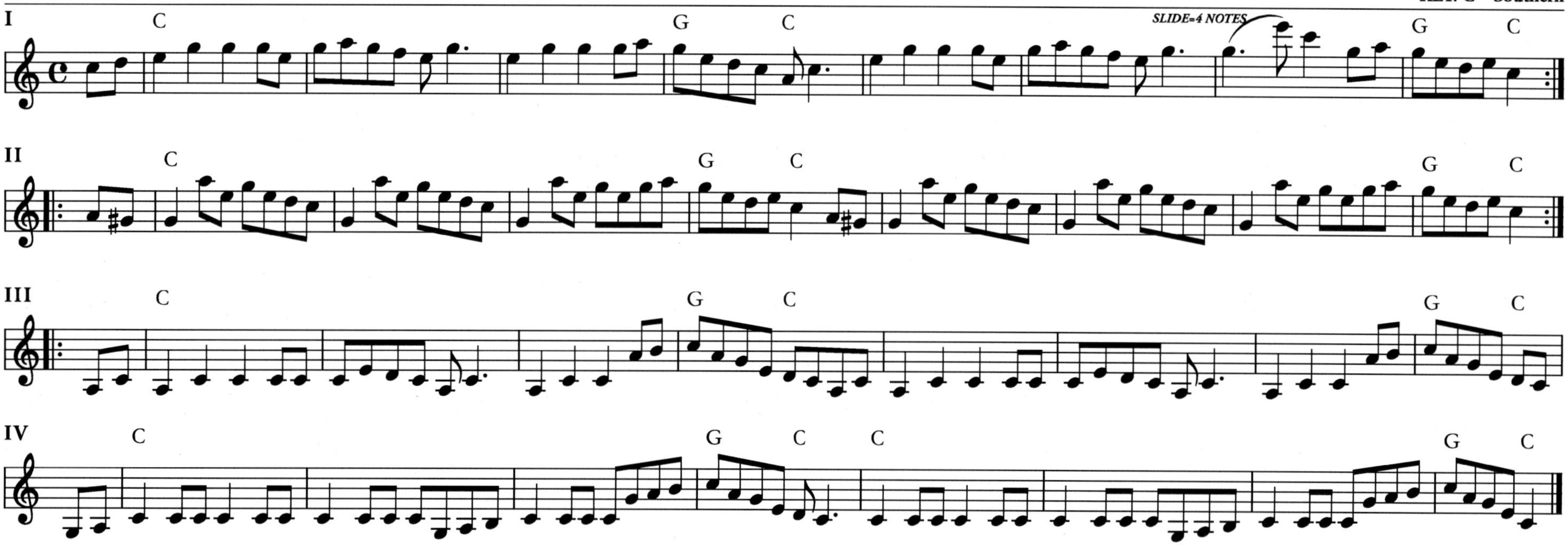

I
C G C
SLIDE=4 NOTES
G C
II
C G C G C
III
C G C G C
IV
C G C C G C

SOURCE: Gid Tanner

THE HELSEYSIDE REEL

KEY: F English

I
F C F C F A F B♭ C F
II
B♭ F B♭ F C F C F B♭ C F

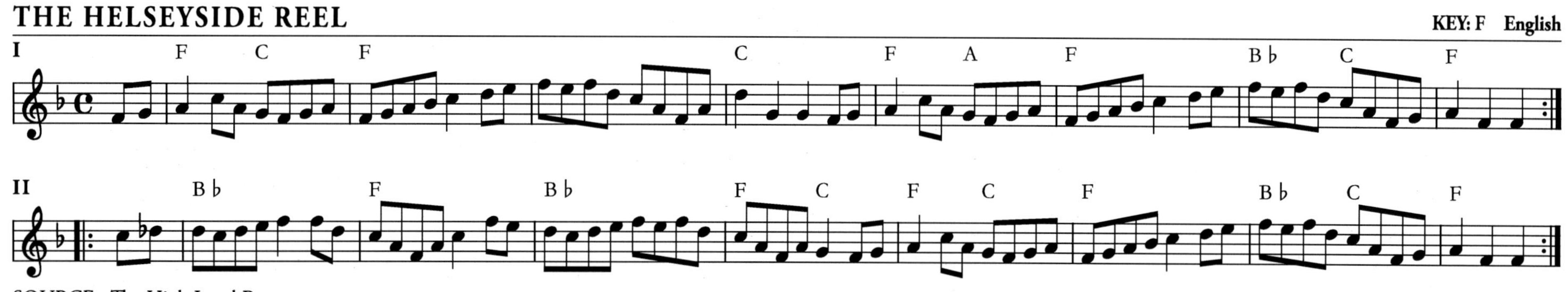

SOURCE: The High Level Ranters

HERE AND THERE

KEY: G Old-Time

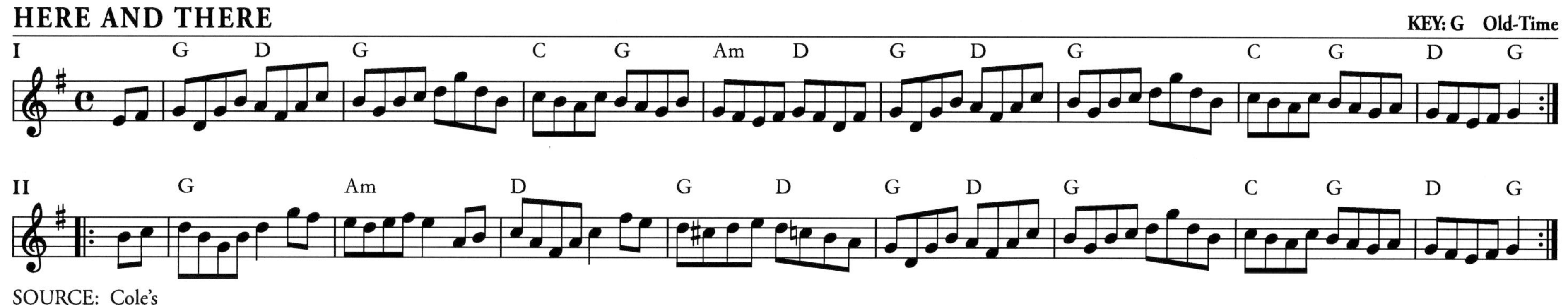

SOURCE: Cole's

HERE AND THERE

KEY: A Old-Time

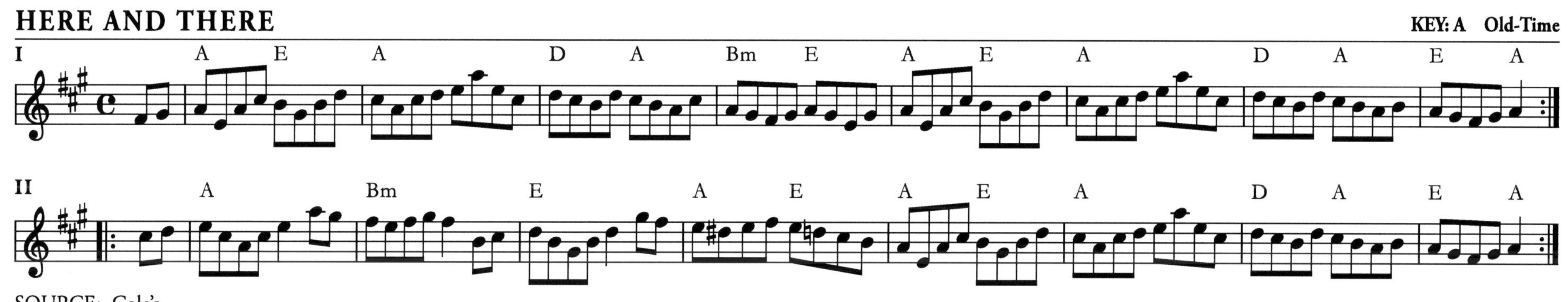

SOURCE: Cole's

HIBERNIAN REEL ☸ HIBERNIA'S PRIDE ☸ FLANNEL JACKET ☸ NEW POLICEMAN ☸ PEELER'S JACKET ☸ THE PEELER'S CAP

KEY: G Northern/Irish

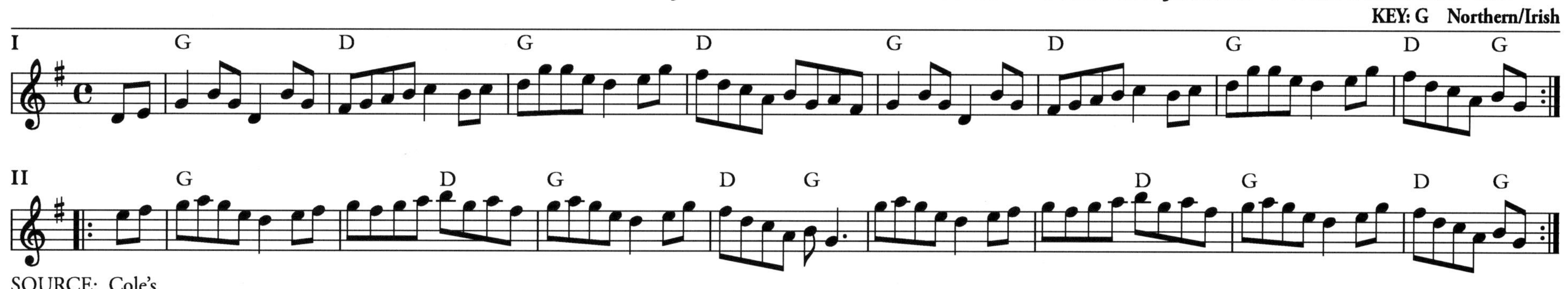

SOURCE: Cole's

HIGH LEVEL HORNPIPE ❁ VELOCIPEDE ❁ BEST SHOT ❁ FLY BY NIGHT ❁ HIGHLAND HORNPIPE ❁ LOUIS QUINN'S ❁ HIGH LEVEL BRIDGE HORNPIPE

KEY: B♭ Old-Time

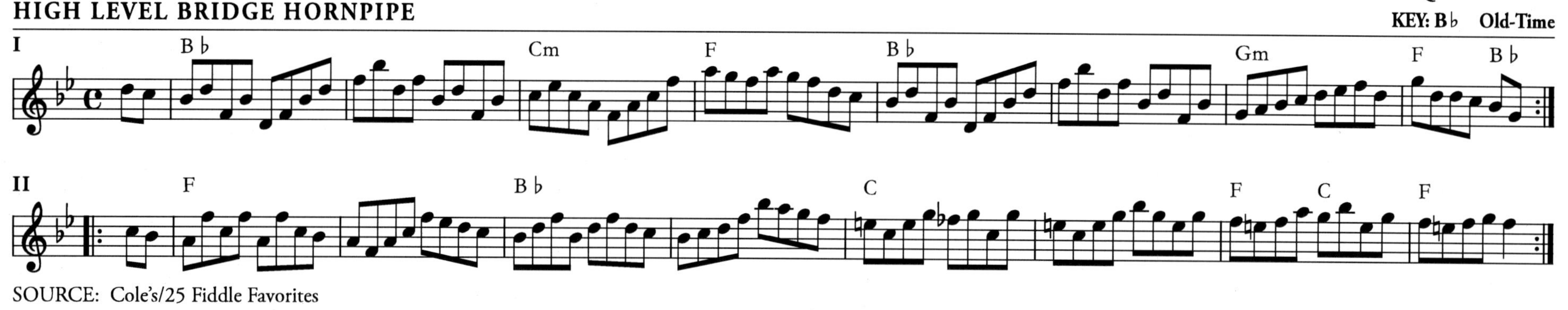

SOURCE: Cole's/25 Fiddle Favorites

HIGH YELLOW

KEY: C Southern

HOBBS' FAVORITE ❁ BOSTON RATTLERS ❁ COLONEL M^cBAIN'S ❁ CONNEMARA STOCKINGS ❁ WINTER APPLES

KEY: C Northern

SOURCE: Cole's

HOBBS' FAVORITE ❁ BOSTON RATTLERS ❁ COLONEL M^C^BAIN'S ❁ CONNEMARA STOCKINGS ❁ WINTER APPLES

KEY: D Northern

I
D Em D A D Em D A D

II
Bm A Bm A Bm A D G A D

SOURCE: Cole's

HOG TROUGH REEL ❁ M^C^MICHEN'S REEL ❁ M^C^MITCHEN'S REEL

KEY: G Bluegrass/Old-Time

SOURCE: Buck Ryan

HOLLOW POPLAR ❁ HOLLOW POPLAR LOG ❁ OLD HOLLOW POPLAR

KEY: G Southern

SOURCE: Cyril Stinnett

PART ORDER: 12134

HOOKER'S HORNPIPE
KEY: G Old-Time
I
G D G C G D G
II
G C G D G C D G
SOURCE: Cyril Stinnett
HORSE'S LEOTARD ☸ MY BROTHER TOM ☸ THE STEPPING STONES
KEY: Em Irish Jig
I
Em D Em D Em D Em D
II
Em D Em G D Em D Em D
Em D Em G D G D Em D Em
HULL'S VICTORY—D
Old-Time
I
D A D A E A
II
D G E A D A D A D

HULL'S VICTORY—F

Old-Time

I
F C F C G C
II
F B♭ G C F C F C F

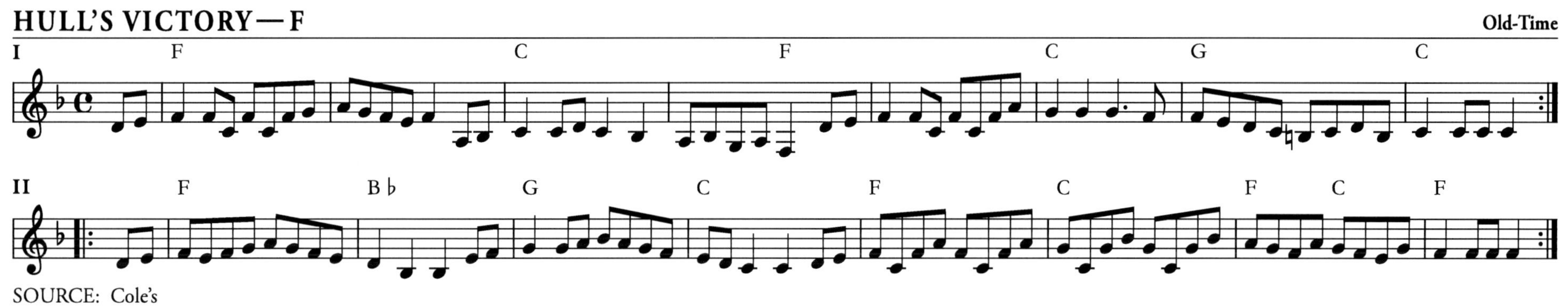

SOURCE: Cole's

HUMORS OF BALLYLOUGHLIN ❁ THE HURLER'S MARCH ❁ FAIRY HURLERS ❁ THE HUMOURS OF DERRYLOUGHLAN

KEY: Am/D Irish Jig

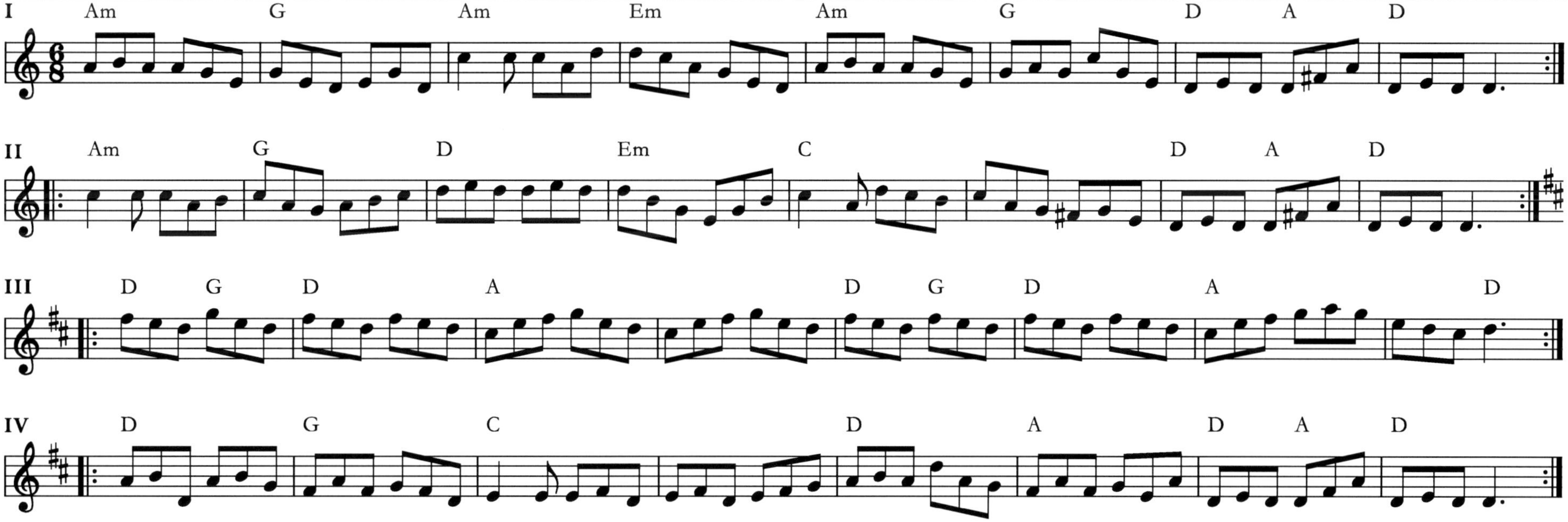

I
Am G Am Em Am G D A D
II
Am G D Em C D A D
III
D G D A D G D A D
IV
D G C D A D A D

SOURCE: Kathleen Collins

HUMORS OF KILKENNY

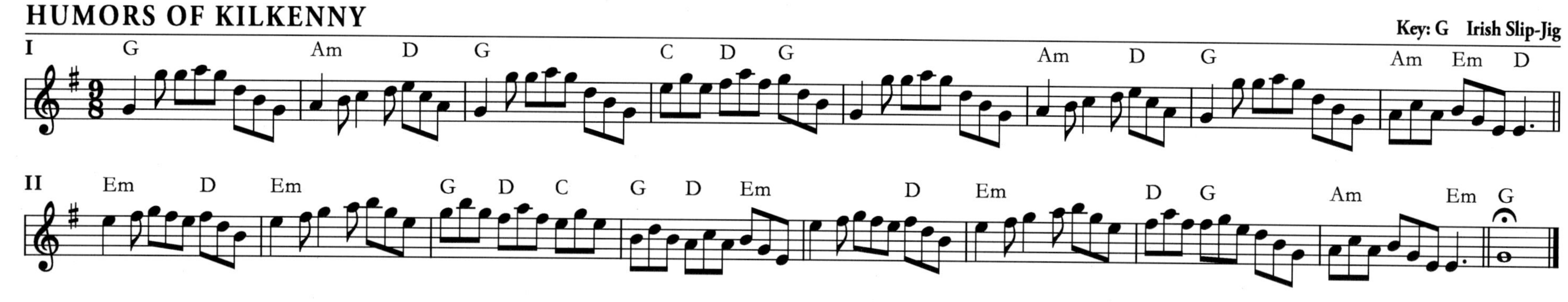

HUMOURS OF WHISKEY ❁ THE BRIDGE OF ATHLONE ❁ CROSSROADS FROLIC ❁ DEEL OF THE DANCE ❁ DEVER THE DANCER ❁ DILLON'S FANCY ❁ HUMORS OF DERRY ❁ THE PEELER'S RETURN ❁ THE POLICEMAN'S RETURN ❁ HUMORS OF WHISKEY ❁ SALLY HEGERTY'S ❁ THE SILVERMORE

HUNDRED PIPERS ❁ SOUTHPORT MORRIS AND MAYPOLE TUNE ❁ THE HAIR FELL OFFMY COCONUT ❁ I'LL EAT NO MORE OF YOUR BARLEY BREAD ❁ MARCH OF THE 49TH FIELD ARTILLERY ❁ THE REGIMENTAL MARCH OF THE WEST KENTS

SOURCE: Conrad Brierre

HUNDRED PIPERS ✵ SOUTHPORT MORRIS AND MAYPOLE TUNE ✵ THE HAIR FELL OFF MY COCONUT ✵ I'LL EAT NO MORE OF YOUR BARLEY BREAD ✵ MARCH OF THE 49TH FIELD ARTILLERY ✵ THE REGIMENTAL MARCH OF THE WEST KENTS

Key: A Northern Jig

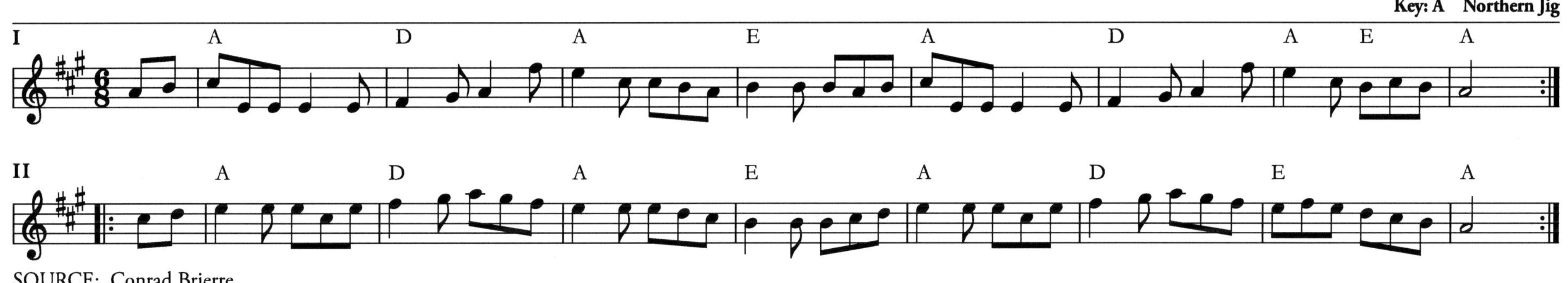

SOURCE: Conrad Brierre

THE HUNTER'S PURSE ✵ THE FIVE-LEAVED CLOVER ✵ THE HAYMAKER ✵ HEEL OF THE HUNT ✵ THE OLD BUSH ✵ FIVE LEAF CLOVER ✵ THE HAWTHORN ✵ INDIAN ON THE ROCK ✵ THE THORNBUSH ✵ MY LOVE IS BUT A LASSIE YET

Key: A Irish

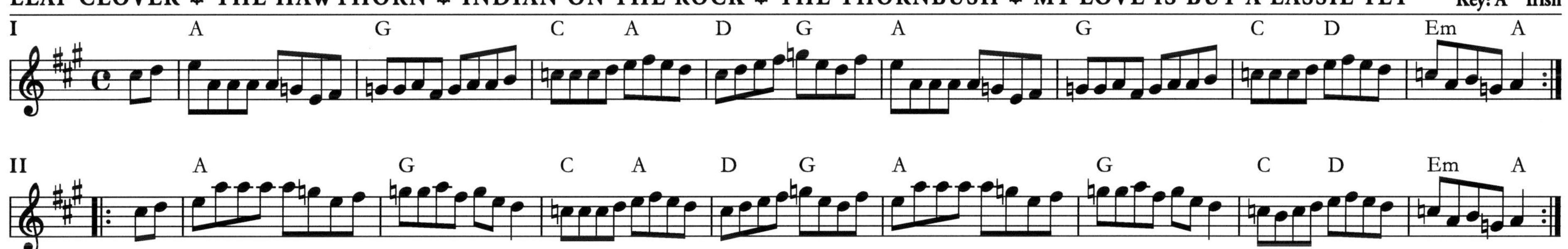

HUNTSMAN'S CHORUS ✵ BUTTERCUPS AND DAISIES

Key: D Old-Time

SOURCE: Bill Spence

ICE ON THE ROAD

Key: Em/G Old-Time

I DON'T LOVE NOBODY ❁ I DON'T WANT TO GET MARRIED ❁ I LOVE A NOBODY

Key: C Old-Time

THE IRISH WASHERWOMAN ❁ THE BIG JIG ❁ HASTE TO THE WEDDING ❁ THE IRISHWOMAN ❁ JACKSON'S DELIGHT ❁ THE WASHERWOMAN ❁ THE WASHING WOMAN ❁ THE WASH WOMAN ❁ CORPORAL CASEY ❁ THE COUNTY COURTSHIP ❁ DARGASON ❁ IRISH WATERMAN ❁ THE MELODY OF CYNWYD ❁ PADDY McGINTY'S GOAT ❁ THE SCHEME ❁ THE SNOUTS AND EARS OF AMERICA ❁ SEDANY ❁ FREE MASONS

Key: G Irish Jig

JACK DANIELSON'S REEL

Key: A Old-Time

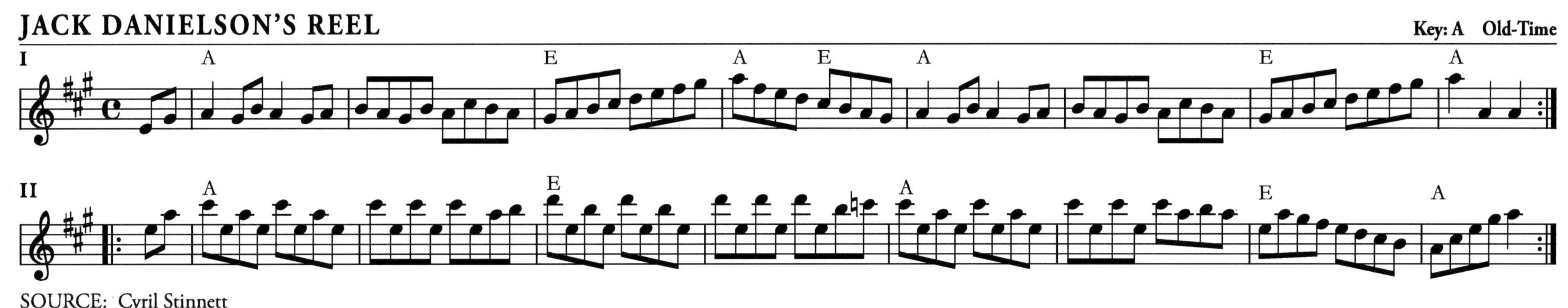

SOURCE: Cyril Stinnett

JACKSON'S ❁ JACKSON'S FAVOURITE ❁ JACKSON'S Nº 1

Key: Em Irish

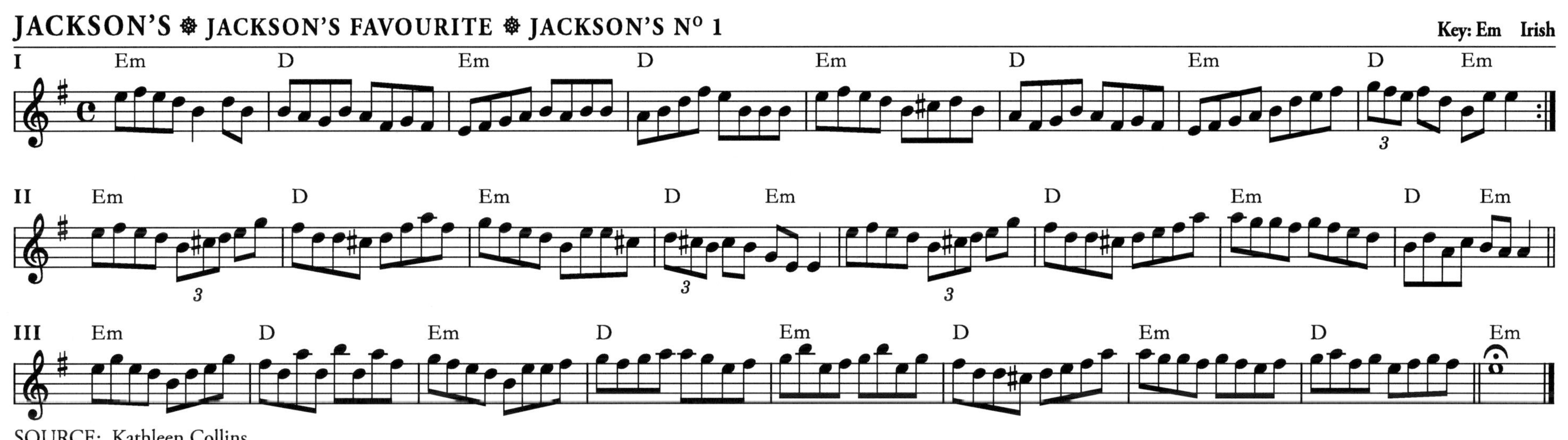

SOURCE: Kathleen Collins

JACKSON'S FANCY ❁ IRISH FANCY

Key: D Irish Jig

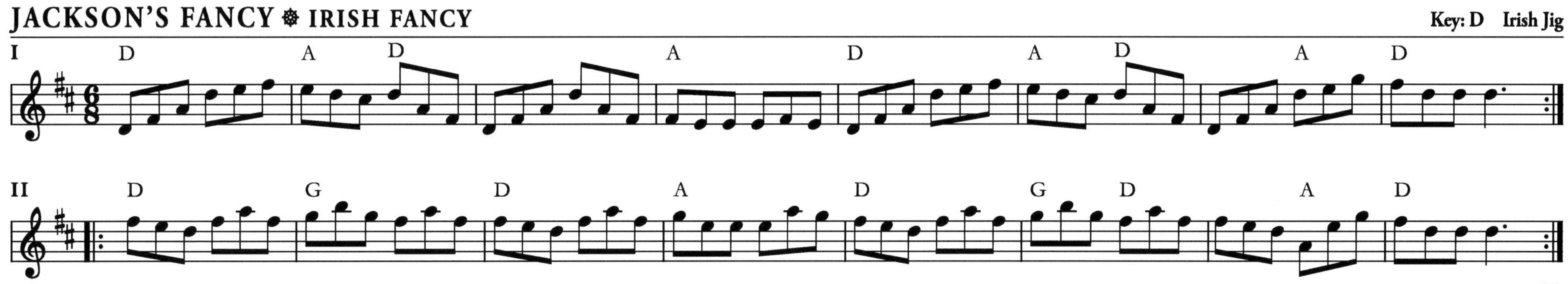

JAWBONE ❁ OLD JAWBONE

JAWBONE ❁ OLD JAWBONE

JAYBIRD ❁ THE PENNSYLVANIA FIFERS

JENNY LIND ❁ JENNY LYNN

Key: G Old-Time

JENNY LIND ❁ JENNY LYNN

Key: A Old-Time

JENNY LIND POLKA ❁ BONNIE POLKA ❁ HEEL AND TOE POLKA ❁ JENNY LINN POLKA ❁ BREAKDOWN DES TETES ❁ HOLE IN HER STOCKING ❁ JENNY LIND'S FAVORITE POLKA ❁ JENNY LIND'S LIEBLINGS–POLKA ❁ REEL LAFRENIERE ❁ SAL WITH THE RUN DOWN SHOES ❁ THE TEMPEST ❁ THE BRIDAL ❁ DOWN TO THE QUAY ❁ JENNY LIND'S ❁ JENNY LIND'S FAVORITE SERENADING ❁ THE JENNY LIND ❁ JENNY LING ❁ JENNY LINN ❁ JOHNNY AND HIS CAMERA ❁ MURPHY'S ❁ QUINN'S IRISH

KEY: G Old-Time

JENNY LIND POLKA ❁ BONNIE POLKA ❁ HEEL AND TOE POLKA ❁ JENNY LINN POLKA ❁ BREAKDOWN DES TETES ❁ HOLE IN HER STOCKING ❁ JENNY LIND'S FAVORITE POLKA ❁ JENNY LIND'S LIEBLINGS–POLKA ❁ REEL LAFRENIERE ❁ SAL WITH THE RUN DOWN SHOES ❁ THE TEMPEST ❁ THE BRIDAL ❁ DOWN TO THE QUAY ❁ JENNY LIND'S ❁ JENNY LIND'S FAVORITE SERENADING ❁ THE JENNY LIND ❁ JENNY LING ❁ JENNY LINN ❁ JOHNNY AND HIS CAMERA ❁ MURPHY'S ❁ QUINN'S IRISH

KEY: D Old-Time

JENNY'S WELCOME TO CHARLIE ❁ THE HIGHWAY TO HOLBURN ❁ JENNIE AND THE WEASEL ❁ JENNIE AND THE WEAVER ❁ THE CORN HILL REEL ❁ JENNY PICKING COCKLES ❁ JENNY AND THE WEAZEL ❁ JENNY'S WELCOME HOME TO CHARLIE

KEY: Dm Irish

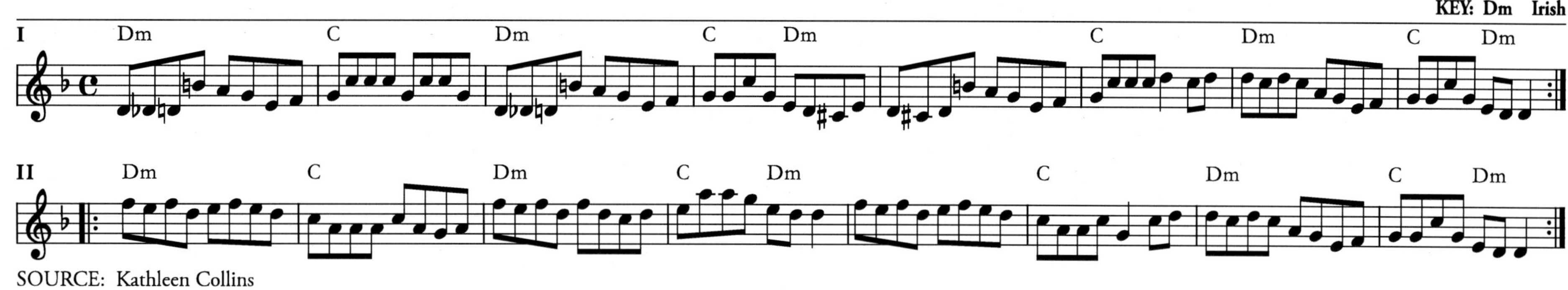

SOURCE: Kathleen Collins

JEUNE MARIE REEL ❁ JEUNES MARIE REEL

KEY: D Northern

JIM KENNEDY'S FAVORITE ❁ THE BUNDLE OF STRAW ❁ FOLLOW ME TO CARPON ❁ THE HARE'S FOOT ❁ THE LOWLANDS OF SCOTLAND ❁ THE SILVERMINES ❁ THE TRALEE LASSES ❁ THE CORRY BOYS ❁ FOLLOW ME TO CARLOW ❁ HARE'S PAW

KEY: Em/G Irish

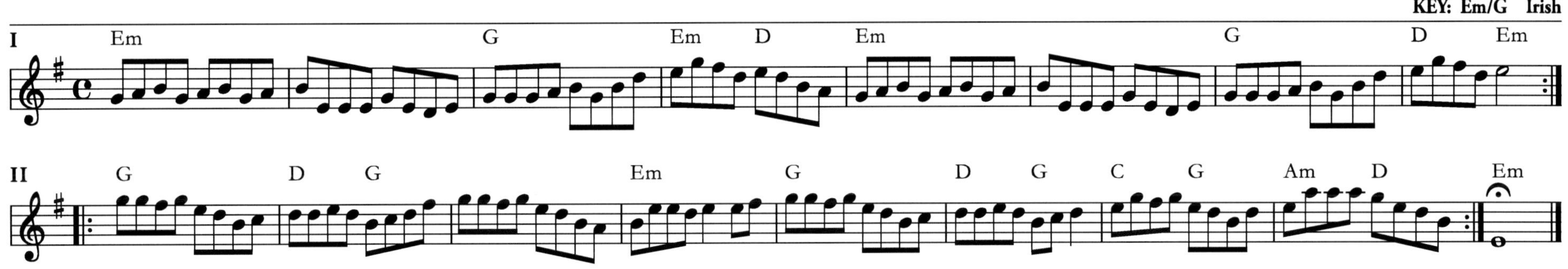

JOE TANZY'S ❁ PAT CARNEY'S REEL ❁ THE BRAES OF GLENDOCHART ❁ MR MENZIES OF CULDARES ❁ PADDY MURPHY'S WIFE

KEY: D Northern/Old-Time

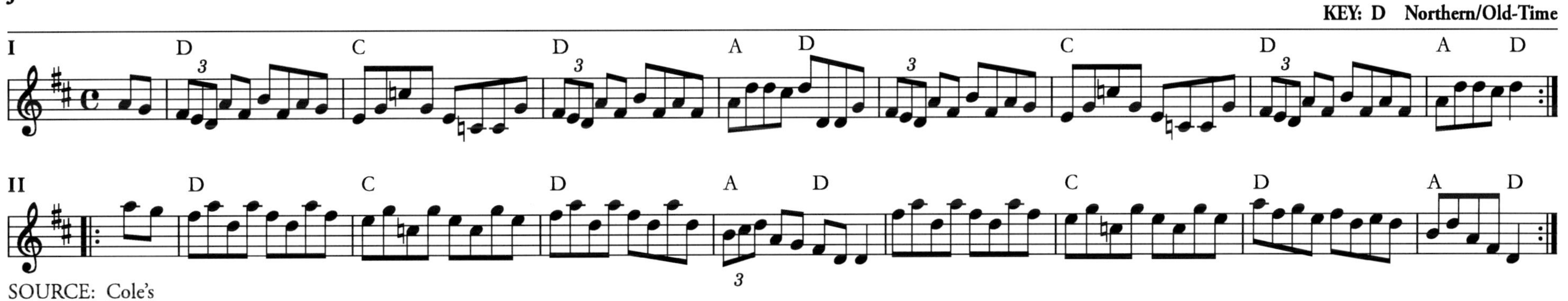

SOURCE: Cole's

JOHAN PÅ SNIPPEN ❁ JOHN FROM THE STICKS ❁ JOHANN PÅ SNIPPEN

KEY: G Scandinavian Schottische

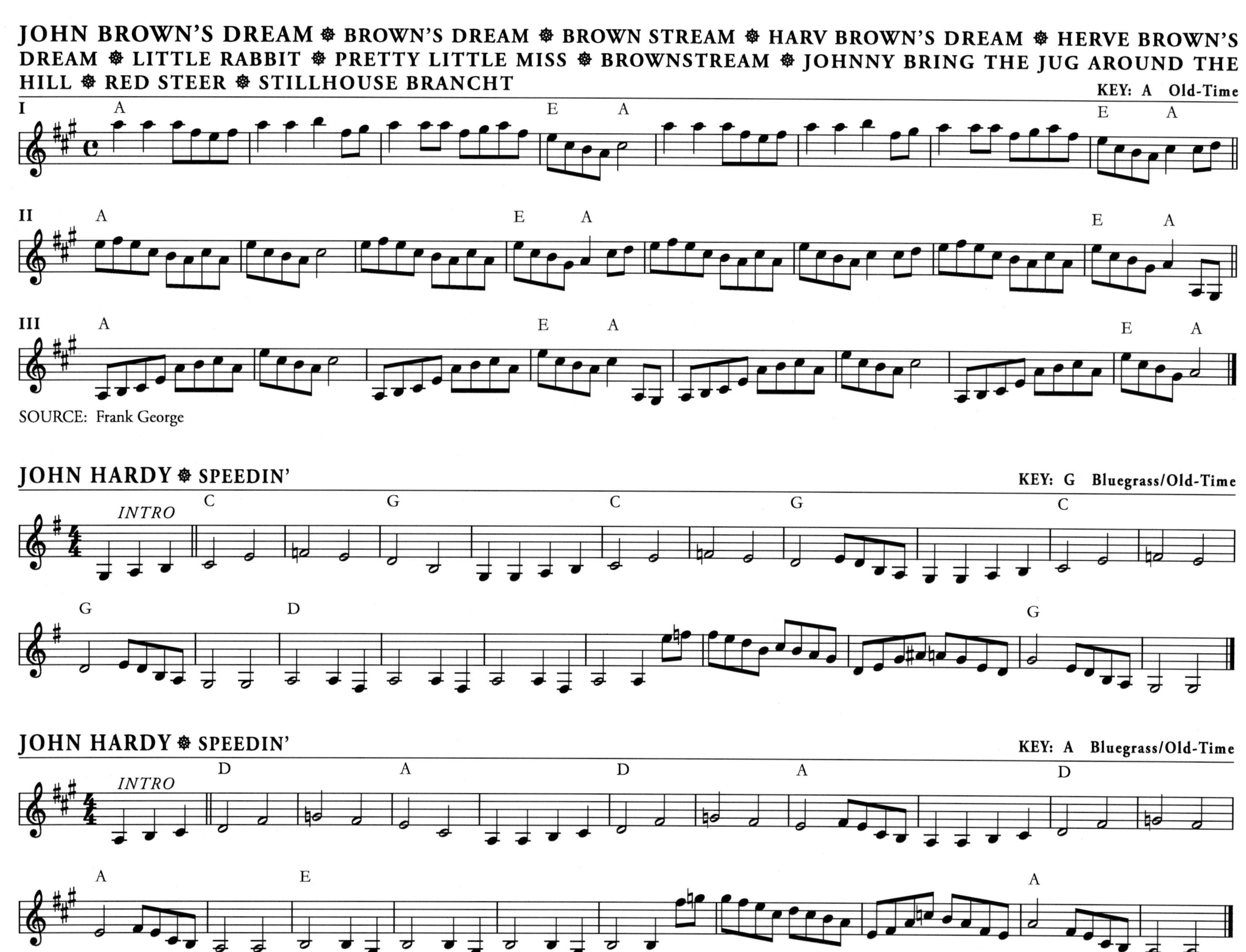
JOHN BROWN'S DREAM ❁ BROWN'S DREAM ❁ BROWN STREAM ❁ HARV BROWN'S DREAM ❁ HERVE BROWN'S DREAM ❁ LITTLE RABBIT ❁ PRETTY LITTLE MISS ❁ BROWNSTREAM ❁ JOHNNY BRING THE JUG AROUND THE HILL ❁ RED STEER ❁ STILLHOUSE BRANCHT
KEY: A Old-Time
I
A E A E A
II
A E A E A
III
A E A E A
SOURCE: Frank George
JOHN HARDY ❁ SPEEDIN'
KEY: G Bluegrass/Old-Time
INTRO
C G C G C
G D G
JOHN HARDY ❁ SPEEDIN'
KEY: A Bluegrass/Old-Time
INTRO
D A D A D
A E A

JOHN PAUL JAMIESON

KEY: G Old-Time

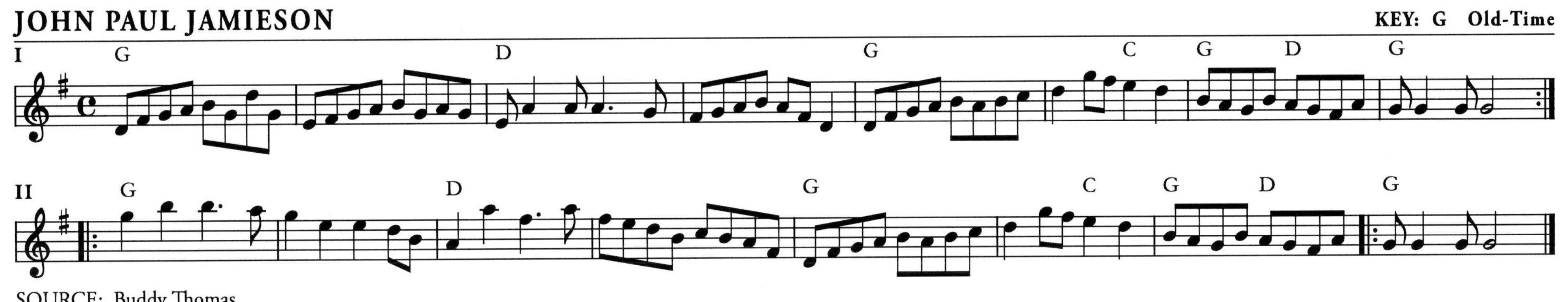

SOURCE: Buddy Thomas

JOHNNY DON'T GET DRUNK ❁ JOHNNY DON'T COME HOME DRUNK

KEY: D Southern

JOHNNY LEARY'S ❁ MAHONEY'S FANCY

KEY: D Irish Jig

SOURCE: Johnny Cronin and Joe Burke

JOHNNY'S GONE TO FRANCE ❁ THE MAIDS OF GALWAY

KEY: Em Irish

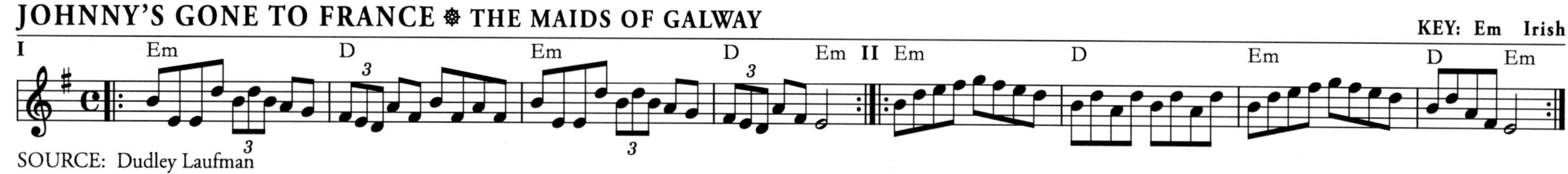

SOURCE: Dudley Laufman

THE JOLLY SEVEN ❁ AROUND THE WORLD ❁ THE CAVAN REEL ❁ MISS KELLY'S

KEY: C/Am Irish

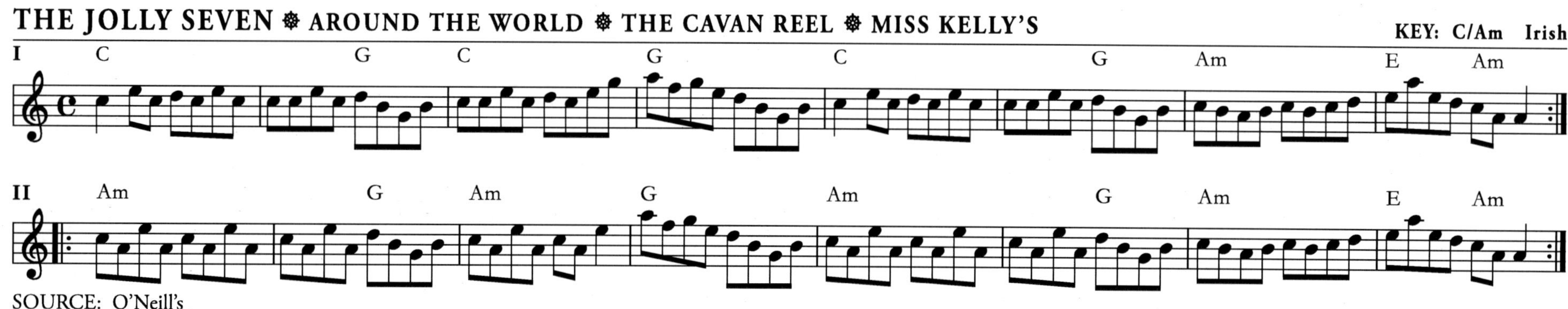

SOURCE: O'Neill's

THE JOY OF MY LIFE ❁ DONNYBROOK FAIR ❁ HUMORS OF DONNYBROOK ❁ THE BOYS FROM THE LOUGH ❁ COROVOTH JIG ❁ THE JOYS OF LIFE ❁ THE JOYS OF MY LIFE ❁ THE JOYS OF YOUTH ❁ OUR OWN LITTLE ISLE ❁ THE CARAVAT ❁ THE JOYS OF LOVE ❁ KISS ME I'M IRISH ❁ OUR LITTLE GREEN ISLE ❁ THE RIVER CREE

KEY: G Irish Jig

THE JUG OF PUNCH ❁ A JUG OF PUNCH ❁ CASEY'S ❁ THE DIAMOND ROCK ❁ THE JUG O' PUNCH

KEY: Dm Irish

SOURCE: Kathleen Collins

JUNE APPLE

KEY: G Bluegrass/Old-Time

JUNE APPLE

KEY: A Bluegrass/Old-Time

KATARONI ❁ CATARONI

KEY: G Irish Jig

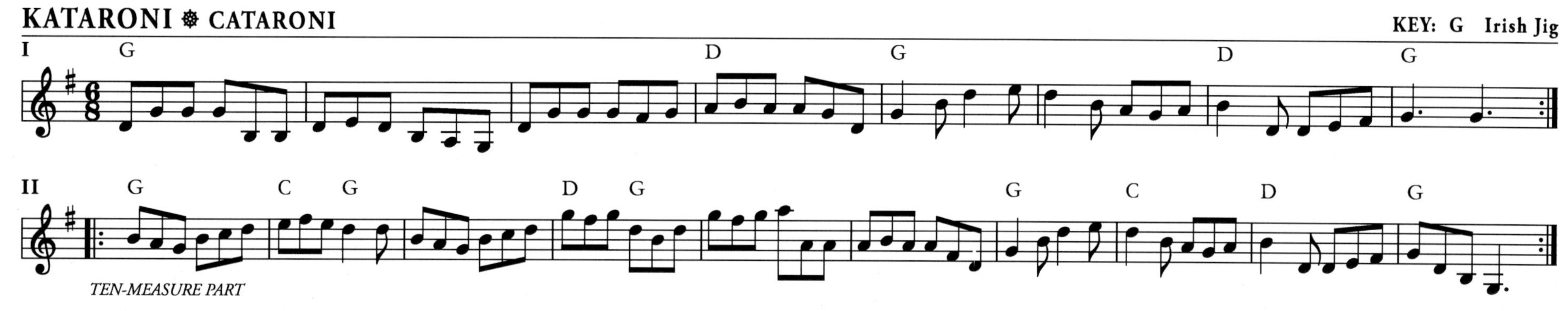

KATYDID

KEY: C Southern

KATY HILL ❁ GOING AROUND THE WORLD

cf SALLY JOHNSON

KEY: G Southern

KAW RIVER

KEY: D Southern

SOURCE: Buddy Thomas

THE KEY WEST HORNPIPE

KEY: G Old-Time

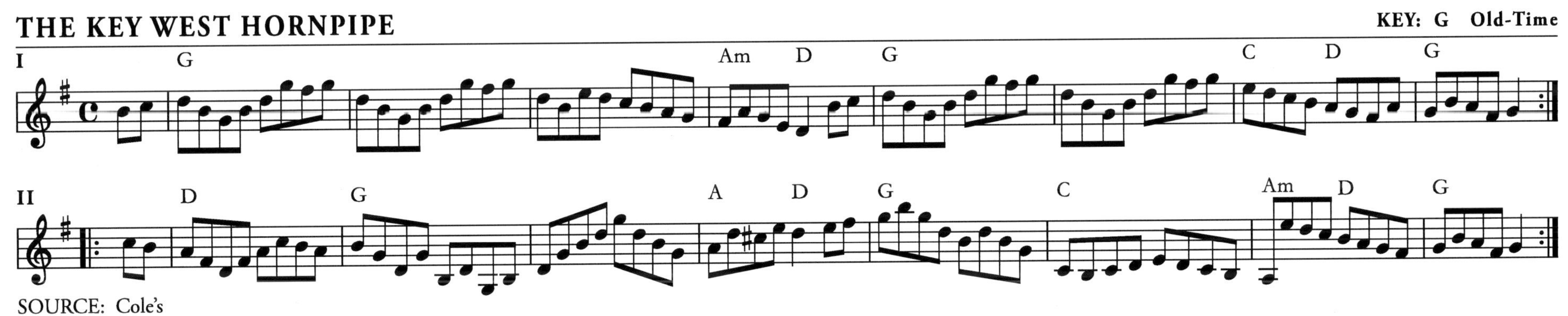

SOURCE: Cole's

KIELY'S REEL ☸ KILEY'S REEL ☸ BUCKLEY'S FAVORITE ☸ HANG FIRE

KEY: A Northern

SOURCE: Donald Commo

THE KILDARE FANCY ❁ DUNDEE ❁ THE DUNDEE HORNPIPE ❁ PANTOMIME REEL—IN F ❁ THE UNION HORNPIPE ❁ DUNDEE CLOG ❁ THE KILDARE

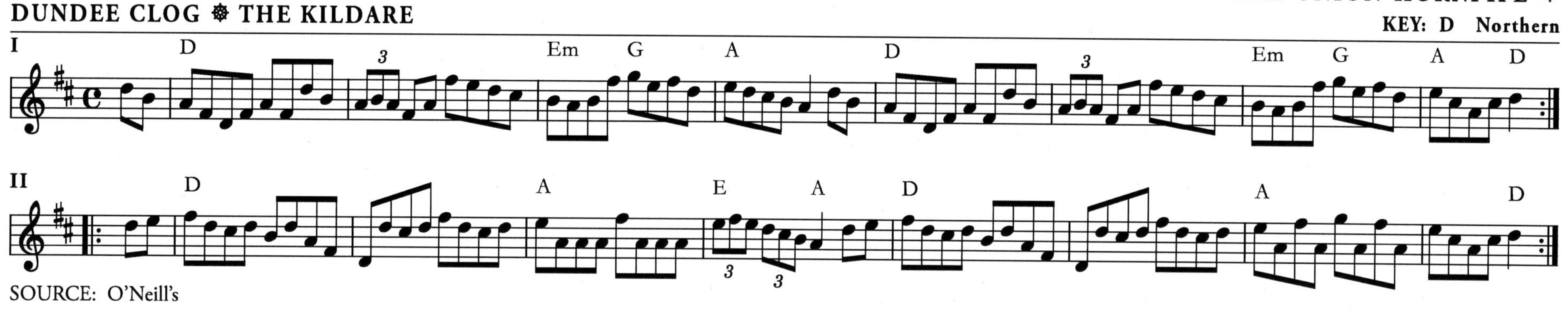

THE KILDARE FANCY ❁ DUNDEE ❁ THE DUNDEE HORNPIPE ❁ PANTOMIME REEL—IN F ❁ THE UNION HORNPIPE ❁ DUNDEE CLOG ❁ THE KILDARE

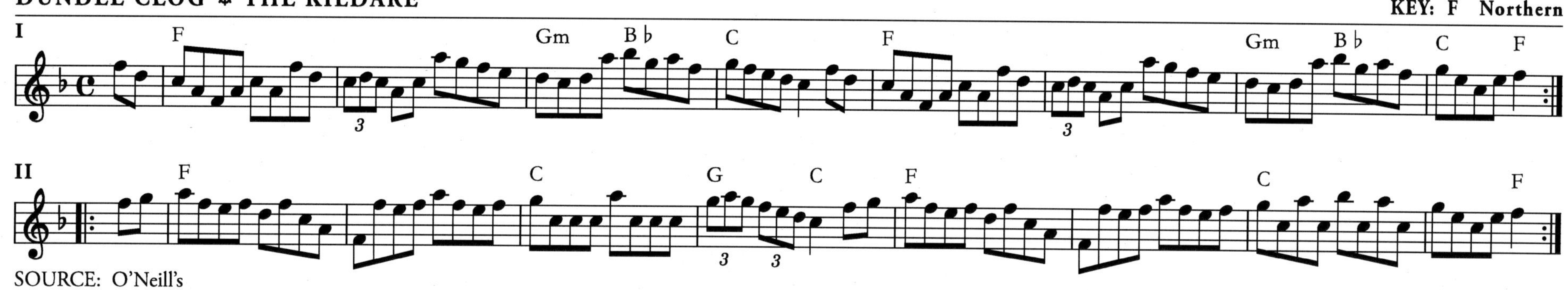

KINGDOM COMING ❁ THE DOODLETOWN FIFER ❁ THE KINGOM ❁ KINGDON COME ❁ LEAPFROG

cf WHEN JOHNNY COMES MARCHING HOME (G) & THE YEAR OF JUBALO *et al*

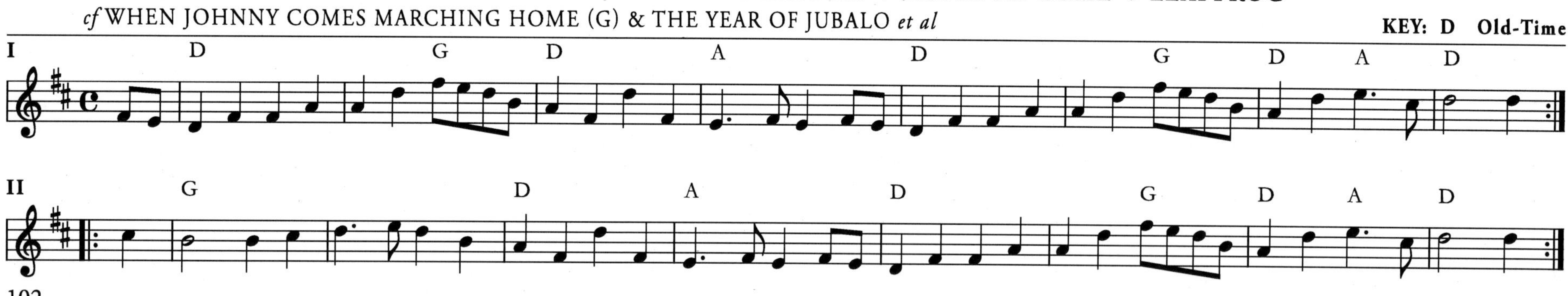

KITCHEN GIRL ❁ KITCHEN GAL
KEY: A/Am Southern
I
A G A G A G A G A
II
Am G Am E Am G Am G Am
SOURCE: Henry Moore
PARTS ARE SOMETIMES REVERSED

KITTY McGEE ❁ KITTY MAGEE ❁ PICKING UP STICKS
KEY: D Old-Time Jig
I
D G D G A D G D A D
II
D G A D G A D A G A D A D
SOURCE: Dudley Laufman

LAMPLIGHTER HORNPIPE ❁ LAMPLIGHTER'S HORNPIPE ❁ MERRY SOLDIER
KEY: A Northern
I
A E A E A
II
A E A E A E A E A
SOURCE: Cole's/Don Messer

LARDNER'S REEL ❁ PRAIRIE HORNPIPE ❁ COWBOY'S ❁ THE HALFWAY HOUSE ❁ KING OF ALL REELS

cf COMING DOWN FROM DENVER *et al*

KEY: A Old-Time

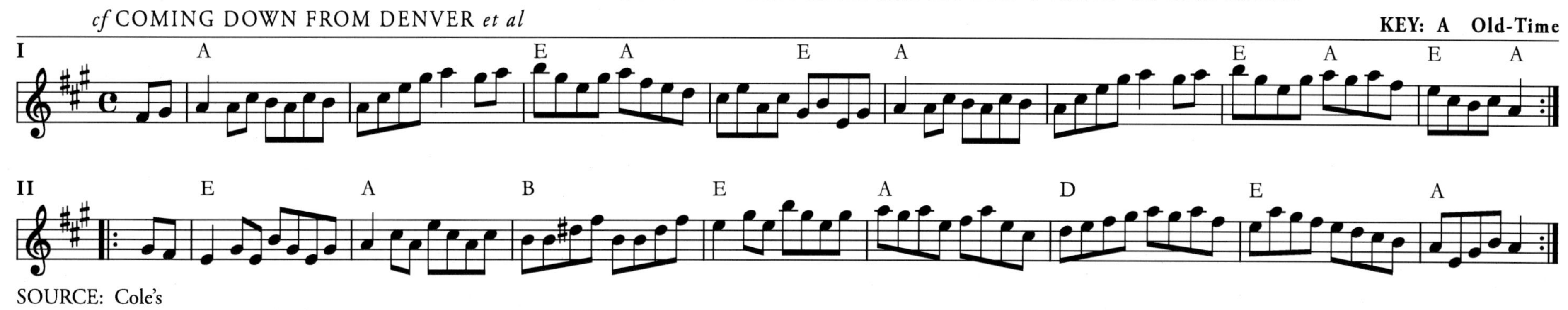

SOURCE: Cole's

The following six tunes and* Geese in the Bog*, along with their alternate titles, make up "The Lark Family." A lot of mixing of titles is to be found among these seven tunes and the roughly fifty titles associated with them.

LARK IN THE MORNING—D ❁ GALWAY TOM ❁ THE HOUSE IN THE GLEN ❁ THE SPOTTED COW ❁ A WESTERN LILT ❁ THE HA'PENNY BRIDGE ❁ THE HUMORS OF MILLINGAR ❁ KELSO RACES

cf GEESE IN THE BOG *et al* & LARK'S MARCH *et al*

Irish Jig

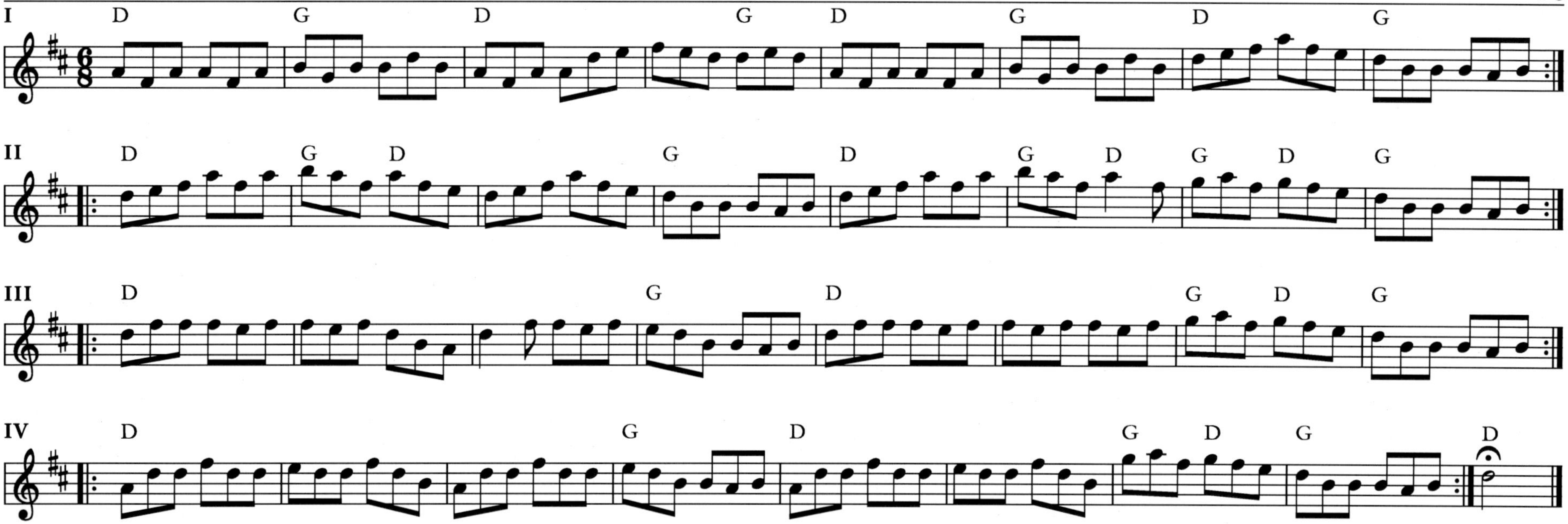

I
D G D G D G D G

II
D G D G D G D G D G

III
D G D G D G

IV
D G D G D G D

LARK IN THE MORNING—Em ❁ COME IN THE EVENING ❁ GALLOWAY TOM ❁ GALWAY TOM ❁ GALWAY TOWN ❁ THE GOAT'S HORN ❁ KELSO RACES ❁ THE LITTLE YELLOW BOY ❁ THE SPOTTED COW ❁ THE THRUSH'S NEST ❁ THE WELCOME ❁ A WESTERN LILT ❁ MORNING LARK

Irish Jig

SOURCE: Cole's

LARK ON THE STRAND—Em/G

Irish Jig

LARK ON THE STRAND—G ❁ THE OLD WOMAN LAMENTING HER EMPTY PURSE ❁ THE STOLEN PURSE ❁ THE LARK IN THE STRAND ❁ THE LARK OF THE STRAND ❁ MULLALY'S ❁ PADDY HUGHES ❁ PADDY THE POST

Irish Jig

LARK ON THE STRAND — G ❁ THE GLEN OF THE SHAMROCKS ❁ MARY GRIFFIN'S JIG ❁ WICKY SEARS ❁ NEARLY KESH ❁ NOEL O'DONOGHUE'S FAVOURITE ❁ OLD KESH ❁ THE PRIMROSE GLEN ❁ THE PRIMROSE VALE ❁ LASS ON THE STRAND ❁ BLOOMING MEADOW

Irish Jig

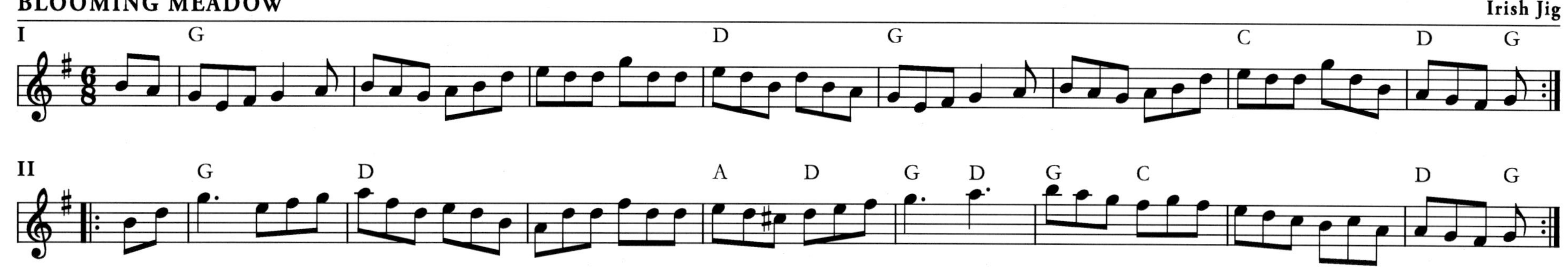

LARK'S MARCH ❁ THE LARK IN THE BOG ❁ TOM BRODERICK'S ❁ BOB THOMPSON'S FAVOURITE ❁ CORAVAT JIG ❁ GREEN MEADOWS ❁ THE HUMORS OF LIMERICK ❁ JACKSON'S TRIP TO LIMERICK ❁ JACKSON'S WALK TO LIMERICK ❁ JACKSON'S COOLA ❁ THE MOUNTAIN LARK ❁ THE PIPER'S FROLIC ❁ TWICE TRICKED ❁ WISEMAN'S FAVOURITE ❁ TUHY'S FROLIC

cf GEESE IN THE BOG *et al* & LARK IN THE MORNING — D *et al*

Key: D Irish Jig

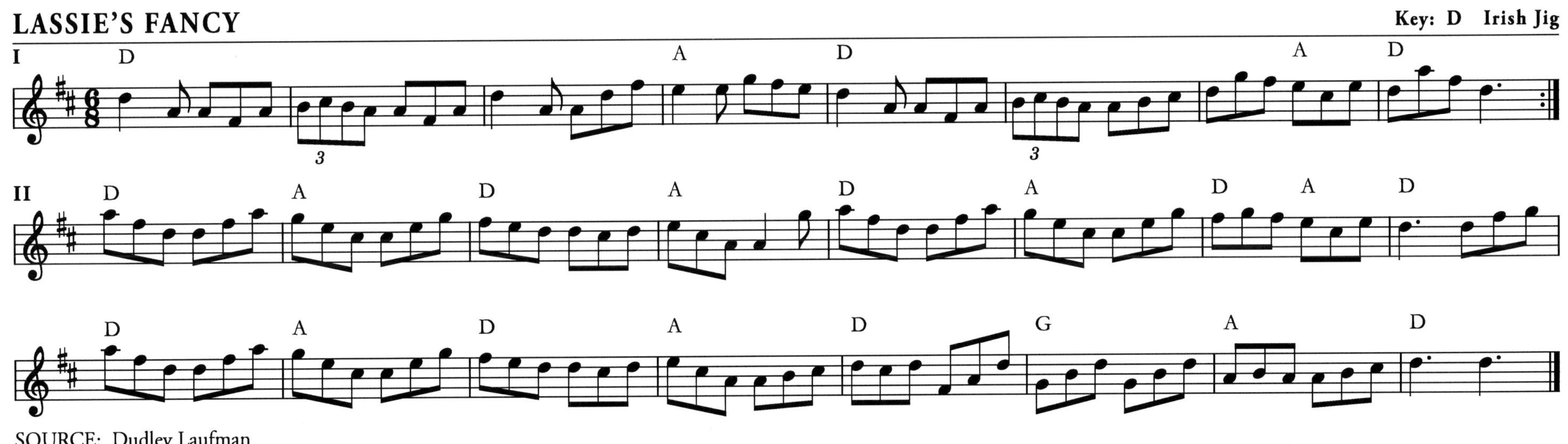
LASSIE'S FANCY
Key: D Irish Jig
I
II
SOURCE: Dudley Laufman

LAST NIGHT'S FUN—D Reel ❁ JOE COOLEY'S Nº 1 ❁ KILLORAN'S REELS
Irish
I
II

LAST NIGHT'S FUN—Em/D Slip Jig ❁ MISS BROWN'S FANCY ❁ PADDY BE EASY
Irish
I
II

THE LAUNDRY BOY ❁ HEJSAN GRABBAR ❁ THE HAPPY BOYS

Key: G/C Scandinavian Schottische

LEATHER BRITCHES ❁ LEATHER BREECHES ❁ OLD LEATHER BRITCHES ❁ JOHN McDONALD'S REEL ❁ MACDONALD'S REEL ❁ SLANTY GART ❁ THE BREECHES ON ❁ THE BRITCHES FULL OF STITCHES ❁ THE IRISH LAD ❁ THE IRISH LAD'S A JOLLY BOY ❁ O, THE BREECHES FULL OF STITCHES ❁ LE PETIT BUCHEUX ❁ REEL McDONNELL

Key: G Old-Time

2ND PART IS OPTIONAL

LEO CARROLL'S HORNPIPE
KEY: B♭ Northern
I
B♭ E♭ B♭ F B♭ E♭ B♭ F B♭
Fine
II
F C7 F C7 F
D.C. al Fine
SOURCE: Reg Hill
THE LEPRECHAUN ☸ THE WORN TORN PETTICOAT ☸ JOHNNY LEARY'S SLIDE ☸ OLD TORN PETTICOAT
KEY: Am Irish Slide
I
Am G Am G Am G Am G Am
II
G Am
1.
G Am G Am
2.
G Am G Am
SOURCE: Johnny Cronin and Joe Burke
LIAM BROWN
KEY: G Irish Polka
I
G D G D G
II
G D G D G
III
G D G D G

LIBERTY ❁ REEL DE TI-JEAN ❁ TIPSY PARSON ❁ TWO-STEP ❁ LIBERTY HORNPIPE ❁ NEW LIBERTY ❁ THE RACCOON AND THE POSSUM ❁ SPANISH POLKA

KEY: D Southern

I
D G D A D

II
D A D G A D

LIGHTNING IN THE WEST

KEY: G Old-Time

LIMERICK LASSES ❁ COPPERS AND BRASS ❁ CROSSING THE FIELD ❁ DUBLIN LASSES ❁ GREEN FIELDS OF ERIN ❁ HEATHER BREEZE ❁ THE HEATHER BLOOM ❁ THE HEATHERY BRAES ❁ THE HEATHERY BRAES OF BALLYHEALY ❁ THE HUMORS OF APPLETOWN ❁ LADY'S PANTALOONS ❁ McNAMARA'S REEL ❁ LIMERICK LADS ❁ PRETTY GIRLS OF MONAGHAN ❁ THE PRETTY LITTLE BOY ❁ WHO MADE YOUR BRITCHES ❁ LADIES' PANTALOONS

KEY: D Irish

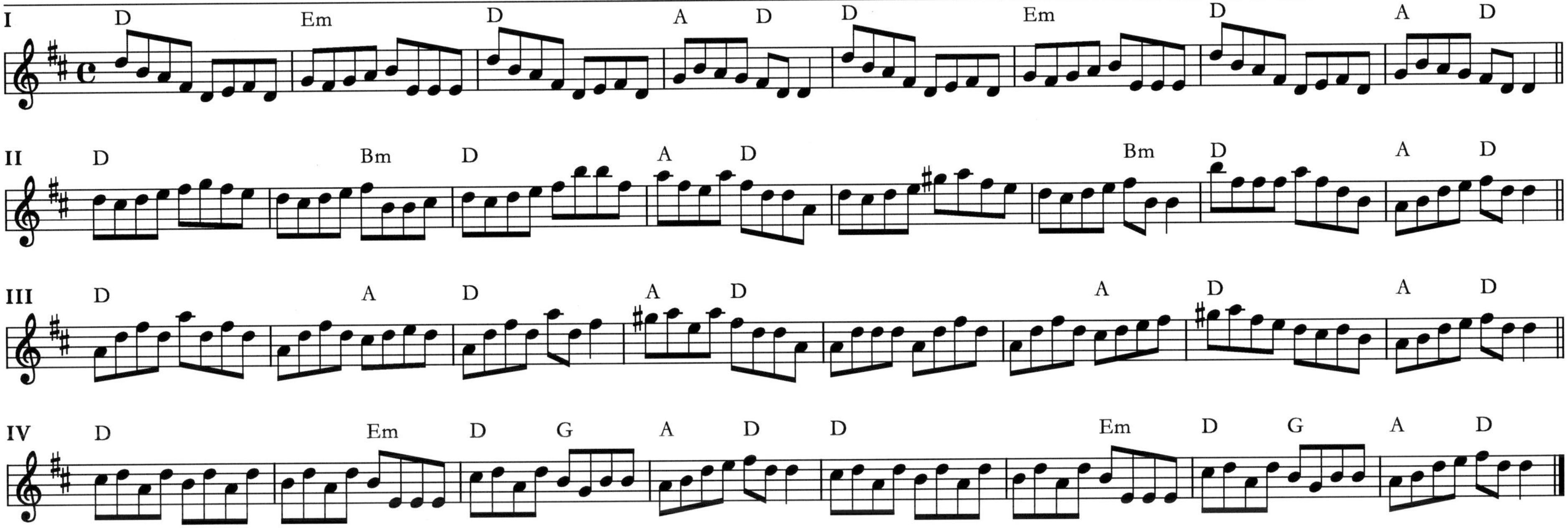

I D Em D A D D Em D A D

II D Bm D A D Bm D A D

III D A D A D A D A D

IV D Em D G A D D Em D G A D

LONESOME ROAD BLUES ❁ GOING DOWN THE ROAD FEELING BAD

KEY: G Bluegrass

LONESOME ROAD BLUES ❁ GOING DOWN THE ROAD FEELING BAD

KEY: A Bluegrass

LONE STAR RAG ❁ STONE'S RAG

KEY: C Texas

SOURCE: Tater Tate

THE LONGFORD COLLECTOR ❁ THE BONNIE BOY ❁ THE LONGFORD BEGGARWOMAN ❁ LADY CLARE'S QUICK STEP ❁ THE LONGFORD BEGGARMAN ❁ THE MAN FROM LONGFORD ❁ THE LONGFORT COLLECTOR ❁ THE LONGFORD RENT COLLECTOR

KEY: G Irish

LOST INDIAN ☸ LONESOME INDIAN ☸ WILD INDIAN

cf CHEROKEE SHUFFLE

KEY: G Bluegrass/Southern

KEY: A Bluegrass/Southern

LUCY CAMPBELL (Irish/Scottish) ☸ THE DEAR MEAL ☸ THE DEAR MEAL IS CHEAP AGAIN ☸ LEAP YEAR ☸ CAIRNGORUM ☸ CHEAP MEAL

KEY: D

LUCY CAMPBELL (Northern/Scottish) ❁ THE DEAR MEAL ❁ THE DEAR MEAL IS CHEAP AGAIN ❁ LEAP YEAR ❁ CAIRNGORUM ❁ CHEAP MEAL

KEY: D

MADAME BONAPARTE ❁ MADAM BONAPARTE ❁ BONAPARTE'S ADVANCE ❁ THE NAVIGATOR'S ❁ NOT TONIGHT JOSEPHINE

KEY: A Irish Hornpipe

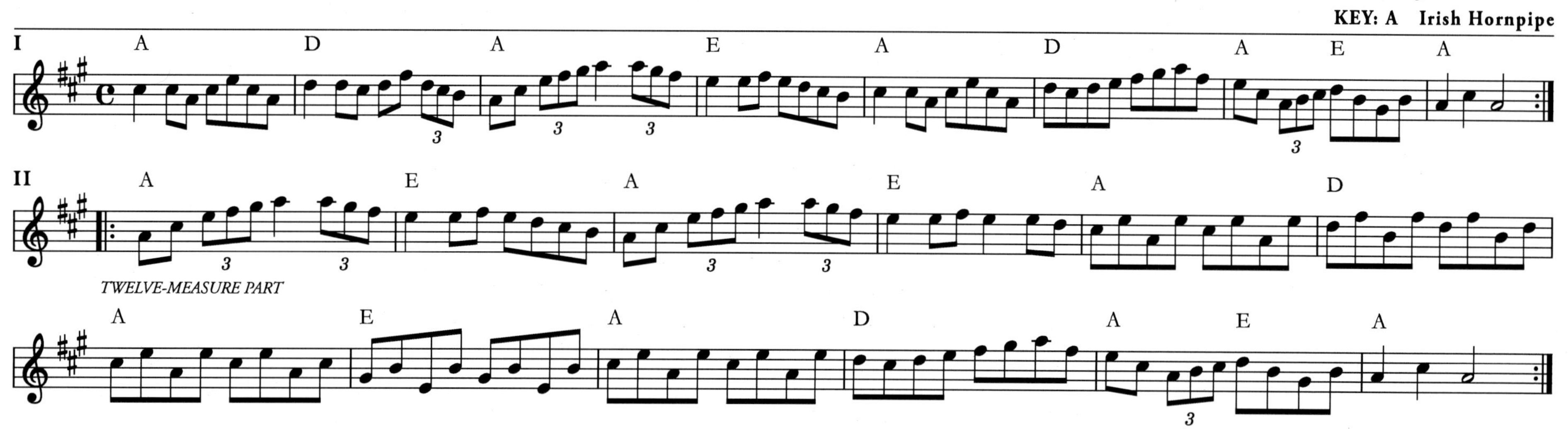

SLIGHT ADJUSTMENTS TO TRIPLETS IN *GFTFG*

MAGGIE BROWN ❁ MISS MARGARET BROWN'S FAVORITE ❁ MARGRETT BROWN'S FAVORITE ❁ MARGARET BROWN'S FAVORITE ❁ MISS BROWN'S ❁ MISS BROWN'S FANCY ❁ MISS MARGARET BROWN (NOW LADY CAMDEN) ❁ PEGGY BROWN ❁ PLANXTY BROWNE ❁ PLANXTY MAGGIE BROWN ❁ THE BUNCH OF CLOVER ❁ CADDEN'S FANCY ❁ MAGGIE BROWN'S FAVOURITE JIG ❁ MAGGIE BROWNE'S FANCY ❁ PLANXTY BROWN ❁ SWEET MAGGIE BROWN ❁ TRIP TO GOREY

KEY: G Irish Jig

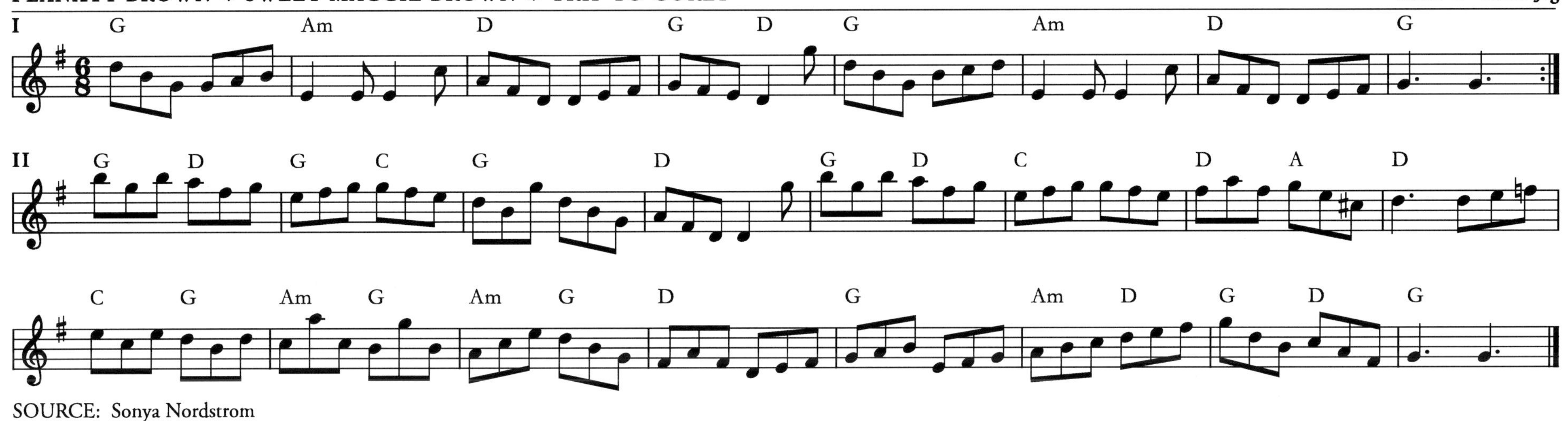

SOURCE: Sonya Nordstrom

MAGPIE

KEY: G Old-Time

MAID OF BALLYDOO

KEY: C Irish Jig

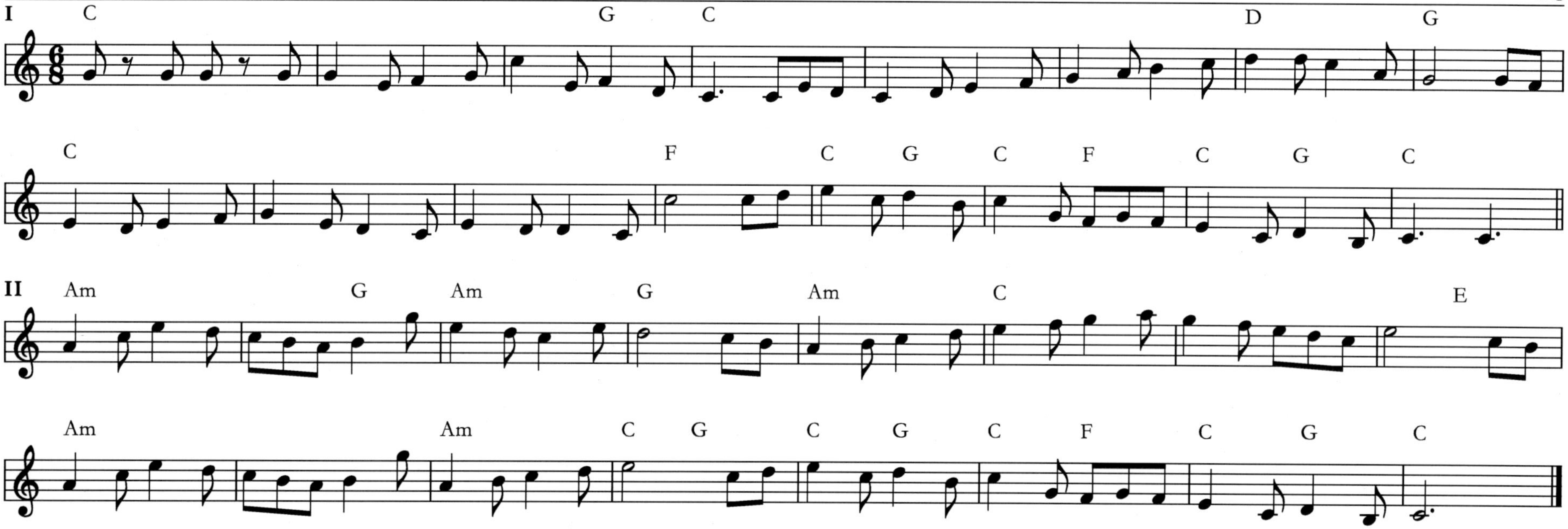
I C G C D G
C F C G C F C G C
II Am G Am G Am C E
Am Am C G C G C F C G C

SOURCE: Libby Larsen

MARMADUKE'S HORNPIPE ❁ THE GOVERNOR'S TUNE ❁ GALWAY HORNPIPE

cf CRICKET ON THE HEARTH *et al* & YEARLING *et al*

KEY: D Old-Time

I D A D A D
II D G D A D G A D

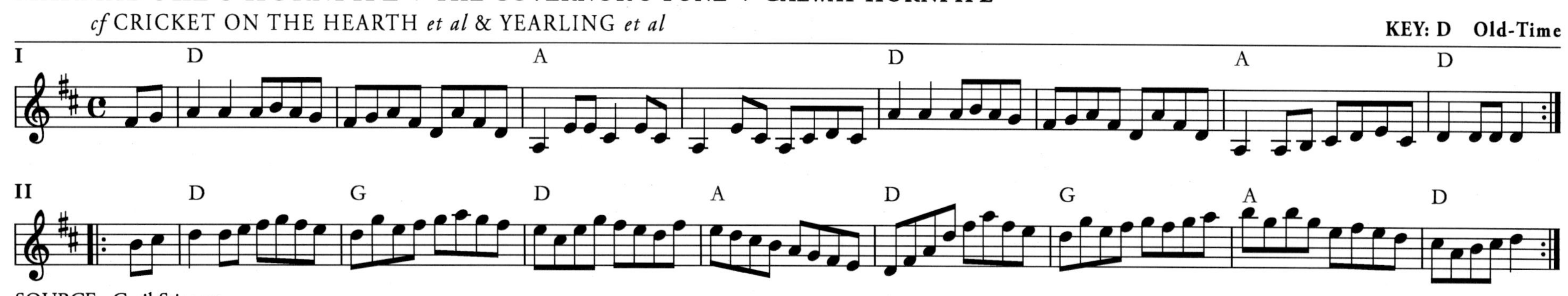

SOURCE: Cyril Stinnett

THE MARQUIS OF WATERFORD ❁ THE MARQUIS OF WATERFORD'S HORNPIPE

KEY: B♭ English Hornpipe

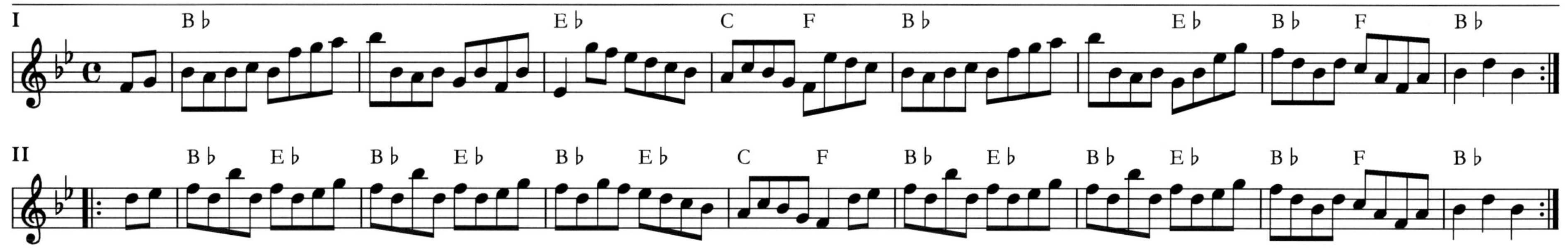

SOURCE: The High Level Ranters

MARTHA CAMPBELL ❁ MARTHIE CAMPBELL'S

KEY: D Old-Time

SOURCE: Buddy Thomas

MARTIN WYNNE'S REEL ❁ BURYING POTEEN ❁ BURYING THE POTEEN ❁ CHEWING ON LARRYS ❁ MARTIN WYNNE'S Nº 2 ❁ MARTIN WYNNE'S FAVOURITE

KEY: D Irish

SOURCE: Johnny Cronin and Joe Burke

MASON'S APRON ❁ CARTON'S REEL ❁ THE COTTAGE BY THE SEA ❁ FORT WORTH ❁ GALLAGHER'S ❁ THE ISLA REEL ❁ JACK OF DIAMONDS ❁ LADY CARBURY ❁ THE MASON LADDIES ❁ MASON'S CAP ❁ PICNIC ROMP ❁ THE RED-HEADED GIRL ❁ WAKE UP SUSAN ❁ WILD HORSE ❁ THE APRON ❁ BRAES OF GLENORCHY ❁ I DON'T LIKE THE GUIDEWIFE ❁ MISS CARBURY ❁ LOWRIE TARREL ❁ MISS CARBERY'S REEL ❁ MISS HOPE'S FAVORITE ❁ REEL DES BRETELLES ❁ ROXBERRY REEL ❁ TOSS THE FEATHER ❁ THE WOODEN SPOON ❁ REEL DE LONGUEUIL ❁ THE GOODWIFE ❁ DROPS OF BRANDY

KEY: A Irish

McGETTRICK'S REEL ❁ THE SMALL HILLS OF OFFALY ❁ SPINDLESHANKS

KEY: G Irish

McGIBBNEY'S FANCY ❁ THE CUCKOO'S NEST ❁ McGIVNEY'S FANCY ❁ McGIBBNEY'S HORNPIPE ❁ EAMONN McGIVNEY'S ❁ JACKY TAR ❁ THE MOWER ❁ JACK A TAR ❁ JACKIE TAR

KEY: Em Irish Hornpipe

I
Em D Em D Em

II
Em D Em D Em

McNABB'S HORNPIPE ❁ CLOONE'S MARCH ❁ CROSSING THE MINCH

KEY: D Northern

SOURCE: 25 Fiddle Favorites

THE MERRY BLACKSMITH ❁ COLLINS' REEL ❁ THE FLAGS OF DUBLIN ❁ PADDY ON THE RAILROAD ❁ PEELER'S JACKET REEL ❁ BOYS OF THE LAKE ❁ CORKONIAN ❁ THE DEVIL'S IN DUBLIN ❁ EMMINENCE BREAKDOWN ❁ IKE FORRESTER'S REEL ❁ MIST ON THE LOCH ❁ THE POLICE JACKET ❁ THE POLICEMAN'S REEL ❁ THE RAILROAD ❁ BOY IN THE GAP ❁ PEELER'S REEL ❁ THE PEELER'S CAP ❁ POLICEMAN'S CAP ❁ THE BLACKENED SMITH ❁ MUSIC OF THE FORGE ❁ SLEIGH RIDE

KEY: D Irish

MICKO RUSSELL'S

KEY: D Irish

Fine

I

D C D A D C D A D

SOURCE: Johnny Cronin and Joe Burke

MIKE MALONEY

KEY: D Northern Jig

MILLER'S REEL ❁ THE DAWN ❁ THE DAWNING OF THE DAY ❁ DUSTY MILLER ❁ MILLER'S HORNPIPE ❁ THE SPIRIT OF 1880 ❁ TWENTY-EIGHTH OF JANUARY ❁ THE TWENTY-SECOND OF FEBRUARY ❁ TWILIGHT IN PORTROE ❁ THE MILLER

KEY: A Irish

SOURCE: Cole's

MINSTREL'S FANCY ❁ McELLIGOTT'S FANCY ❁ THE BUCK FROM THE MOUNTAIN ❁ CLOG DU COURONNEMENT ❁ HANOVER HORNPIPE ❁ THE MINSTREL'S FAVOURITE ❁ MINSTREL'S HORNPIPE ❁ THE PIONEER CLOG ❁ BILLY CAPLES'S ❁ THE BUCK ON THE MOUNTAIN ❁ THE HANOVER

KEY: D Old-Time

SOURCE: David Carr

MISSISSIPPI SAWYER ☸ DOWNFALL OF ADAM ☸ THE DOWNFALL OF PARIS ☸ FISH ON A SNAG ☸ MISSISSIPPI JUBILEE ☸ LOVE FROM THE HEART

KEY: D Southern

MISSOURI QUICK-STEP ☸ RACHEL ☸ TEXAS QUICK-STEP

cf TEXAS TWO-STEP *et al*

KEY: D Southern

SOURCE: Cyril Stinnett

MOLL ROE'S ☸ COME UNDER MY DIMITY ☸ COURTING IN THE KITCHEN ☸ DITHERUM DOODLE ☸ HER BLUE EYES, THEY GLEAM AND THEY TWINKLE ☸ I'LL TAKE A GLASS WITH A FRIEND ☸ LATE ON A SATURDAY NIGHT ☸ MOLL ROE IN THE MORNING ☸ THE MUNSTERMAN'S FLATTERY ☸ THE NIGHT OF THE FUN ☸ ONE BUMPER AT PARTING ☸ THOUGH LATE WAS I PLUMP ☸ MALL RUA ☸ SWEET MOLLY ROE ☸ THE MARKET STAKE ☸ LOVE IS THE CAUSE OF MY FOLLY ☸ THE DEVIL AND THE PLAINTIFF ☸ JOHNNY D'S ☸ MAURA RUA ☸ THE NIGHT BEFORE LARRY WAS STRETCHED ☸ RED HAIRED MARY ☸ RENT IN ARREARS ☸ THE WHEELS OF THE WORLD

KEY: D Irish Slip-Jig

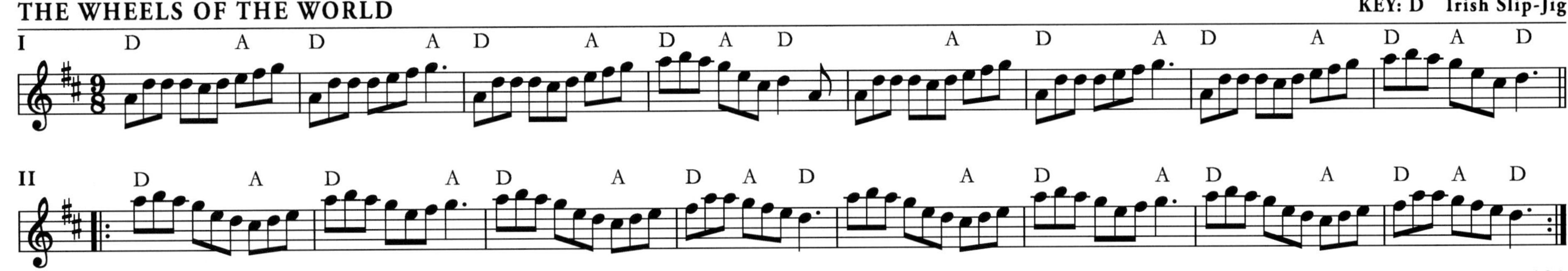

MOLL ROE'S

KEY: G Irish Slip-Jig

MONSIGNOR'S BLESSING ❁ FATHER KELLY'S REEL ❁ OVER THE BOG ROAD ❁ IRISH GIRL

KEY: D Irish

SOURCE: Kathleen Collins

MORNING DEW ❁ THE HARE AMONG THE HEATHER ❁ THE HARE IN THE HEATHER ❁ SUNDEW

KEY: Em Irish

SOURCE: Kathleen Collins

MOUNTAINTOP ❁ MOUNTAIN TOP ❁ THE CROOKED WAY TO DUBLIN ❁ DILLON BROWN ❁ DOON REEL ❁ HOLLY BUSH ❁ QUINN'S REEL ❁ THE DUNNE HILLS ❁ DOONE HILL

KEY: G Irish

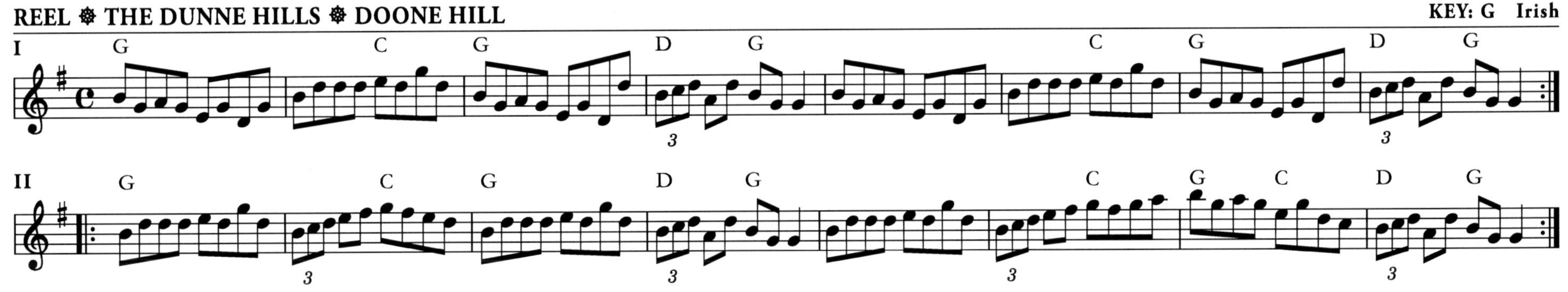

MOUSE IN THE CUPBOARD ❁ THE MERRY OLD WOMAN ❁ THE RAKES OF NEWCASTLE WEST ❁ REPEAL OF THE UNION ❁ TUMBLE THE TINKER ❁ WALLOP THE POTLID ❁ THE WALLS OF ENNISCORTHY ❁ THE WALLS OF LISCARROLL ❁ DUIGNAN'S OLD JIG

KEY: G Irish Jig

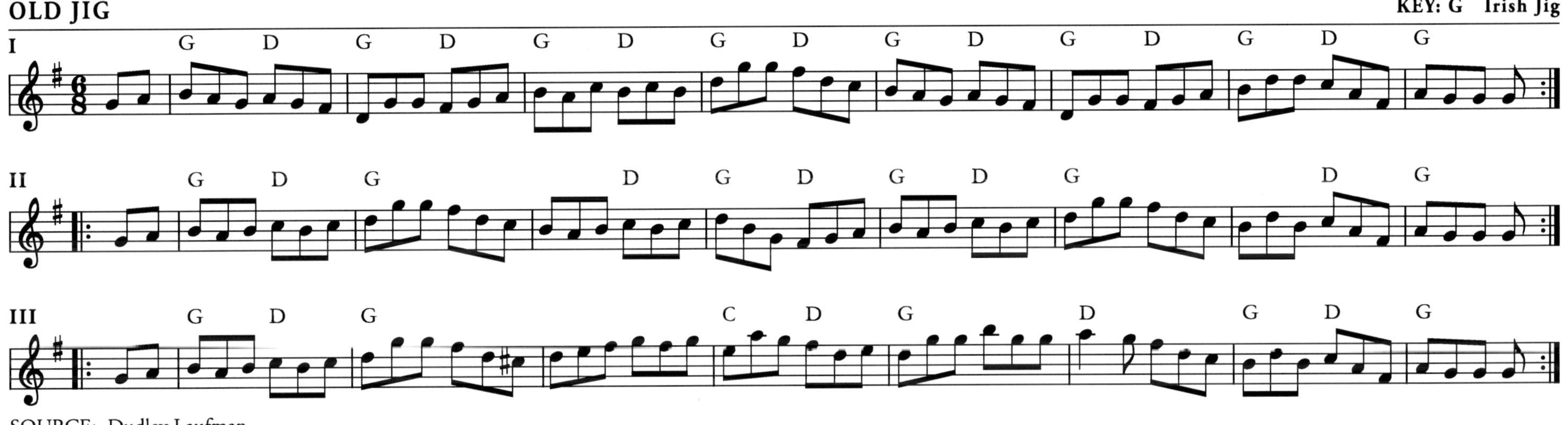

SOURCE: Dudley Laufman

MRS BOLLICK'S

KEY: G Irish

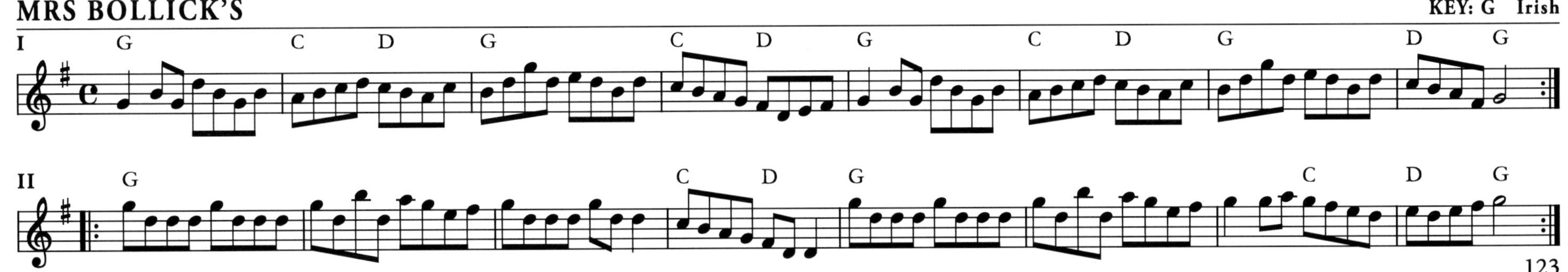

MUG OF BROWN ALE ❁ BUTCHER'S MARCH ❁ THE CLARE JIG ❁ THE COORACLARE ❁ DELANEY'S DRUMMERS ❁ GINGER'S FAVOURITE ❁ THE JUG OF BROWN ALE ❁ PADDY IN LONDON ❁ THE RAFFLE JIG ❁ THE SPOONFUL OF TREACLE ❁ WINTER APPLES ❁ THE BASKET OF SHAMROCKS ❁ THE CAVAN LASSIES Nº 2 ❁ THE CLARE ❁ GINGER'S FAVORITE ❁ THE MILLER OF GLENMIRE ❁ THE MUG OF ALE

KEY: Am   Irish Jig

SOURCE: Donna Hinds

MY BROTHER'S LETTER

KEY: A   Northern

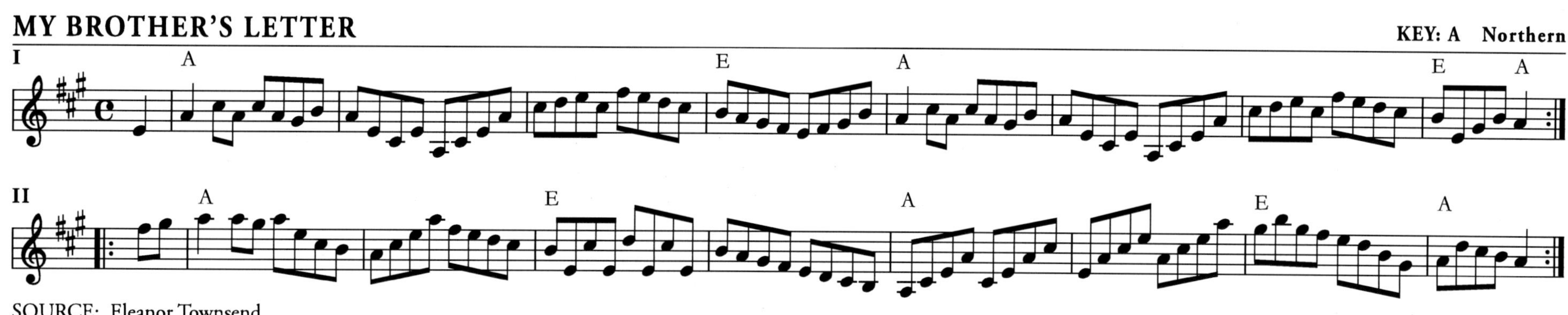

SOURCE: Eleanor Townsend

NAKED AND BARE

KEY: G   Irish Jig

SOURCE: The Boys of the Lough

NELLIE'S JIG

KEY: G Old-Time

NEW BROOM ❁ DEMOCRATS A-RISING

KEY: G Texas

SOURCE: Dick Barrett

NEW CENTURY HORNPIPE—IRISH ❁ CENTURY HORNPIPE

cf NEW CENTURY HORNPIPE--OLD TIME

KEY: D

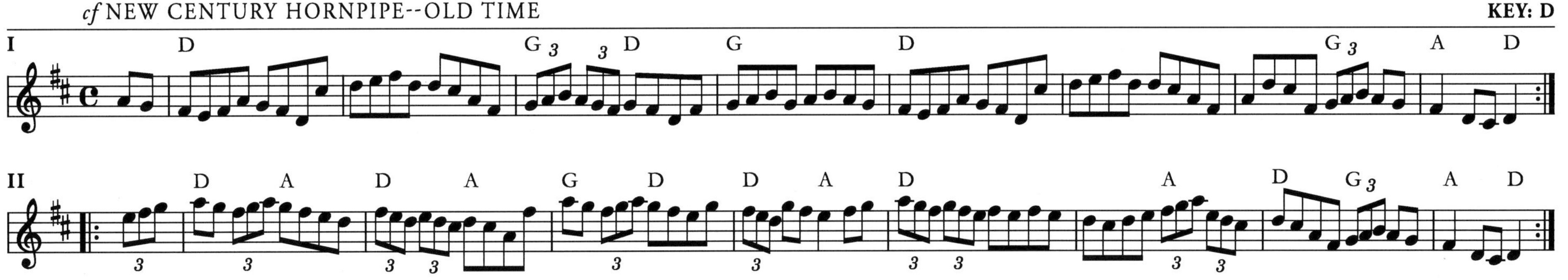

SOURCE: Kathleen Collins

NEW CENTURY HORNPIPE—OLD TIME ❁ THE NEW CENTURY

cf NEW CENTURY HORNPIPE--IRISH

KEY: D

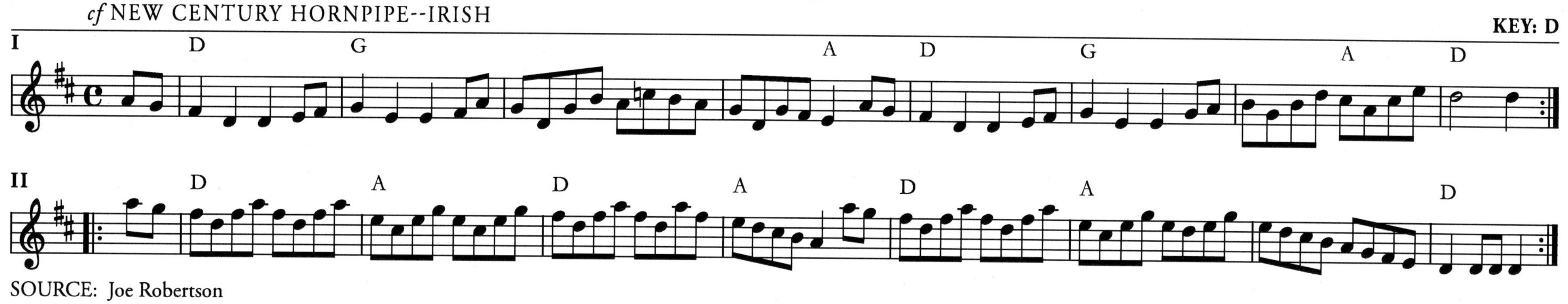

SOURCE: Joe Robertson

THE NEW COPPER PLATE ❁ LORD WELLINGTON ❁ THE NEW COPPERPLATE ❁ WELLINGTON'S REEL ❁ HARDYMANS FIGHT

KEY: G Irish

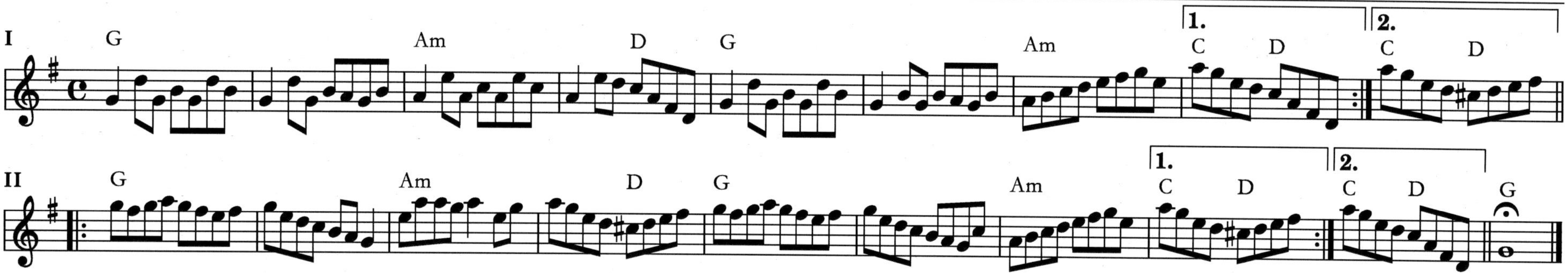

I

II

NEWFOUNDLAND BREAKDOWN

KEY: D Old-Time

I

II

SOURCE: George Stinson

NIAGARA HORNPIPE

KEY: B♭ Old-Time

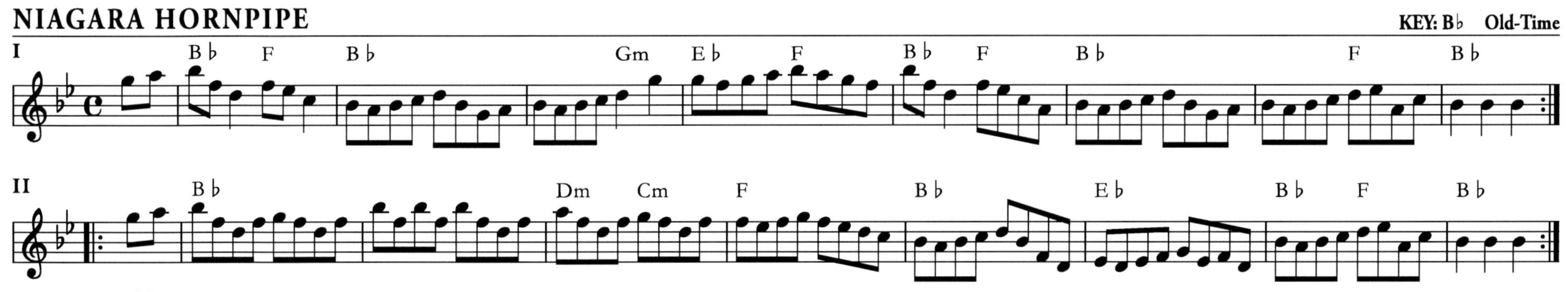

SOURCE: Cole's

NINE MILES OUT OF LOUISVILLE

KEY: G Old-Time

SOURCE: Buddy Thomas

NOTHING TO IT

cf I DON'T LOVE NOBODY

KEY: G Old-Time

SOURCE: Doc Watson

OFF SHE GOES ☸ LANCER'S QUADRILLE ☸ DANSE DES SUTINS ☸ LA GIGUE DU BONHOMME ☸ THE LAUNCH ☸ OFF SHE GOES FOR BUTTER AND CHEESE ☸ PEEL THE WILLOW ☸ RUSTIC REEL ☸ RUSTIC DANCE ☸ UP SHE GOT AND OFF SHE WENT ☸ DOGGIE DOGGIE ☸ DOGGIE DOGGIE BARK AT THE CAT ☸ HUMPTY DUMPTY ☸ THE LANCER'S ☸ TO MIRAMICHI ☸ OFF WE GO ☸ SINGLE ☸ WALTER BULWER'S OFF SHE GOES

KEY: D Old-Time Jig

I
D G A D G D A D G A D A D
II
D G D A D G D A D

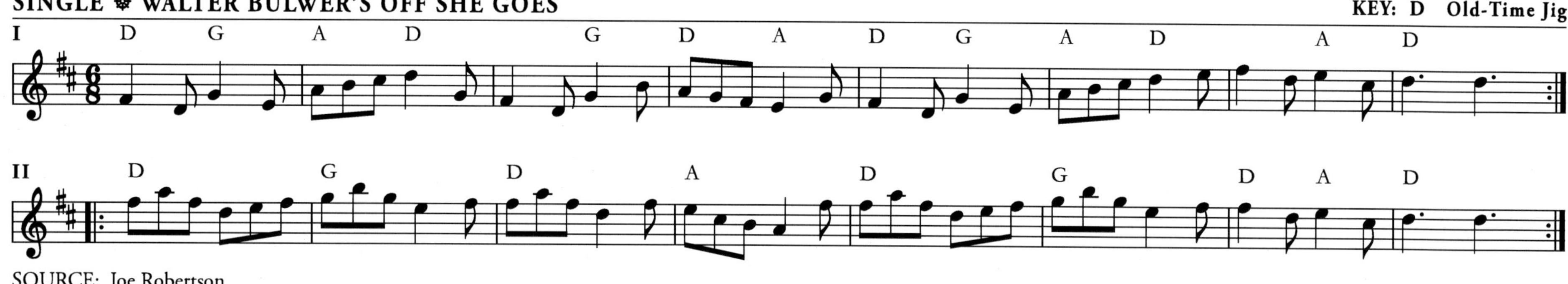

SOURCE: Joe Robertson

OFF TO CALIFORNIA—G ☸ PORTSMOUTH HORNPIPE—A ☸ THE WHISKEY HORNPIPE ☸ GOING TO CALIFORNIA ☸ HUMORS OF CALIFORNIA ☸ INDIAN COTTON JIG ☸ WHISKEY YOU'RE THE DEVIL ☸ WHISKEY IN THE JAR ☸ BUTTERMILK AND CIDER ☸ FIREMAN'S REEL ☸ GYPSY HORNPIPE ☸ MISS JOHNSON'S HORNPIPE ☸ OLD TOWSER ☸ POSSUM UP A GUM STUMP

cf FIREMAN'S REEL *et al*

KEY: G Irish

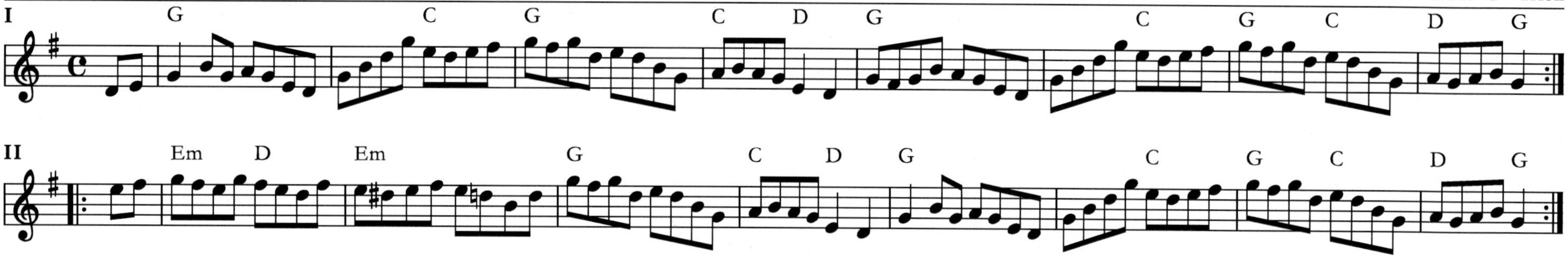
I
G C G C D G C G C D G
II
Em D Em G C D G C G C D G

OFF TO CALIFORNIA—G

KEY: A Irish

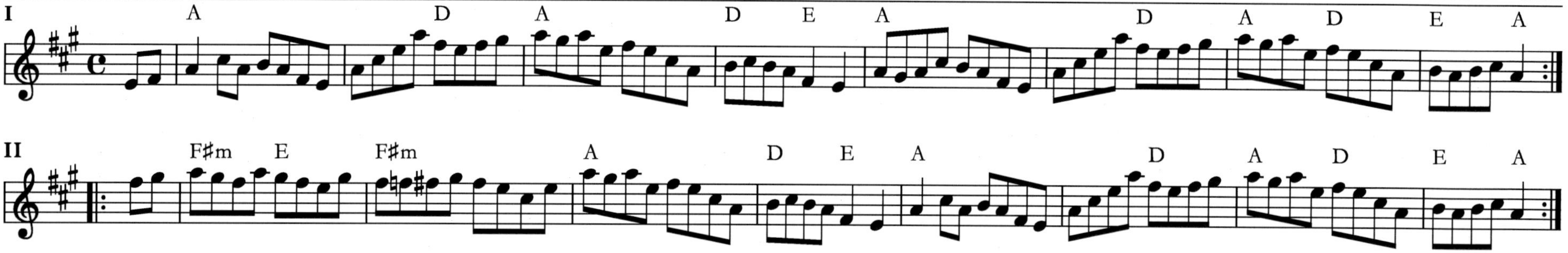
I
A D A D E A D A D E A
II
F♯m E F♯m A D E A D A D E A

O'KEEFE'S

KEY: D Irish Slide

SOURCE: Johnny Cronin and Joe Burke

OKLAHOMA REDBIRD—C

Texas

OKLAHOMA REDBIRD—D

Texas

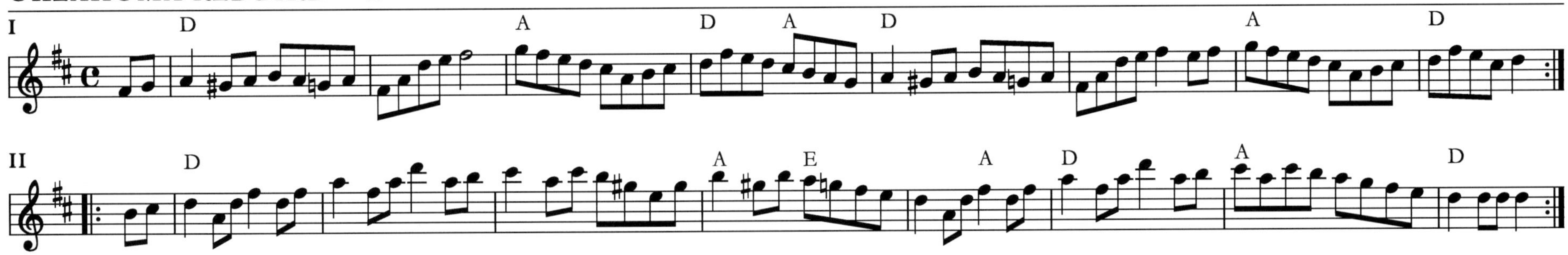

OKLAHOMA REDBIRD—G

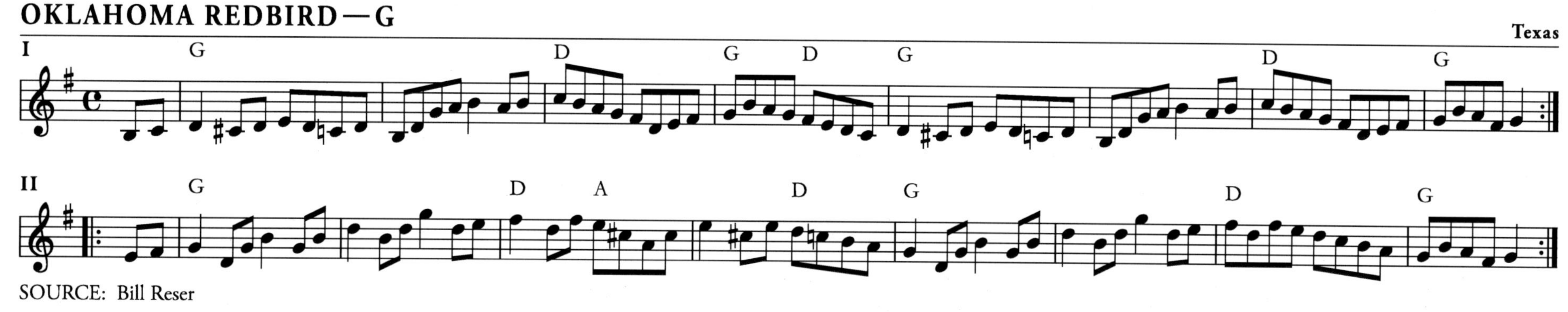

SOURCE: Bill Reser

OKLAHOMA REDBIRD—A

SOURCE: Bill Reser

OKLAHOMA REDBIRD—B♭

SOURCE: Bill Reser

THE OLD COPPER PLATE ❁ THE COPPER PLATE ❁ THE COPPERPLATES ❁ LEITRIM ❁ THE PEWTER TEAPOT

KEY: Am Irish

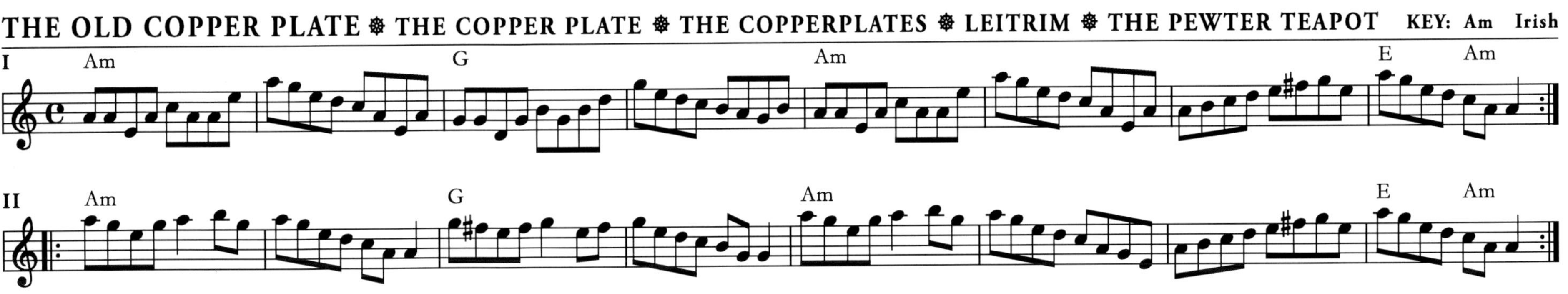

SOURCE: Johnny Cronin and Joe Burke

THE OLD COUNTRYMAN'S REEL ❁ COUNTRYMAN'S REEL ❁ THE FLOWERS OF CAHIRCIVEEN

KEY: B♭ Old-Time

SOURCE: Cyril Stinnett

OLD FRENCH

cf RAMBLER'S HORNPIPE *et al*

KEY: D/A Northern

THE OLD GRAY MARE CAME A-TEARIN' OUT OF THE WILDERNESS ☸ DOWN IN ALABAM ☸ THE OLD GRAY MARE ☸ THE OLD GREY MARE KICKING OUT OF THE WILDERNESS ☸ OUT OF THE WILDERNESS ☸ JOHNNY STOLE A HAM ☸ OLD YELLER DOG ☸ OLD BLIND DOG ☸ THE WHITE HORSE

KEY: G Southern

OLD JOE CLARK ☸ GEORGIA BUCK ☸ OLD JOE CLARKE ☸ ROCK, ROCK OLD JOE CLARK

KEY: G Bluegrass/Southern

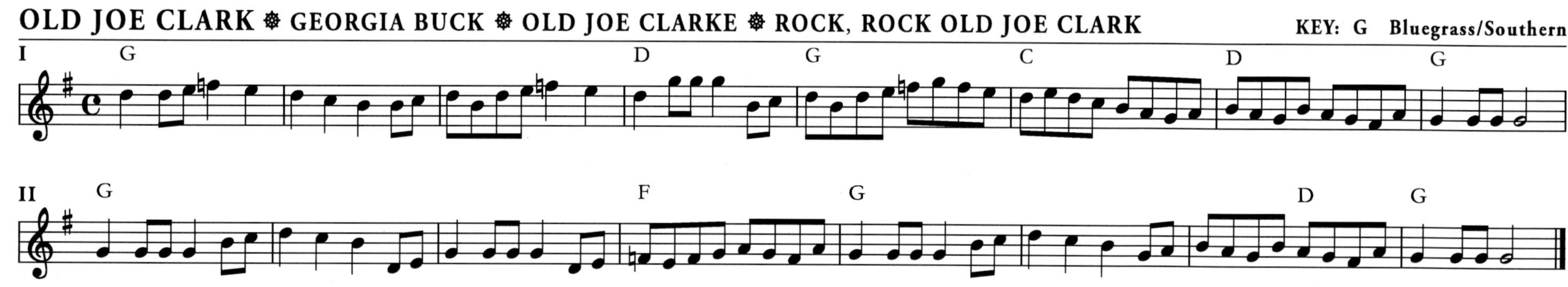

OLD JOE CLARK ☸ GEORGIA BUCK ☸ OLD JOE CLARKE ☸ ROCK, ROCK OLD JOE CLARK

KEY: A Bluegrass/Southern

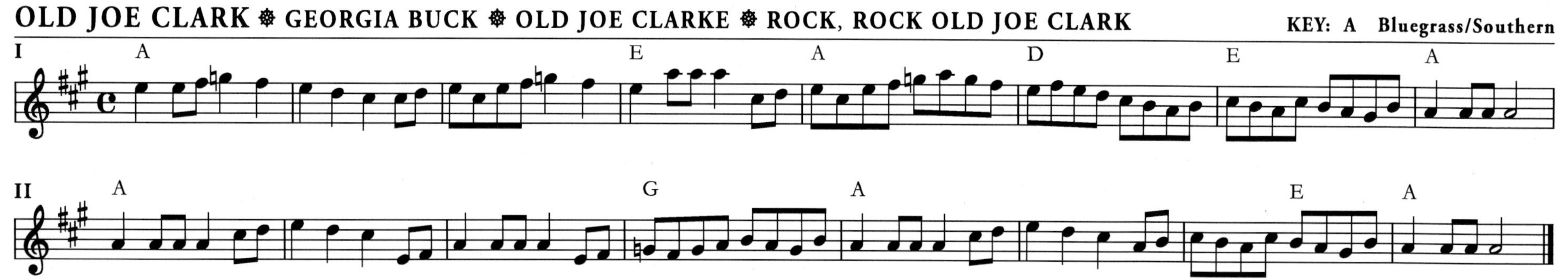

OLD MOLLY HARE ❁ FISHER LADDIE ❁ GRANDMA BLAIR ❁ LADY OF THE LAKE ❁ MOLLY HARE ❁ LARGO'S FAIRY DANCE ❁ OLD GRANNY BLAIR ❁ RUSTIC DANCE ❁ THE FAIRY REEL ❁ BLUE EAGLE RAG

KEY: D Southern

I D G A D G A D II D G D A D G A D

OLD MOTHER FLANAGAN ❁ MOTHER FLANAGAN ❁ OLD MOTHER FINNEGAN ❁ SUKIE FLANAGAN ❁ SOOKA FLANAGAN

cf CHARMING MOLLY BRANNIGAN *et al* & GREEN FIELDS OF AMERICA *et al*

KEY: A Old-Time

OLD ZIP COON ❁ THE OLD BOG HOLE

cf TURKEY IN THE STRAW *et al*

KEY: C Southern

SOURCE: Frank George

OLD ZIP COON ❁ THE OLD BOG HOLE

cf TURKEY IN THE STRAW *et al*

ON THE WAVES

THE ORPHAN ❁ MISS CASEY ❁ HUMORS OF TRALEE ❁ STOLEN CHILD

OVER THE WATERFALL ❁ THE FELLOW THAT LOOKS LIKE ME ❁ PUNKIN HEADLIGHT

KEY: D Old-Time

PADDY ON THE TURNPIKE—G ❁ BUNCH OF KEYS ❁ JENNY ON THE RAILROAD ❁ PADDY ON THE HANDCAR ❁ PATTY ON THE TURNPIKE ❁ FLOWERS OF LIMERICK ❁ HALF PAST FOUR ❁ INDIAN NATION ❁ THE MILLS ARE GRINDING ❁ OLD TOWN REEL ❁ PADDY ON THE HANDLECAR ❁ REEL DU PLOMBIER ❁ TELEPHONE REEL ❁ PIGEON ON THE GATEPOST ❁ THE OLD ❁ PLUMBER'S ❁ LADY ELMER'S ❁ CAIRNGORM BROOCH ❁ CARIGOIM ❁ CARIGOAM BROACH ❁ CARIGON BROACH ❁ MISS BETTY ANN GORDON ❁ MISS WELLINGTON'S ❁ THE YELLOW HEIFER

KEY: G Bluegrass/Irish/Northern

PADDY ON THE TURNPIKE—Gm

cf PADDY ON THE TURNPIKE—G *et al*

Irish

PADDY WHACK JIG ☸ THE GREEN JOKE ☸ PADDY O'WHACK ☸ PADDY WACK ☸ PADDYWHACK ☸ TOMMY RECK'S ☸ WHEN HISTORY'S MUSE

KEY: A Old-Time

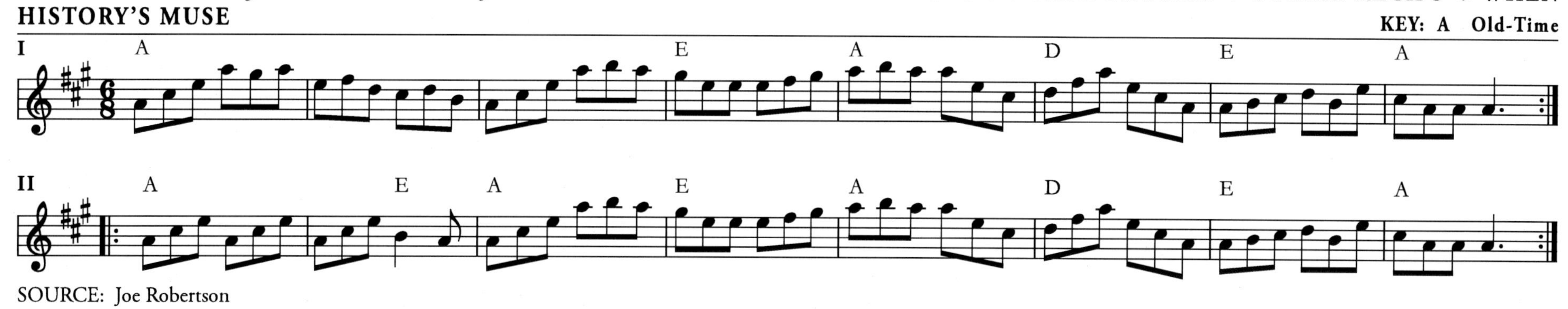

SOURCE: Joe Robertson

PARTIE DU QUADRILLE

KEY: C/G Northern

PETER STREET ☸ BLANCHLAND RACES ☸ TIMOUR THE TARTAR ☸ SWEET PETER STREET ☸ MILLER'S FROLICS ☸ PETER STREET DANCE ☸ BABE IN THE WOODS ☸ BABES IN THE WOOD ☸ NANO'S FAVORITES ☸ PETER'S STREET ☸ TIMOR THE TARTAR ☸ TIMUR THE TARTAR

KEY: A Irish

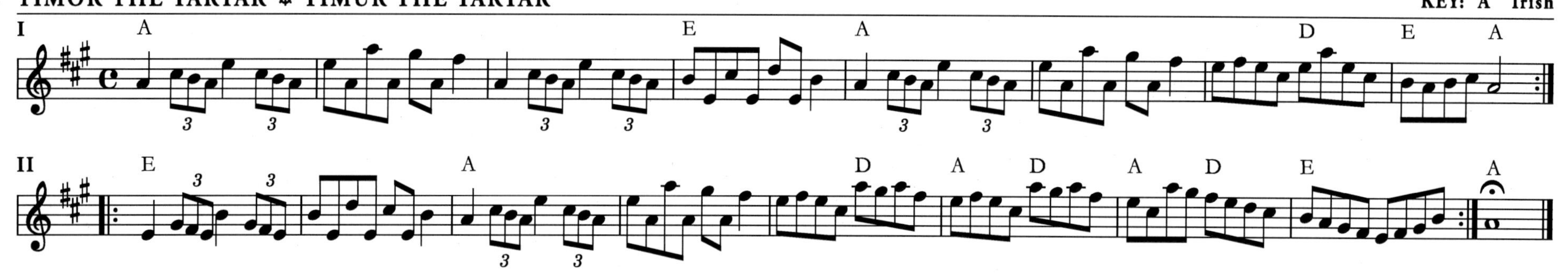

PET OF PIPERS ❁ DOUGHERTY'S FANCY ❁ THE PET OF THE PIPERS ❁ DOHERTY'S FANCY ❁ THE HUMORS OF BALLINAFAD ❁ KIP'S JIG ❁ KIPS ❁ NYANZA INDIAN BAY ❁ PET OF THE PIPES

KEY: G Irish Jig

SOURCE: Delores White

PET OF PIPERS ❁ DOUGHERTY'S FANCY ❁ THE PET OF THE PIPERS ❁ DOHERTY'S FANCY ❁ THE HUMORS OF BALLINAFAD ❁ KIP'S JIG ❁ KIPS ❁ NYANZA INDIAN BAY ❁ PET OF THE PIPES

KEY: A Irish Jig

SOURCE: Delores White

PETRONELLA ❁ PATTERNELLY ❁ PATRONELLA ❁ PATRONELLO ❁ PATRONELLA MARCH

KEY: D Old-Time

PETRONELLA ✽ PATTERNELLY ✽ PATRONELLA ✽ PATRONELLO ✽ PATRONELLA MARCH
KEY: F Old-Time
LA PIEDRERA
KEY: G Mexican Polka
intro
SOURCE: Santiago Jiminez
PIG ANKLE RAG
KEY: D Old-Time
SOURCE: Gus Cannon

PIGEON ON THE GATE—A ☸ PRIDE OF THE BALL ☸ JACK TAR ☸ PIGEON ON THE GATE POST ☸ PIGEON ON THE PIER ☸ THE STURGEON TEA ☸ THE TWIN SISTERS ☸ PIGEON AT THE GATE ☸ THE PIDGEON ON THE GATE ☸ PIDGEON ON THE GATEPOST

cf PIGEON ON THE GATE—Em *et al*

Irish

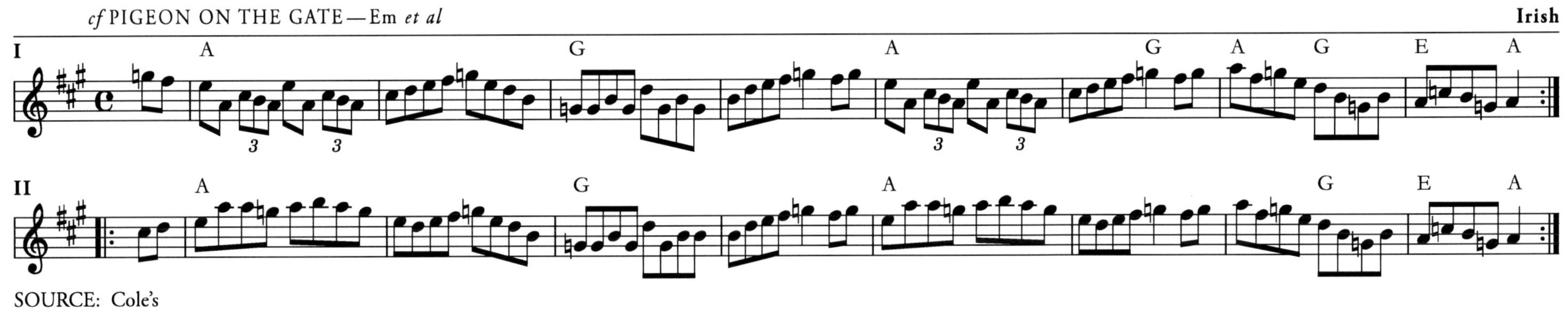

SOURCE: Cole's

PIGEON ON THE GATE—Em ☸ THE ATHOL BRAES ☸ THE DRINKING REEL ☸ THE DRUNKEN TAILOR ☸ GALLAGHER'S BEST ☸ LAGAN SLASHERS ☸ LEAGUE AND SLASHER ☸ PIGEON ON THE PIER ☸ REIDY'S REEL ☸ THE SCOTCH BRAES ☸ THE WANDERING TINKER ☸ BANK OF IRELAND

cf PIGEON ON THE GATE—A *et al*

Irish

PIKE'S PEAK ☸ PROSPERITY SPECIAL ☸ RAT CHEESE UNDER THE HILL

KEY: C Southern

PIPE ON THE HOB ❁ THE LONELY LAD ❁ THE PORTROE JIG ❁ PADDY CANNY'S JIG ❁ THE LOVELY LAD ❁ THE PIPE ON THE HOB Nº 1

KEY: D Irish Jig

THE PLAINS OF BOYCE ❁ THE PLAINS OF BOYLE ❁ PRETTY MAGGIE MORRISEY ❁ ROSCOMMON AIRPORT ❁ THE WEXFORD

KEY: D Irish Hornpipe

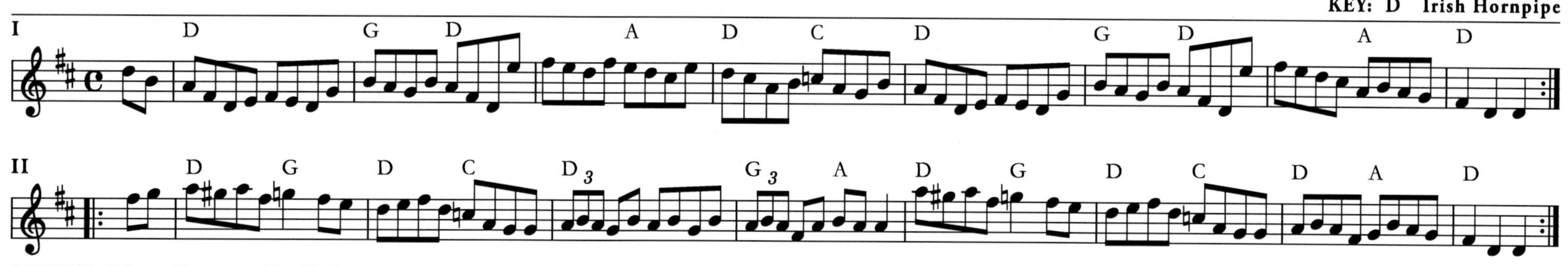

SOURCE: Johnny Cronin and Joe Burke

POP GOES THE WEASEL

KEY: D Old-Time Jig

SOURCE: Cole's

POP GOES THE WEASEL

KEY: G Old-Time Jig

SOURCE: Cole's

POSSUM UP A GUM STUMP

KEY: G Southern

POSSUM UP A 'SIMMON TREE ❁ LITTLE SALLY ANN ❁ NANCY ANNE ❁ SALLY ANN THE GAL I LIKE

KEY: A Southern

SOURCE: Buddy Thomas

PRESIDENT GARFIELD'S (OLD-TIME) ❁ THE BLUE WATER ❁ BLUE WATER HORNPIPE (BLUEGRASS) ❁ GARFIELD'S (OLD-TIME) ❁ NEWCASTLE CLOG (CAPE BRETON) ❁ HIGH LEVEL ❁ LAMENT FOR PRESIDENT GARFIELD (IRISH)

KEY: B♭

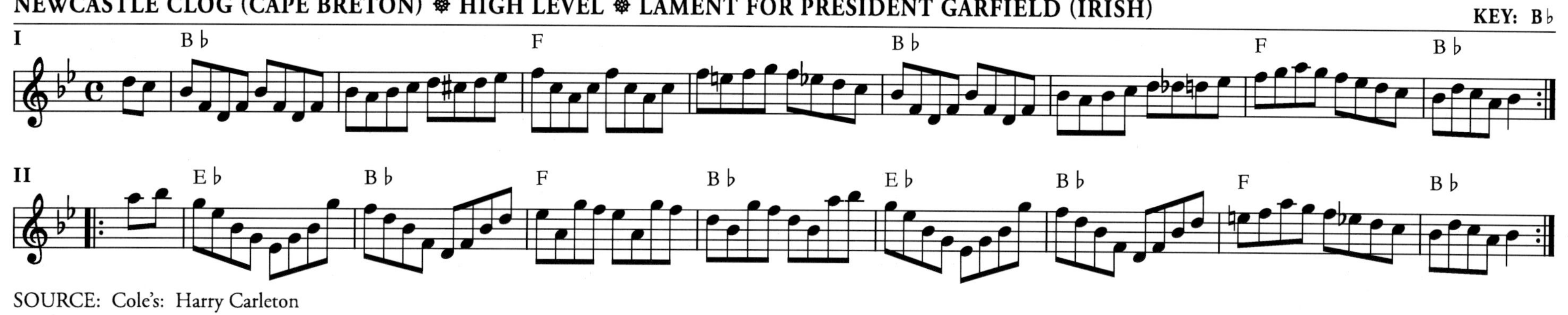

SOURCE: Cole's: Harry Carleton

PRESIDENT GRANT'S ❁ PRESIDENT GRANT'S HORNPIPE

KEY: B♭ Old-Time Hornpipe

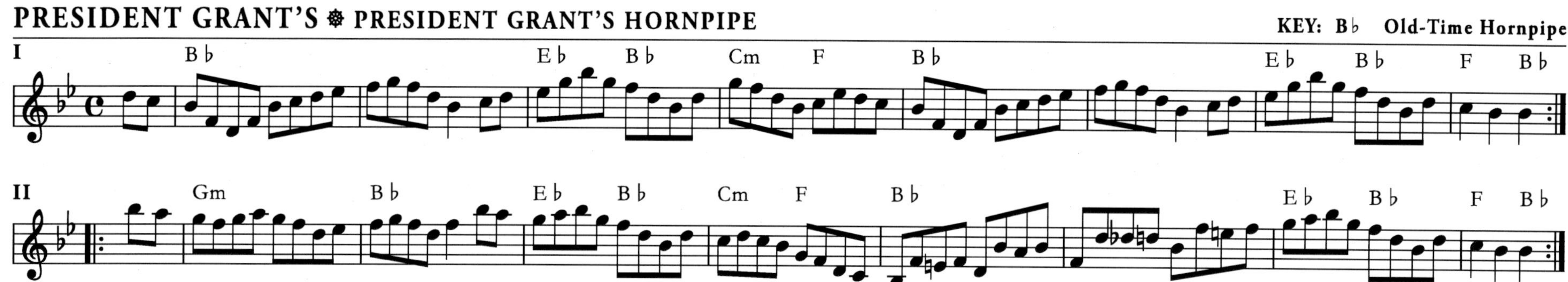

SOURCE: Cole's: Harry Carleton

PRETTY LITTLE DOG ❁ LITTLE DOG

KEY: Am Southern

PRETTY LITTLE INDIAN

KEY: A Southern

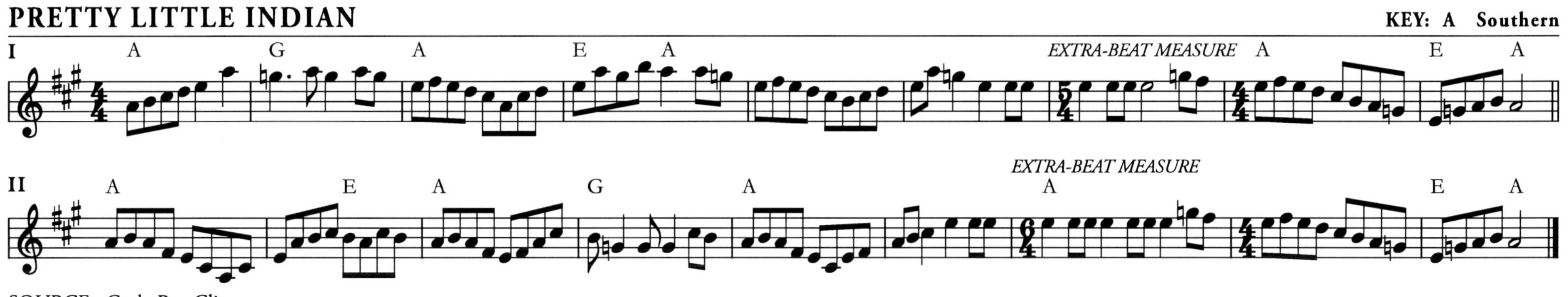

SOURCE: Curly Ray Cline

PRETTY MAGGIE MORRISSEY ❁ PEGGY MORRISSEY ❁ BRIGHTON HORNPIPE ❁ THE FIVE POUND NOTE ❁ O'NEILL'S HORNPIPE ❁ WEXFORD HORNPIPE ❁ HENNESSEY'S HORNPIPE-IN A ❁ DUNPHY'S REEL ❁ LOCH GARMAN McNAMARA'S

KEY: G Irish Hornpipe

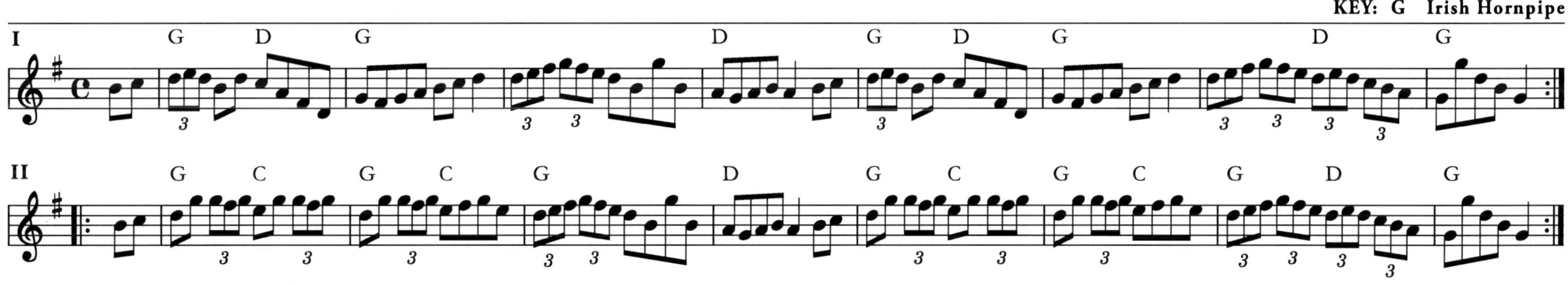

KEY: A Irish Hornpipe

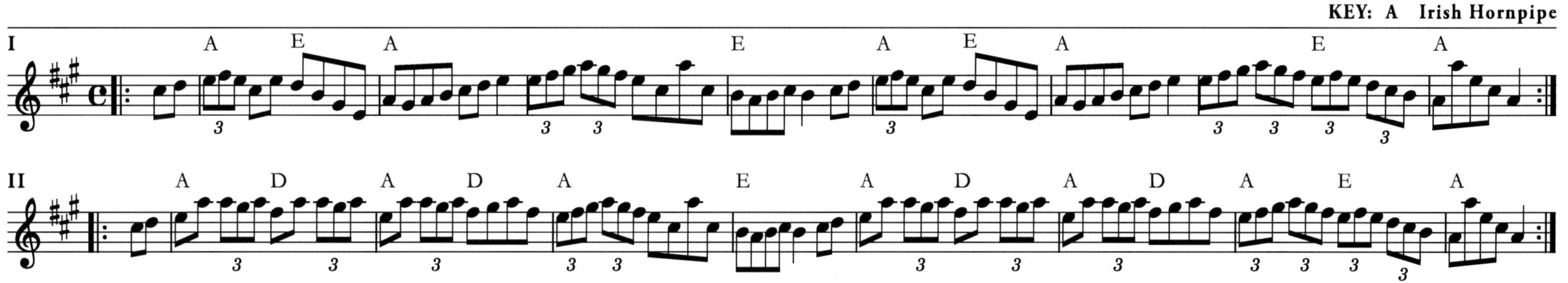

PRIVATE ASS AND CART ✵ THE BONNY BUNCH OF FERNS ✵ CALLAHAN'S REEL ✵ THE CAT THAT ATE THE SIDECOMB ✵ THE DOON REEL ✵ HOT AWAKE ✵ NELLIE DONOVAN ✵ KEADY PIPER ✵ KATE KELLY'S FANCY ✵ O'KEEFE'S REEL ✵ THE RAVELLED HANK OF YARN ✵ TWIN KATY'S

KEY: D Irish

PROUDLOCK'S HORNPIPE ✵ LEWIS PROUDLOCK'S ✵ BELLE ISLE'S MARCH ✵ THE BELLISLE MARCH ✵ BELLISLE'S MARCH ✵ GENERAL MONK'S MARCH ✵ GENERAL MONK'S GOOSESTEP ✵ GENERAL MONCK'S MARCH ✵ MONCK'S MARCH ✵ MONK'S MARCH

KEY: F English

SOURCE: The High Level Ranters

PROUDLOCK'S HORNPIPE

KEY: G English

I
G D G C G D G D G D G C G D G
3 3 3 3

II
G D G D G D G C G D G
3 3

SOURCE: The High Level Ranters

QUEEN OF THE WEST ❁ REEL AUX CHEVEUX BLANCS ❁ REEL DE GASPÉ ❁ SUMNER'S HORNPIPE ❁ THE TOSS POT ❁ THE TOSSPOT ❁ THE VERMONT ❁ VERMONT HORNPIPE—IN A

KEY: D Northern

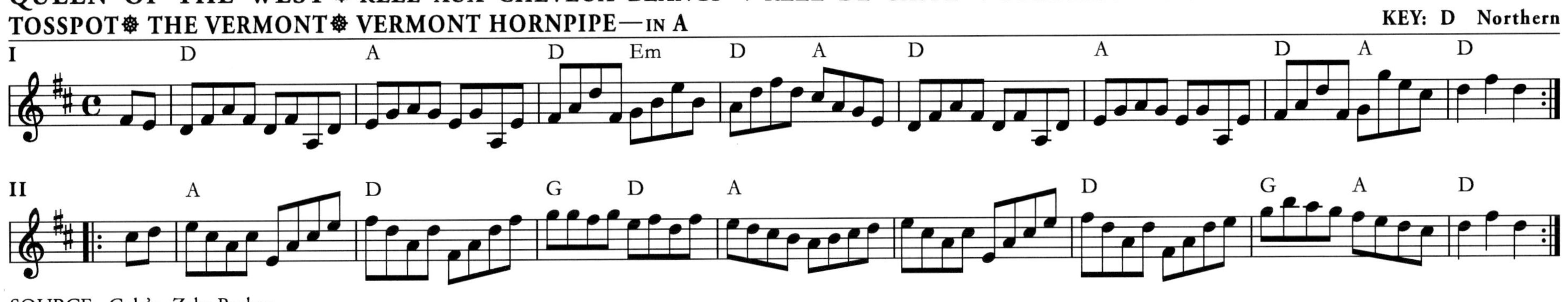

SOURCE: Cole's: Zeke Backus

KEY: A Northern

SOURCE: Cole's: Zeke Backus

RABBIT IN A PEA PATCH

KEY: D Southern

RAGGEDY ANNE ❁ RAGTIME ANNIE ❁ RAGGED ANN RAG ❁ RAGGED ANNIE

KEY: D Southern

THE RAKES OF KILDARE ❁ BARN DOOR JIG ❁ THE BARNDOOR JIG ❁ THE CRANBALLY FARMER ❁ THE FAIR OF DRUMLISH ❁ THE GALBALLY FARMER ❁ GET UP EARLY ❁ THE OLD BARNDOOR ❁ LET US LEAVE THAT AS IT IS ❁ WE WILL SOON HAVE A DEVIL OF A MORNING ❁ JIM M^c^BRIDE'S ❁ LEAVE THAT AS IT IS ❁ M^c^BRIDE'S ❁ THE OLD BARN DOOR ❁ THE RACE OF KILDARE ❁ THE RAKES OF KILDARE RETREAT MARCH

KEY: Am Irish Jig

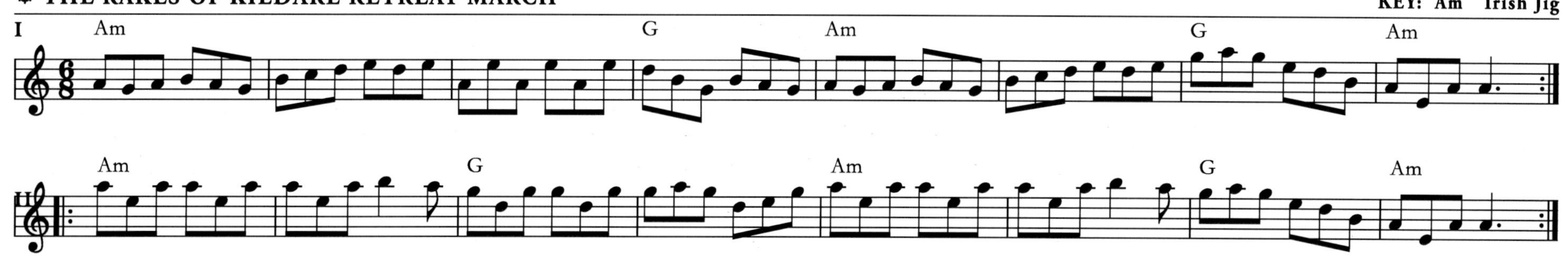

RAMBLER'S HORNPIPE ❁ THE LITTLE OLD MAN ❁ THE RAMBLER'S ❁ REEL DE ST-TITE

cf OLD FRENCH

KEY: D/A Northern

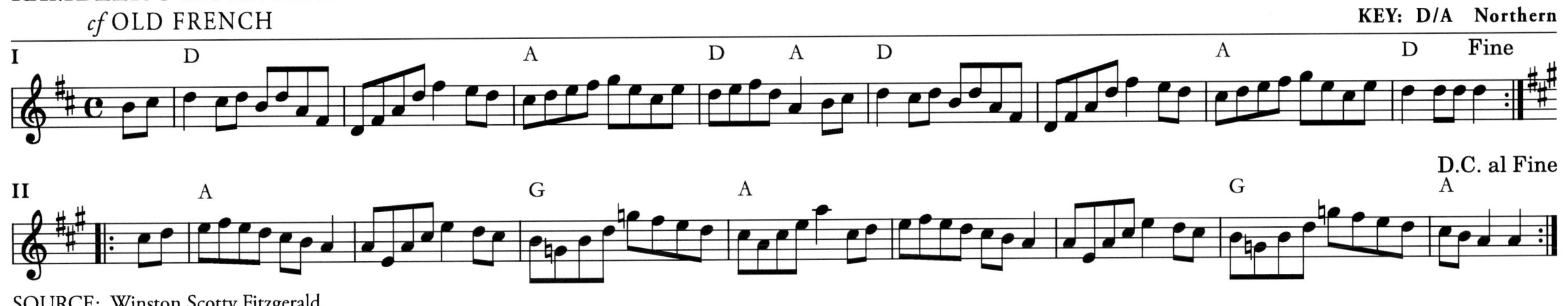

SOURCE: Winston Scotty Fitzgerald

REAVY'S REEL ❁ THE HUNTER'S HOUSEMAID

KEY: G Irish

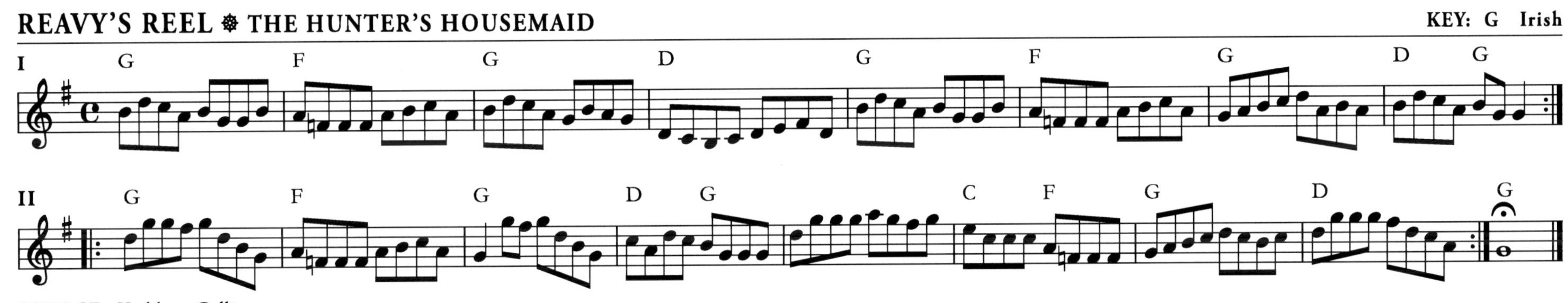

SOURCE: Kathleen Collins

RED APPLE RAG

KEY: G Texas

SOURCE: Arthur Smith

REDBIRD

KEY: A Old-Time

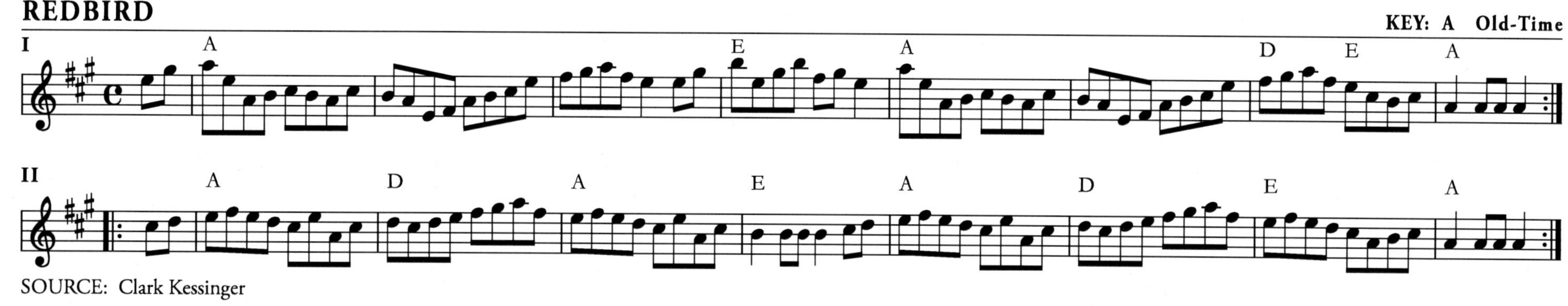

SOURCE: Clark Kessinger

REDDIGAN'S

KEY: G Irish

RED-HAIRED BOY ❁ GILDEROY ❁ GILROY ❁ LITTLE BEGGAR MAN ❁ LITTLE RED-HAIRED BOY ❁ OLD SOLDIER WITH A WOODEN LEG ❁ RED-HAIRED IRISHMAN ❁ RED-HEADED BEGGAR BOY ❁ SOLDIER WITH A WOODEN LEG ❁ WOODEN LEG ❁ THE RED-HAIRED LAD ❁ THE RED-HEADED IRISHMAN ❁ THE DUCK CHEWED TOBACCO ❁ THE FIRST OF MAY ❁ JOHNNY DHU ❁ THE LITTLE RED FOX ❁ THE OLD SOLDIER ❁ LOVELY CHARLIE ❁ THE AULD RIGADOO ❁ THE BEGGAR MAN ❁ DANNY PEARL'S FAVOURITE ❁ GUILDEROY ❁ INDIAN ATE A WOODCHUCK ❁ THE JOLLY BEGGARMAN ❁ THE JOLLY BEGGAR ❁ THE OLD RIGADOO ❁ THY REDHAIRED LAD

KEY: A Bluegrass/Old-Time

RED LINE HORNPIPE ❁ RED LION HORNPIPE ❁ RED LYON HORNPIPE—A

KEY: G Old-Time

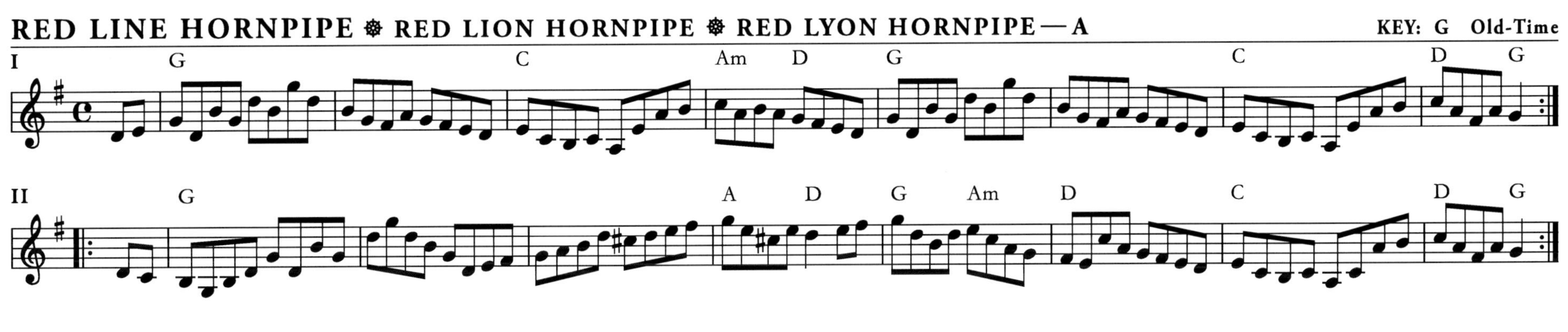

RED LINE HORNPIPE ❁ RED LION HORNPIPE ❁ RED LYON HORNPIPE—A

KEY: A Old-Time

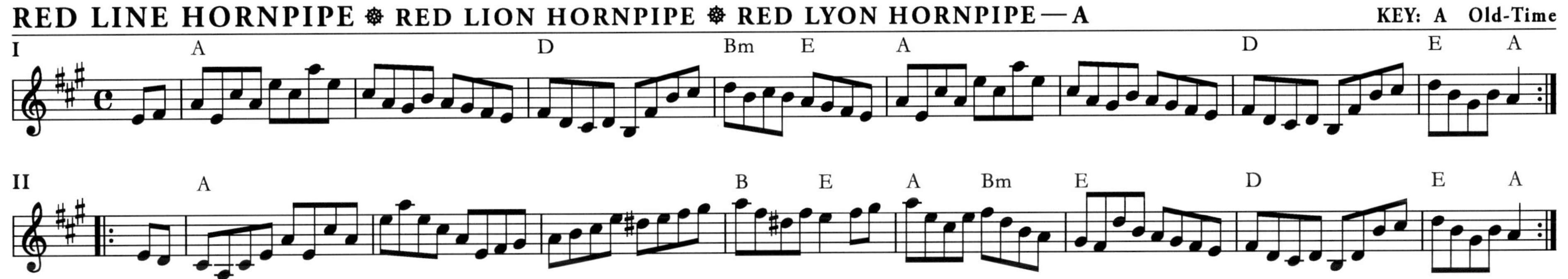

REDWING ❁ THE REDWING POLKA ❁ RED WING ❁ UNION MAID ❁ INDIAN MAID ❁ REEL DU MOULIN ❁ CHARLIE CHAPLIN ❁ LITTLE REDWING ❁ PRETTY REDWING

KEY: G Old-Time

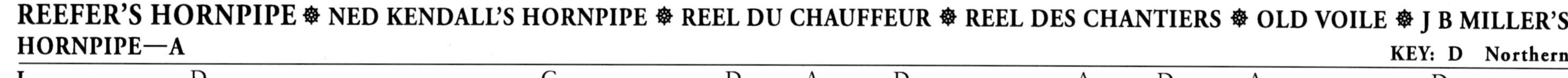

REEFER'S HORNPIPE ☸ NED KENDALL'S HORNPIPE ☸ REEL DU CHAUFFEUR ☸ REEL DES CHANTIERS ☸ OLD VOILE ☸ J B MILLER'S HORNPIPE—A

KEY: D Northern

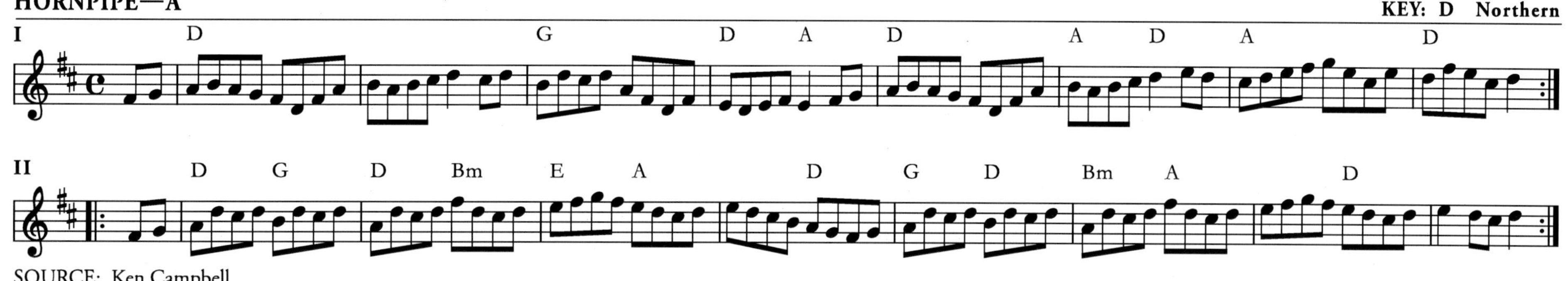

SOURCE: Ken Campbell

REEFER'S HORNPIPE

KEY: A Northern

SOURCE: Ken Campbell

LA REEL DU CULTIVATEUR ☸ THE FARMER'S REEL ☸ GARDENER'S REEL

KEY: C Northern

REUBEN ❁ REUBEN'S TRAIN ❁ TRAIN 45 ❁ OLD REUBEN'S

KEY: D Bluegrass/Old-Time

RICKER'S ❁ RICHER'S HORNPIPE—A

KEY: D Old-Time

KEY: A Old-Time

RICKETT'S HORNPIPE ☸ ILLINOIS RICKETT'S HORNPIPE ☸ MANCHESTER HORNPIPE ☸ RICKETS HORNPIPE ☸ THE SAILOR'S HORNPIPE ☸ TANNER'S HORNPIPE ☸ RABBIT IN THE PEA PATCH ☸ THE NEW COLLEGE HORNPIPE ☸ ONE-EYED FIDDLER ☸ RAKER'S HORNPIPE ☸ TEXARKANA HORNPIPE ☸ TOMORROW MORNING ☸ YARMOUTH HORNPIPE ☸ THE ALDRIDGE ☸ BOTTOM OF THE PUNCH BOWL ☸ THE MANCHESTER ☸ PIBDDAWNS ALDRIDGE ☸ PIBDDAWNS WRECSAM ☸ RICKETS ☸ RICKETTS ☸ THE SPANISH ☸ THE WREXHAM ☸ THE YARMOUTH ☸ MERTHYR HORNPIPE—IN A

KEY: D Old-Time

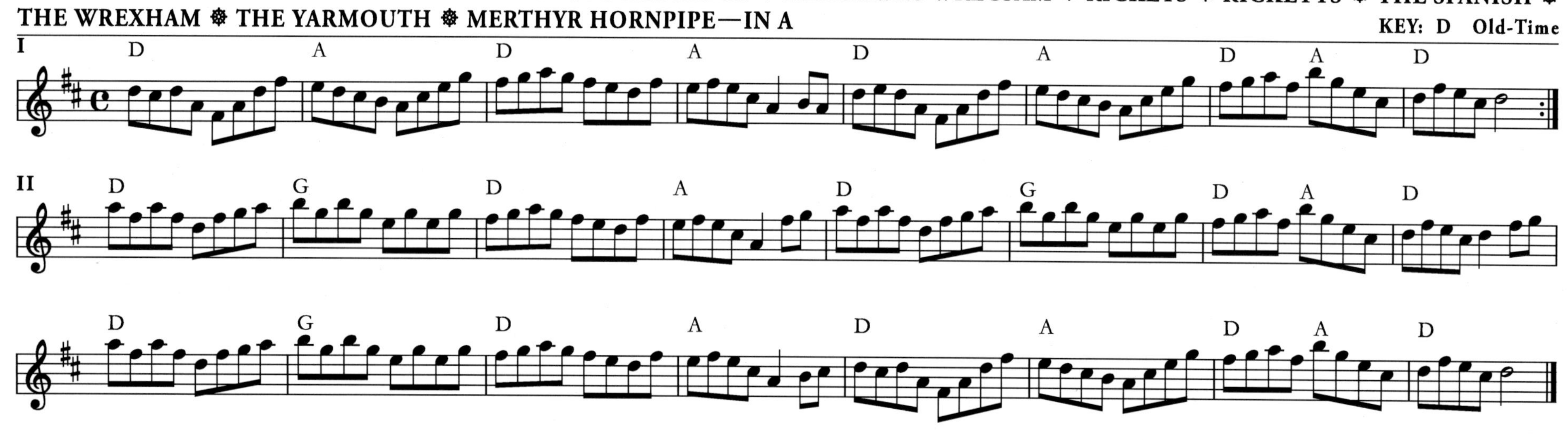

KEY: A Old-Time

THE RIGHTS OF MAN ❁ HIGH COULD CAT ❁ THE RIGHT OF MAN ❁ THE RIGHTS OF HUMANKIND ❁ THE RIGHTS OF WOMANKIND

KEY: Em Irish Hornpipe

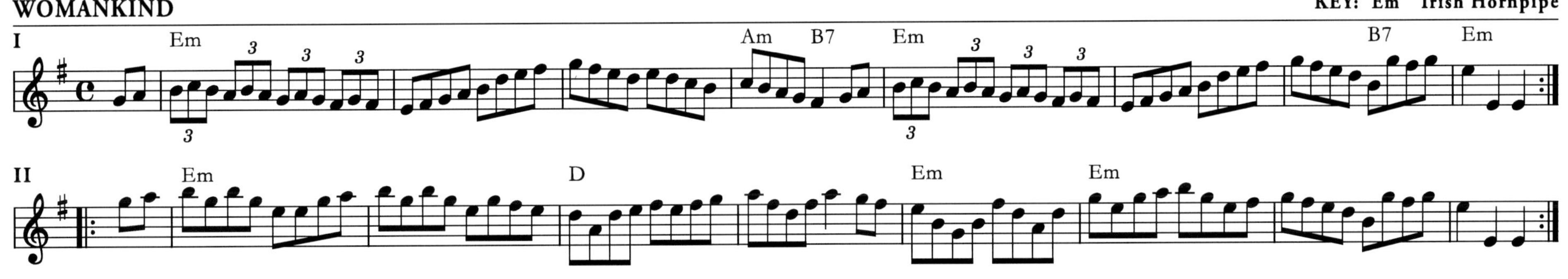

RIPPLING WATERS JIG ❁ RIPPLING WATER JIG ❁ THE RIPPLING WATER

KEY: G/D Northern

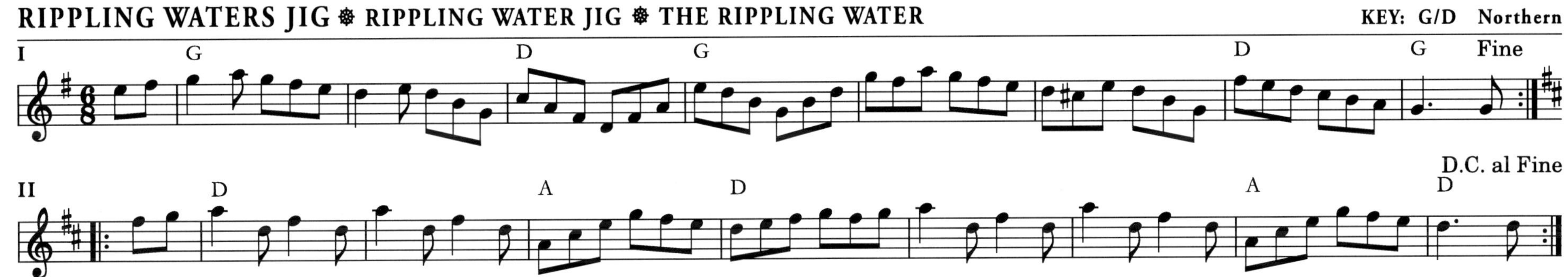

ROARING MARY ❁ FOXIE MARY

KEY: D Irish

ROBINSON COUNTY ☸ ROBERTSON
KEY: D Southern
I
D G D D G D D
II
D A D A D
ROCK THE CRADLE JOE
KEY: D Southern
I
D G A D
II
A D G D A D G A D
ROCKY PALLET ☸ PEAS AND CORNBREAD ☸ ROCKY PALACE ☸ POSSUM AND TATERS
KEY: C Southern
I
C G C G C
II
C G C G C
III
C F C G C F G C

THE ROCKY ROAD TO DUBLIN—G

Southern

SOURCE: Wilson Douglas

ROCKY ROAD TO DUBLIN—A ❁ BLACK BURKE ❁ PROMENADE SIDE-STEP ❁ PROMENADE STEP ❁ THE ROCKY ROAD

Irish Slip-Jig

RORY O'MOORE

KEY: F Northern Hornpipe

SOURCE: John Campbell

ROSEMARY LANE ❁ McCANN'S JIG

KEY: D Irish Jig

SOURCE: Kathleen Collins

THE ROSE TREE ❁ THE ROSETREE ❁ THE DAINTY BESOM MAKER ❁ I'LL CLOOT MHY JOHNNY'S GREY BREECKS ❁ JOHNNY'S GREY BREEKS ❁ MAGEE'S ❁ THE OLD LEA RIGG ❁ LITTLE MARY CULLINAN ❁ LITTLE SHIELA CONNELLAN ❁ MAUREEN FROM GIBERLAND ❁ MOORE'S FAVORITE ❁ PHELIM O'NEILL ❁ PORT LAIRGE ❁ THE ROSE TREE IN FULL BEARING ❁ THE ROSE TREE OF PADDY'S LAND ❁ THE GIMBLET ❁ FORGIVE THE MUSE THAT SLUMBERED ❁ I'D MOURN THE HOPES THAT LEAVE ME ❁ PADDY'S LAND ❁ CUPS AND SAUCERS ❁ THE FALSE KNIGHT ON THE ROAD ❁ LET'S PET THE POPE ❁ LILTED MARCH ❁ LITTLE MAY CULLINANE ❁ MOORE'S FAVOURITE ❁ NANCY HOGAN'S GOOSE ❁ O, I COURTED A FARMER'S DAUGHTER ❁ PORTLAIRGE

KEY: D English

THE ROUTE ❁ JENNY ON THE RAILROAD ❁ OLD MOTHER FLANNIGAN ❁ COLONEL CROCKET ❁ COLONEL CROCKETT

KEY: A Old-Time

RUN BOY RUN ❁ THE PATEROLLER SONG ❁ RUN JOHNNY RUN

KEY: D Southern

RUSHES AND PEPPERS ❁ RUSH AND THE PEPPER

KEY: D Old-Time

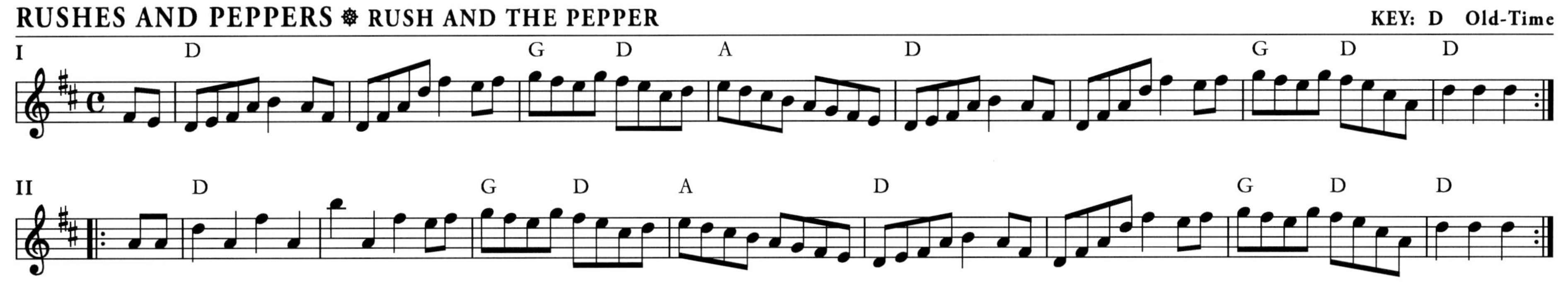

RUTLAND'S REEL

cf SUGAR IN THE GOURD

KEY: Am/C Bluegrass/Texas

RYE STRAW ☸ JOKE ON THE PUPPY ☸ ALABAMA WALTZ ☸ BIG FISH ☸ BLACK MY BOOTS AND GO SEE THE WIDOW ☸ DOG SHIT A RYE STRAW ☸ DOG IN THE RYE STRAW ☸ DOG IN THE STRAW ☸ THE DOG IN DIFFICULTY ☸ ILLINOIS WHISKEY ☸ LADY'S FANCY ☸ LADIES FANCY ☸ PREACHER'S FAVORITE ☸ THE UNFORTUNATE PUP ☸ THE UNFORTUNATE DOG ☸ WHOOP FROM ARKANSAS

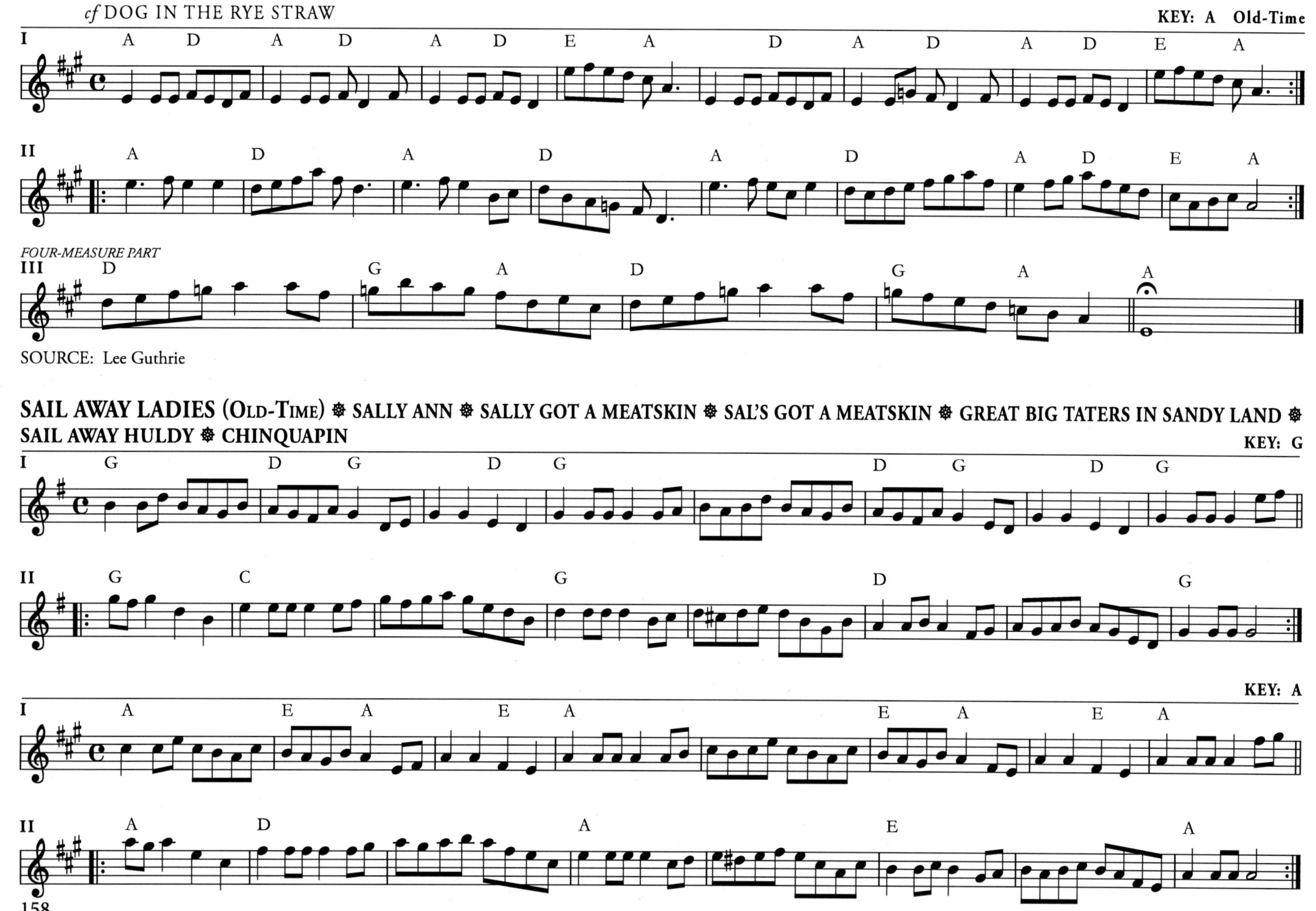

SAIL AWAY LADIES (Bluegrass)

cf SAIL AWAY LADIES (OLD-TIME) *et al*

KEY: G

SAIL AWAY LADIES (Bluegrass)

cf SAIL AWAY LADIES (OLD-TIME) *et al*

KEY: A

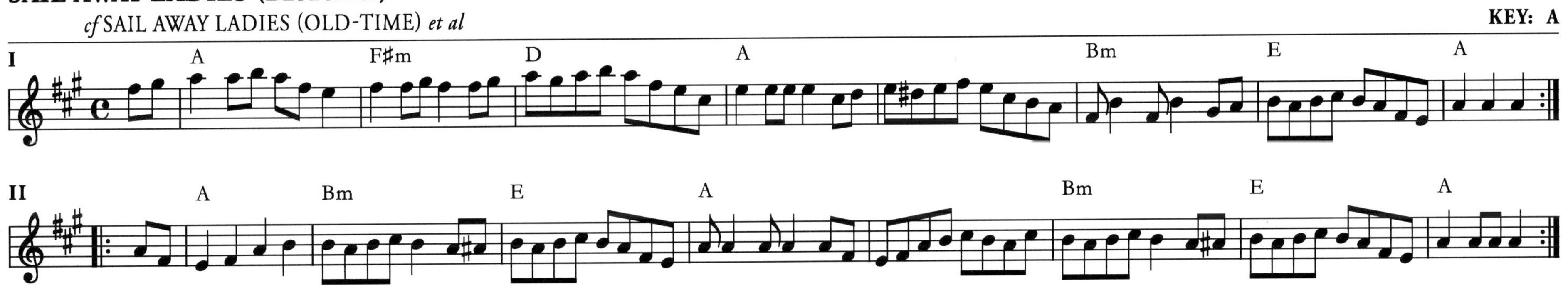

THE SAILOR'S HORNPIPE—C

Old-Time

THE SAILOR'S HORNPIPE—D

Old-Time

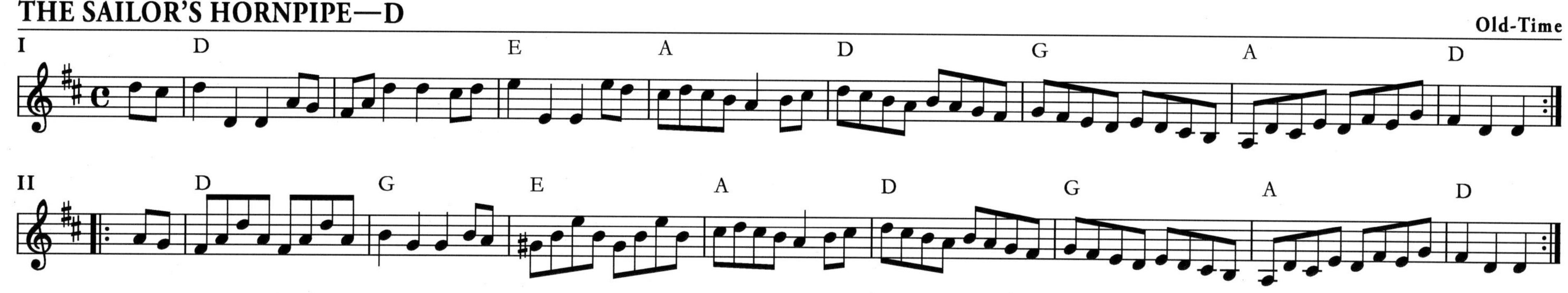

THE SAILOR'S HORNPIPE—F

Old-Time

THE SAILOR'S HORNPIPE—G (Irish) ☸ THE COLLEGE HORNPIPE— B♭ Northern ☸ DUKE WILLIAM'S HORNPIPE ☸ JACK'S THE LAD ☸ LANCASHIRE HORNPIPE ☸ REEL DES MATELOTS

THE SAILOR'S HORNPIPE—A (Irish) ☸ THE COLLEGE HORNPIPE— B♭ Northern ☸ DUKE WILLIAM'S HORNPIPE ☸ JACK'S THE LAD ☸ LANCASHIRE HORNPIPE ☸ REEL DES MATELOTS

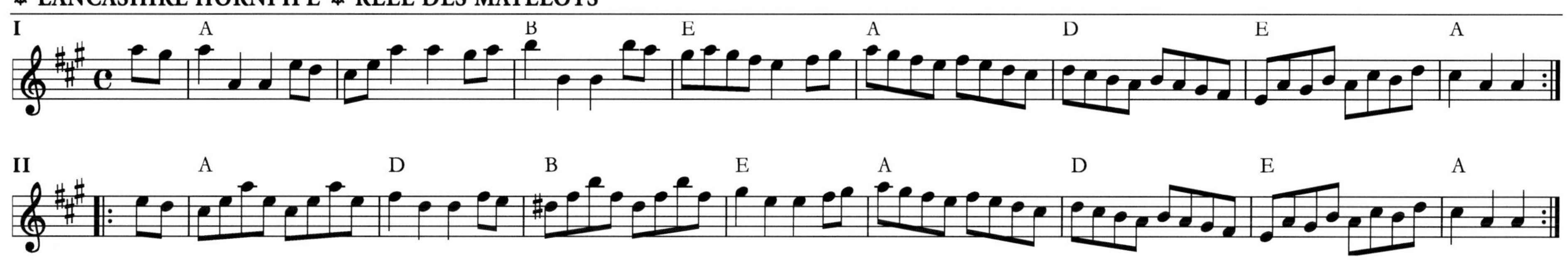

THE SAILOR'S HORNPIPE—B♭ (Irish) ☸ THE COLLEGE HORNPIPE— B♭ Northern ☸ DUKE WILLIAM'S HORNPIPE ☸ JACK'S THE LAD ☸ LANCASHIRE HORNPIPE ☸ REEL DES MATELOTS

ST ADELLE'S REEL ☸ STE ADELE'S REEL

KEY: G Northern

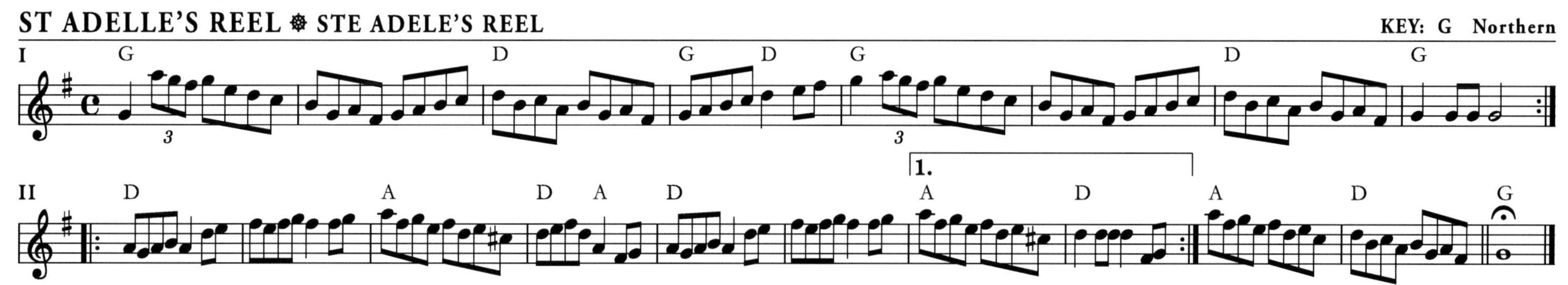

ST ANNE'S REEL ❁ ESQUIMAULTS REEL ❁ QUADRILLE DU LOUP GAROU ❁ LA REEL DE LA BAIE STE ANNE ❁ REEL DES ESQUIMAULTS ❁ STE AGATHE ❁ REEL DE STE ANNE ❁ SAINT ANN'S ❁ SATAN'S ❁ STAN'S REEL

KEY: D Northern

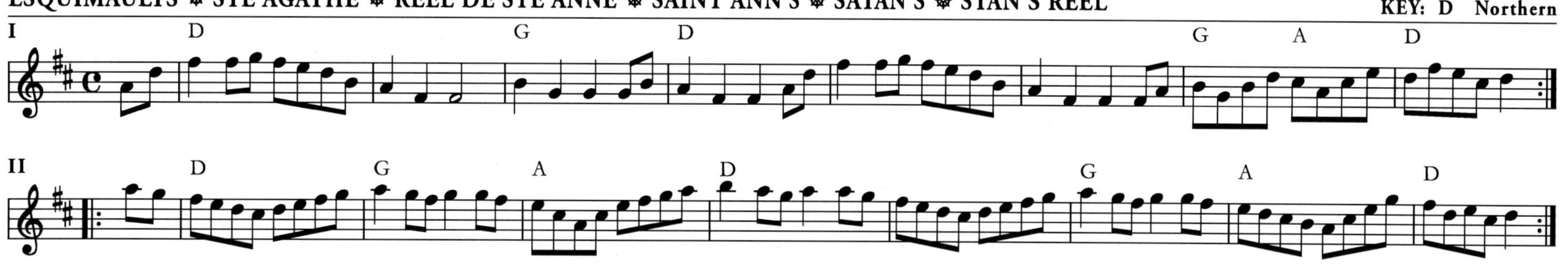

SALLY GOODIN ❁ SALLY GOODING ❁ SALLY GOODWIN ❁ BROKE-LEGGED CHICKEN ❁ SALLY GOODIN' ❁ SALLIE GOODIN ❁ SALLY GOODMAN

KEY: A Bluegrass/Old-Time

SALLY JOHNSON ❁ SALLY ANN JOHNSON'S

cf KATY HILL

KEY: G Bluegrass/Old-Time

THIRD PART IS OPTIONAL

SALT CREEK ❁ SALT RIVER ❁ PATEROLLER

KEY: A Bluegrass/Old-Time

SALTY RIVER REEL ❁ SALT RIVER REEL

KEY: A Old-Time

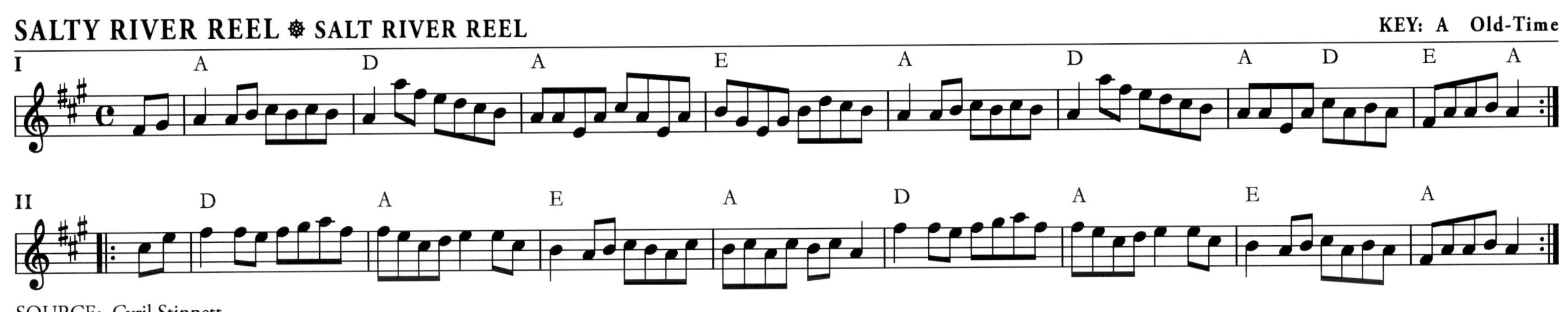

SOURCE: Cyril Stinnett

SANDY RIVER BELLE

KEY: C Bluegrass/Southern

SOURCE: Bill Spence

SANDY RIVER BELLE

KEY: D **Bluegrass/Southern**

SOURCE: Bill Spence

SANDY ROAD

cf FIDDLER'S DREAM *et al*

KEY: G **Bluegrass**

SARATOGA HORNPIPE ☸ SARATOGA REEL

KEY: F **Old-Time**

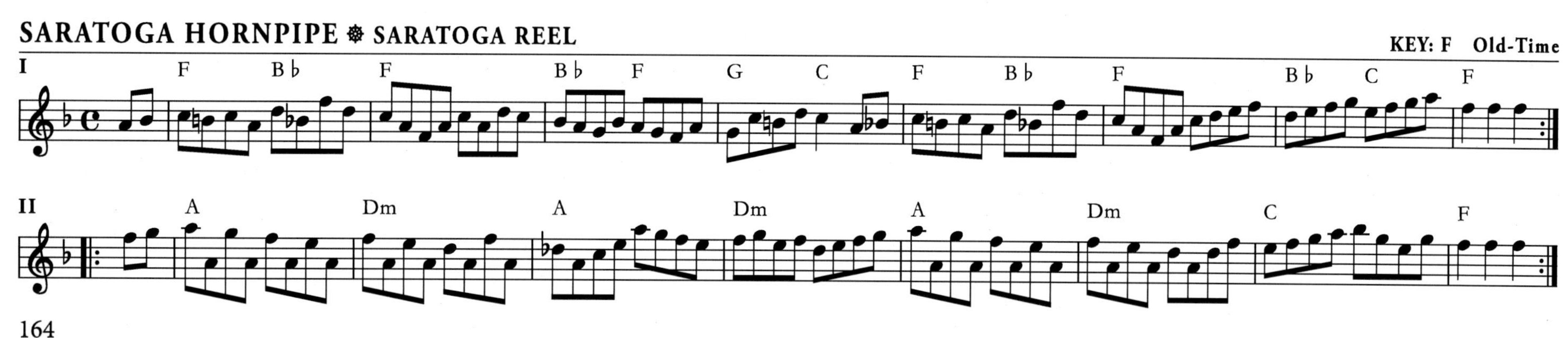

SAY OLD MAN ❁ SAY OLD MAN ❁ CRIPPLED TURKEY ❁ LADY'S FANCY ❁ OH, SAY, OLD MAN, CAN YOU PLAY A FIDDLE ❁ SAY OLD MAN, CAN YOU PLAY THE FIDDLE

KEY: Em/E Bluegrass/Old-Time

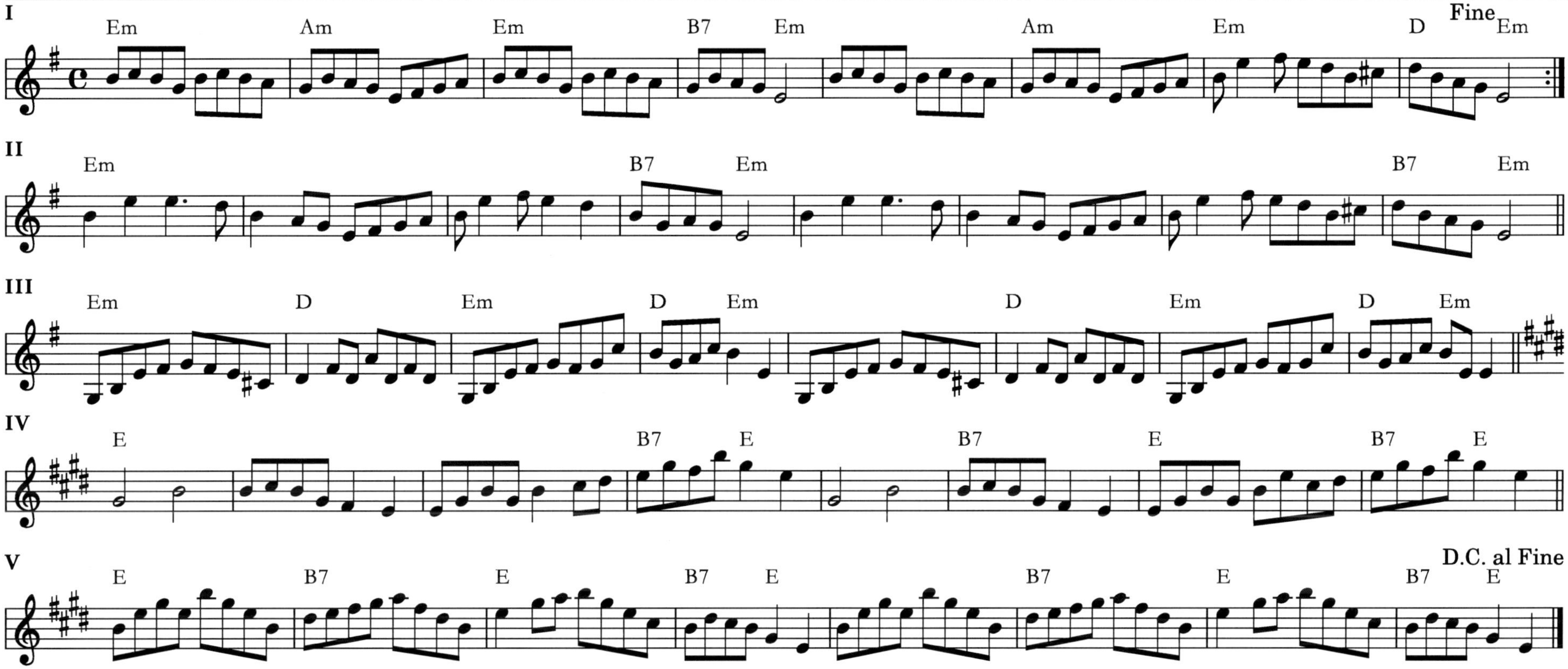

I
Em Am Em B7 Em Am Em D Fine Em
II
Em B7 Em B7 Em
III
Em D Em D Em D Em D Em
IV
E B7 E B7 E B7 E
V
E B7 E B7 E B7 E B7 E
D.C. al Fine

SOURCE: Howdy Forrester

THE SCHOLAR ❁ THE SOUTH SHORE HORNPIPE

KEY: D Irish Hornpipe

I
D G D A D G A D
II
D A D A D

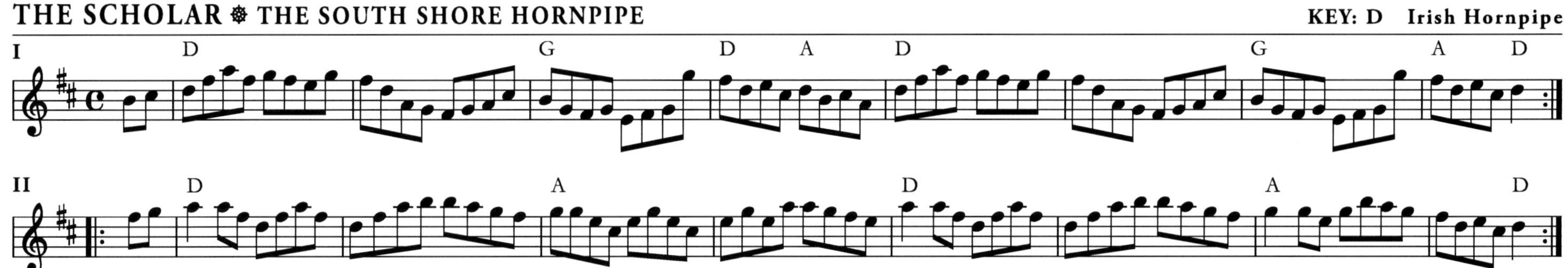

SCOTLAND THE BRAVE ❁ MY BONNIE LASSIE-O
KEY: D Scottish
SEAN RYAN'S HORNPIPE
KEY: D Irish
SOURCE: Kathleen Collins
SEAN RYAN'S JIG
KEY: D Irish
SOURCE: Kathleen Collins

SERGEANT EARLY'S DREAM ❁ THE DISTRACTION ❁ KATHLEEN COLLINS'

KEY: Dm Irish

SOURCE: Kathleen Collins

SERGEANT EARLY'S DREAM ❁ THE DISTRACTION ❁ KATHLEEN COLLINS'

KEY: Am Irish

SOURCE: Kathleen Collins

SETH'S REEL ❁ STEPH'S REEL

cf CAMPBELL'S FAREWELL TO RED GAP

KEY: A Scottish

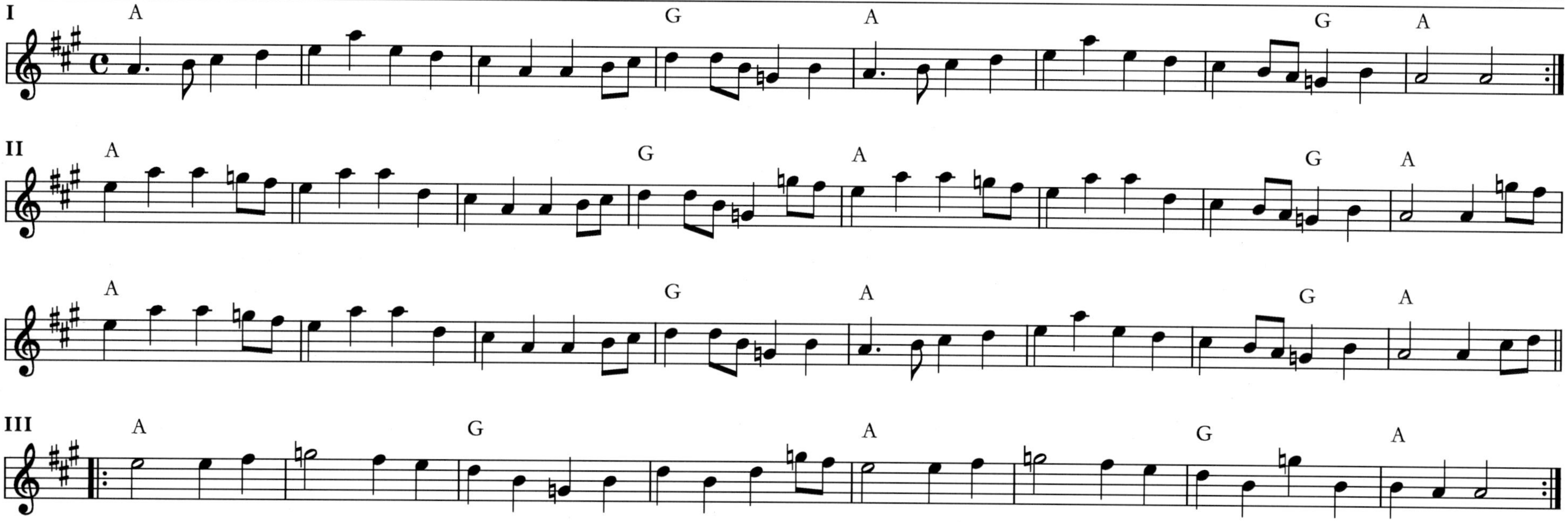
I
A G A G A
II
A G A G A
A G A G A
III
A G A G A

SHEEP AND HOGS WALKING THROUGH THE PASTURE

KEY: G Southern

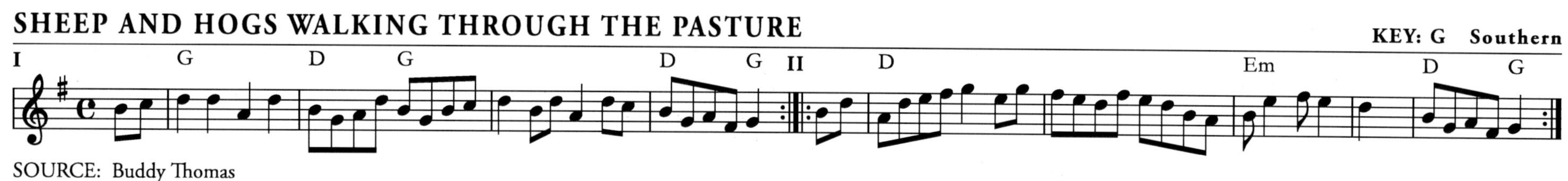

I
G D G D G
II
D Em D G

SOURCE: Buddy Thomas

KEY: A Southern

I
A E A E A
II
E F♯m E A

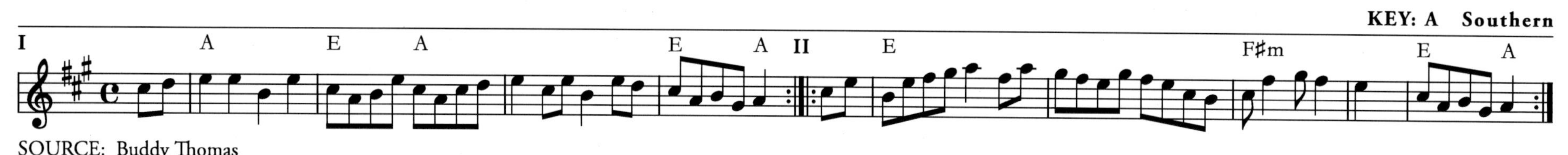

SOURCE: Buddy Thomas

SHELBOURNE REEL

KEY: B♭ Northern

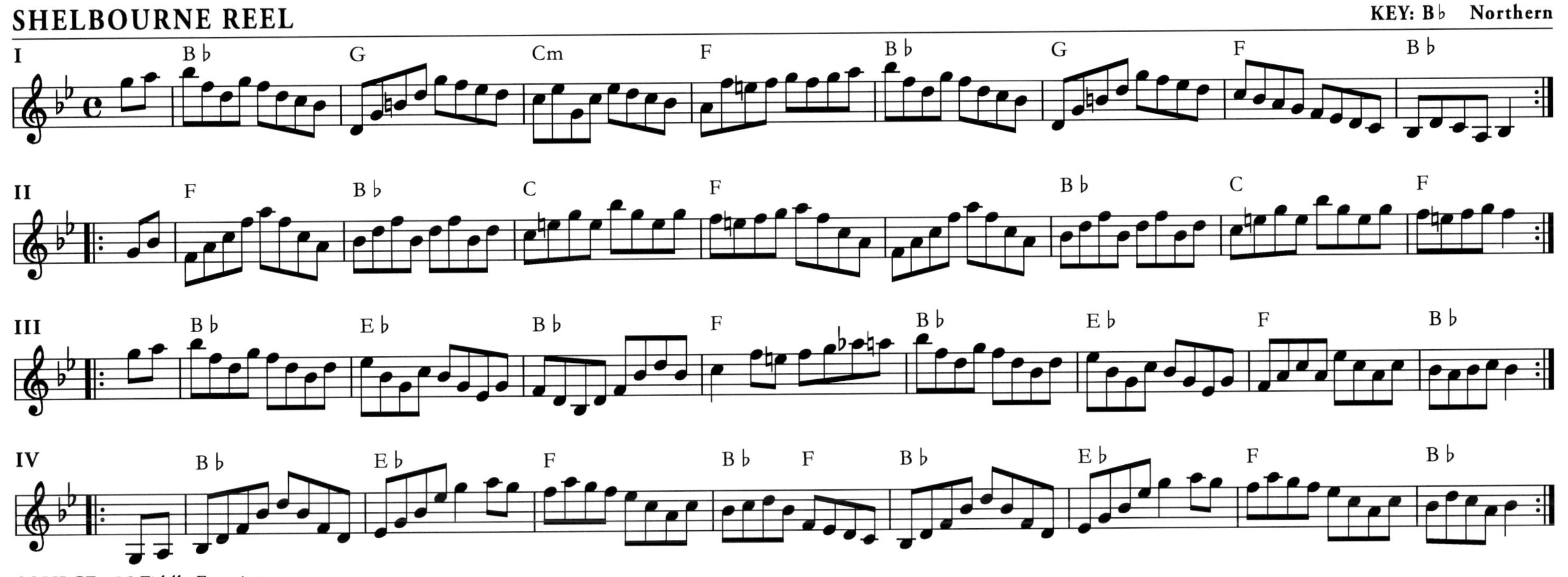

SOURCE: 25 Fiddle Favorites

SHIPS ARE SAILING ☸ ALL DA SHIPS IR SAILIN ☸ ALL THE SHIPS ARE SAILING ☸ THE SEALS ARE SHAPING ☸ THE SHIPS A SAILING ☸ TAKE HER OUT AND AIR HER

KEY: Em Scottish

I
Em D Em G D Em D Em D Em

II
Em D Em D Em D G D Em D Em

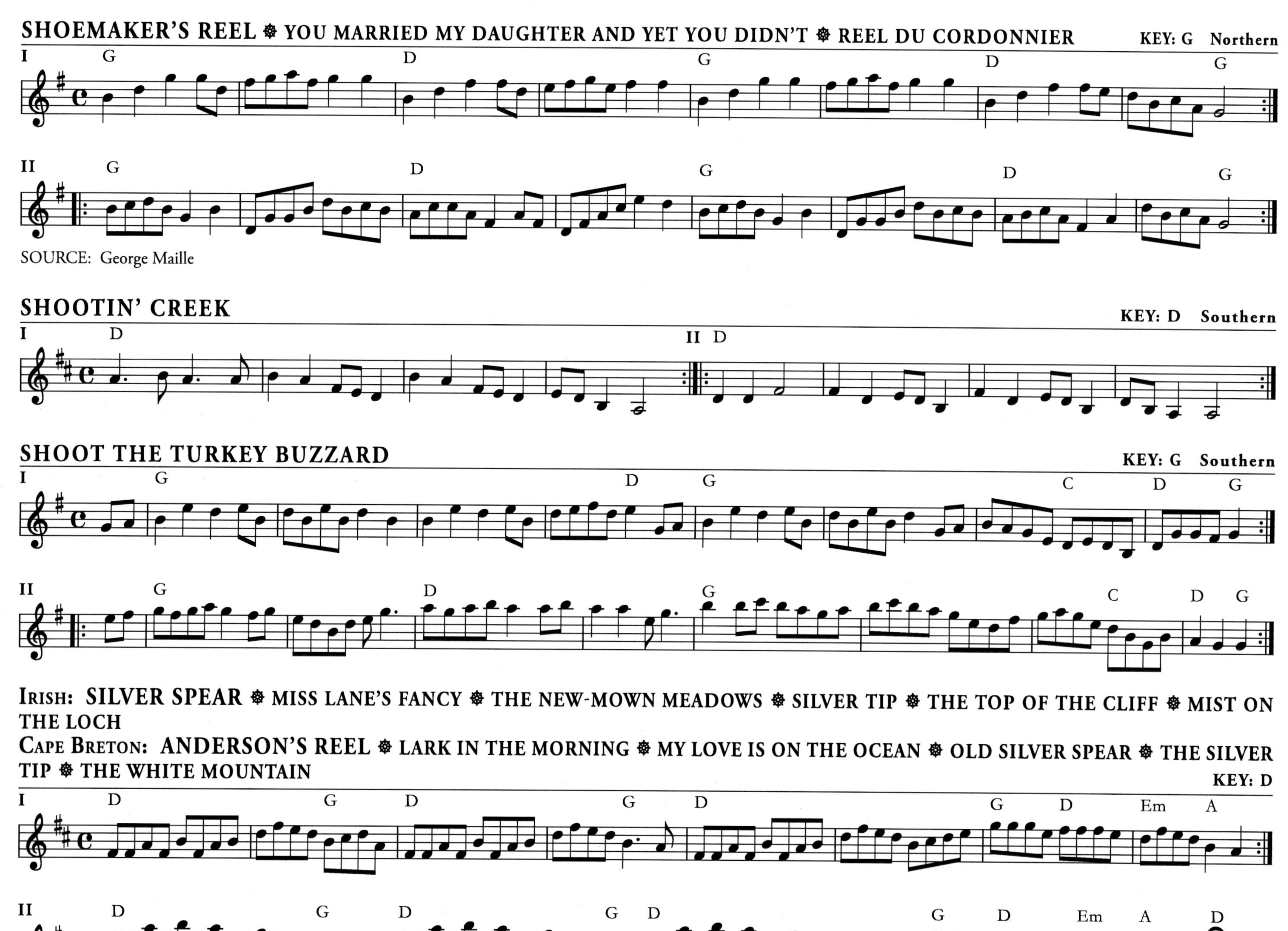

SHOEMAKER'S REEL ❁ YOU MARRIED MY DAUGHTER AND YET YOU DIDN'T ❁ REEL DU CORDONNIER
KEY: G Northern
I G D G D G
II G D G D G
SOURCE: George Maille
SHOOTIN' CREEK
KEY: D Southern
I D
II D
SHOOT THE TURKEY BUZZARD
KEY: G Southern
I G D G C D G
II G D G C D G
IRISH: SILVER SPEAR ❁ MISS LANE'S FANCY ❁ THE NEW-MOWN MEADOWS ❁ SILVER TIP ❁ THE TOP OF THE CLIFF ❁ MIST ON THE LOCH
CAPE BRETON: ANDERSON'S REEL ❁ LARK IN THE MORNING ❁ MY LOVE IS ON THE OCEAN ❁ OLD SILVER SPEAR ❁ THE SILVER TIP ❁ THE WHITE MOUNTAIN
KEY: D
I D G D G D G D Em A
II D G D G D G D Em A D
3
3
3

SILVER STAR HORNPIPE ❁ THE STAR HORNPIPE ❁ THE TWILIGHT STAR
KEY: G Old-Time
I G D G D G
II G C A D G D G C A D G
SOURCE: Cole's
SINKING CREEK
KEY: G Bluegrass
I G F G D G II G F G F G
SOURCE: The Dillards
SIX PENNY MONEY ❁ THE MADCAP ❁ SIXPENNY MONEY ❁ THE SIX-PENNY MONEY
KEY: D Irish Jig
I D G D A D G D A
II D G D A D G D A D G D A D G A D
SLEEPY-EYED JOE ❁ SLEEPY JOE
KEY: A Texas
I A E A E A
II A E A E A

THE SMALL HILLS OF OFFLAY ☸ THE SMALL HILLS OF OFFALY ☸ THE LITTLE HILLS OF OFFALY
KEY: D Irish
SMASH THE WINDOWS ☸ ROARING JELLY ☸ SMASH THE WINDOW ☸ GIGUE DE CHICOUTIMI ☸ LA GIGUE DES BELLES FILLES ☸ REEL STADACONA
KEY: D Northern Jig
SNORING MRS GOBEIL ☸ RONFLEUSE GOBEIL
KEY: C Northern

SNOW DEER

KEY: D Old-Time

SNOW DEER

KEY: G Old-Time

SNOWFLAKE BREAKDOWN ❅ SNOWFLAKE REEL

KEY: D Bluegrass/Old-Time

SOURCE: 25 Fiddle Favorites

SNOWFLAKE HORNPIPE

KEY: A Old-Time

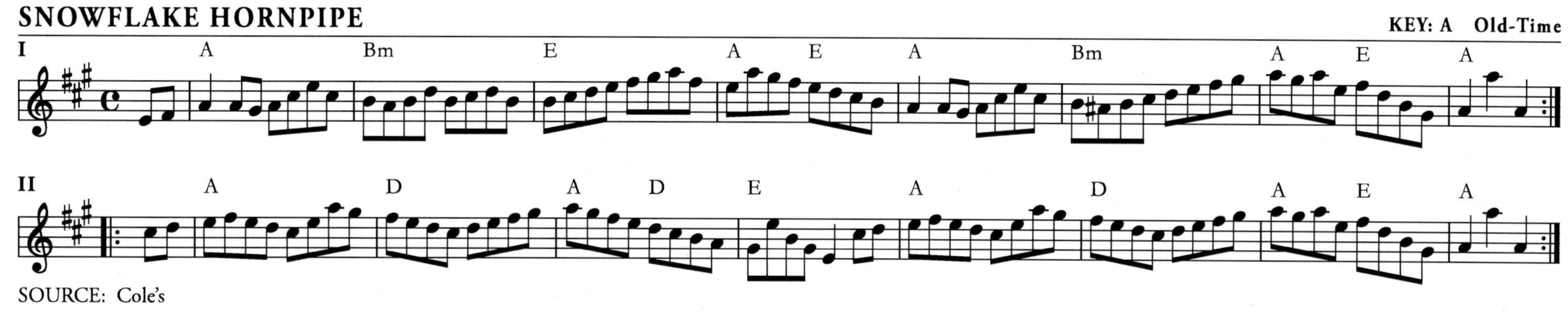

SOURCE: Cole's

SOLDIER'S JOY ❁ FRENCH FOUR ❁ I LOVE SOMEBODY ❁ THE KING'S HEAD ❁ LOVE SOMEBODY ❁ LOVE SOMEBODY, YES I DO ❁ NEW SOLDIER'S JOY ❁ SAILOR'S HORNPIPE ❁ THE SOLDIER'S JOY HORNPIPE ❁ WILD BILL REEL ❁ YELLOW PEACHES REEL ❁ AM MY MAMMA'S DARLIN' CHILD ❁ THE KING'S HORNPIPE ❁ JOHN WHITE ❁ LA JOI DE SOLDAT ❁ THE MILANESE COUNTRY DANCE ❁ PAYDAY IN THE ARMY ❁ ROCK THE CRADLE LUCY ❁ CHICKEN IN THE BREAD TRAY ❁ THE CLAP DANCE ❁ DA SOLDIER'S JOY ❁ THE GOWER ❁ LUMBERS ❁ THE MORRIS REEL ❁ PIBDDAWNS GWYR ❁ REEL DES POMPIERS ❁ REEL DU VAGABOND ❁ SEKSMANNSRIL

KEY: D Old-Time

SOPPIN' THE GRAVY
KEY: D Texas
SORENSON'S RHINELANDER
KEY: G/C Scandinavian
Fine
D.C. al Fine
SOURCE: Leroy Larsen
SOURWOOD MOUNTAIN ❁ I'VE GOT A WOMAN ON SOURWOOD MOUNTAIN
KEY: G Southern

SPANISH JIG
KEY: C Old-Time
SOURCE: Dudley Laufman
SPEED THE PLOUGH ☸ DROGHAN HILL ☸ THE DOON REEL ☸ GLENGARRY ☸ GOD SPEED THE PLOUGH ☸ GOD SPEED THE PLOW ☸ THE NAVAL PILLAR ☸ OFF IN THE MORNING ☸ REEL MATANE ☸ TIRE LA LANGUE ☸ QUIGLEY'S
KEY: A Irish
SPEED THE PLOW
cf SPEED THE PLOUGH et al
KEY: A Old-Time
SOURCE: Levi Masse
PARTS ARE OFTEN REVERSED
SPOTTED PONY
KEY: D Southern

STAR OF MUNSTER ❁ THE BRIGHT STAR OF MUNSTER ❁ MUNSTER ❁ MUNSTER'S STAIRS ❁ THE STARS OF MUNSTER

KEY: Am Irish

SOURCE: Kathleen Collins

STAR OF MUNSTER ❁ THE BRIGHT STAR OF MUNSTER ❁ MUNSTER ❁ MUNSTER'S STAIRS ❁ THE STARS OF MUNSTER

KEY: Gm Irish

SOURCE: Kathleen Collins

STATEN ISLAND HORNPIPE ❁ THE ARRANMORE FERRY ❁ BURNS'S HORNPIPE ❁ NONE SO PRETTY ❁ THE STATEN ISLAND FERRY ❁ THE STATEN ISLAND

KEY: D Old-Time

SUCCESS TO THE FLEET

SUGAR IN THE GOURD—A

SOURCE: Frank George

SUGAR IN THE GOURD—Am

cf RUTLAND'S REEL

THE SUNSHINE HORNPIPE ❁ ST ELMO'S HORNPIPE ❁ SHUNSTER HORNPIPE ❁ THE PANSY BLOSSOM ❁ SHUNTER'S HORNPIPE—A

KEY: A Old-Time

SOURCE: Cole's

SWALLOWTAIL JIG ❁ THE DANCING MASTER ❁ DROMEY'S FANCY ❁ FROM THE NEW COUNTRY ❁ GIGUE DE BARNABE ❁ SWALLOW'S NEST ❁ THE CUSTOM HOUSE ❁ THE NEW COUNTRY ❁ FROM THE NEW WORLD ❁ FROM THE NEXT COUNTRY ❁ THE SWALLOW TAIL❁ THE SWALLOW'S TAIL

KEY: Em Northern

SOURCE: John Campbell

SWAMPLAKE BREAKDOWN ❁ SHULL CREEK

KEY: G Old-Time

SOURCE: Enoch Cameron

SWEDISH WALKING TUNE ❁ GÅRDEBYLÅTEN ❁ BOFFMAN'S REEL

KEY: G Scandinavian

SWINGING ON THE GATE ❁ KATHERINE BRENNAN'S FAVORITE ❁ CHARLIE HARRIS'S

KEY: G Irish

TEETOTALER ❁ THE DEVIL IN GEORGIA ❁ GOLDEN GRIP ❁ JOHNNY'S FAVORITE ❁ TEETOTALER'S FANCY ❁ TEETOTALER'S REEL ❁ TEMPERANCE REEL ❁ GIGUE DU PERE LAUZON ❁ KINGSPORT ❁ OH MY FOOT ❁ OLD TIDDLEY-TOE ❁ GOL GRIER ❁ ROCKY ROAD TO DENVER ❁ SIX HAND REEL ❁ WHERE'S MY OTHER FOOT? ❁ PEELER'S JACKET ❁ TEMPERENCE REEL ❁ BOWL OF COFFEE ❁ PROHIBITION ❁ THE ROAD TO NEWBRIDGE ❁ THE TEATOTALER'S FANCY ❁ TEATOTLERS ❁ THE TEETH OF TAILORS ❁ THE TEMPERANCE

KEY: G Old-Time

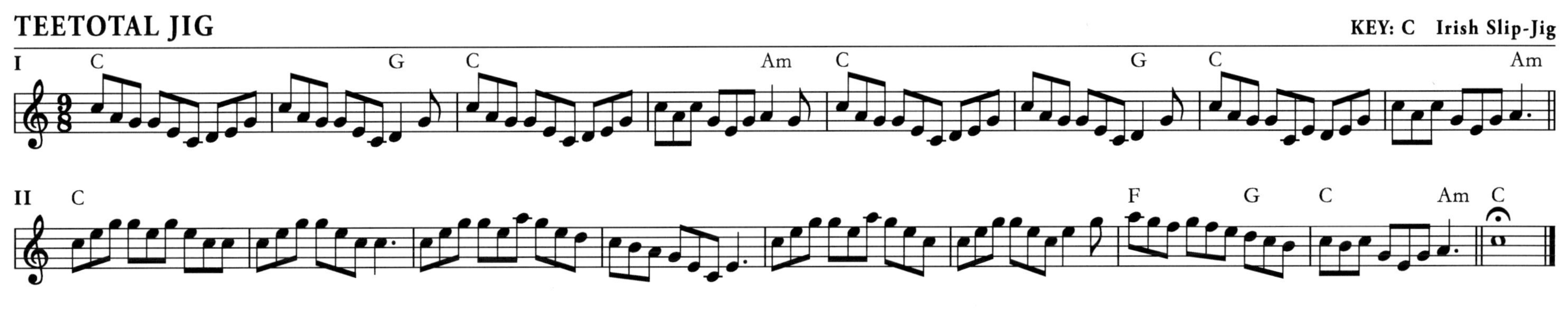
TEETOTAL JIG
KEY: C Irish Slip-Jig
I
C G C Am C G C Am
II
C F G C Am C

TELEGRAPH HORNPIPE
KEY: G/D Old-Time
I
G D G D G
Fine
II
D G A D A D G A
1. D
2. D
D.C. al Fine

TELEPHONE HORNPIPE
KEY: D Old-Time
I
D A D G A D
II
A D F♯ Bm Em D A Bm G A D

TENNESSEE FIDDLER

KEY: G Bluegrass/Southern

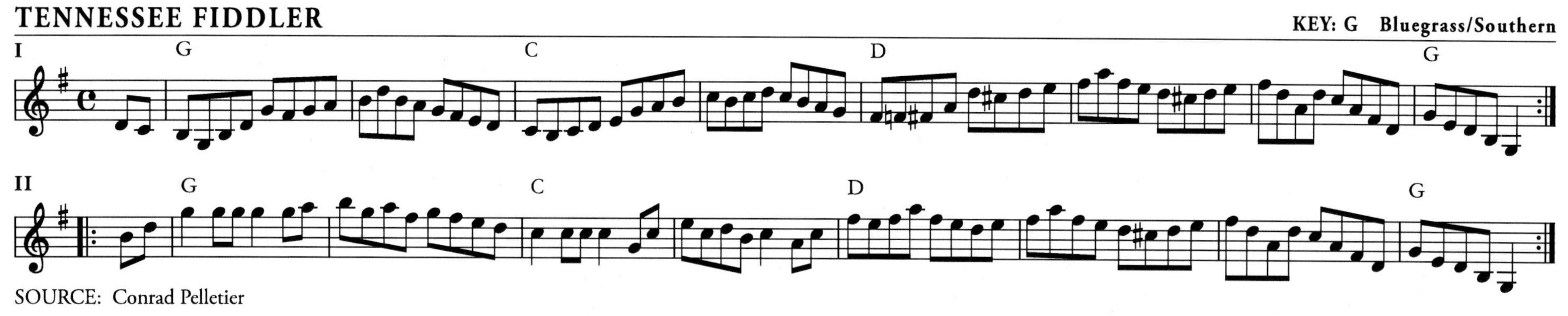

SOURCE: Conrad Pelletier

THE TEN-PENNY BIT ❁ PADDY O'RAFFERTY ❁ BILLY'S AWAKE ❁ THE THREE LITTLE DRUMMER BOYS ❁ THE THREE LITTLE DRUMMERS ❁ TEN PENNEY BIT

KEY: Am Irish Jig

TEXAS ❁ TEXAS 147

KEY: A Old-Time

TEXAS GALES ☸ TEXAS GALS

KEY: C Texas

TEXAS TWO-STEP ☸ BLACK JACK ☸ TEXAS QUICKSTEP ☸ TEXAS GALLOP ☸ ST LOUIS QUICKSTEP ☸ CHEROKEE POLKA ☸ RACHEL

cf MISSOURI QUICKSTEP *et al*

KEY: C Old-Time

THE TIN WEDDING ☸ PEERLESS HORNPIPE

KEY: C Irish/Old-Time

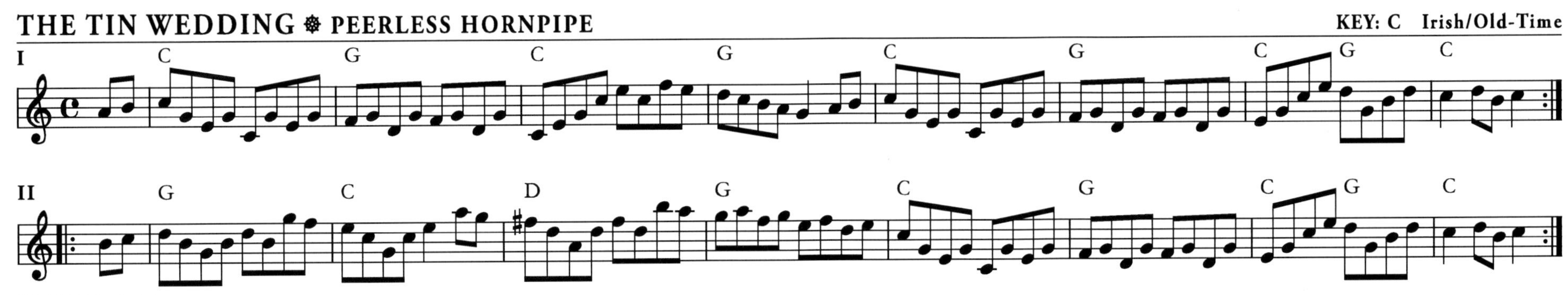

SOURCE: Cole's

TOM BILLY'S JIG ❁ O'KEEFE'S ❁ PADDY'S ❁ PORT THOM BILLY

KEY: A Irish

TOMMIE JIG

KEY: G Old-Time

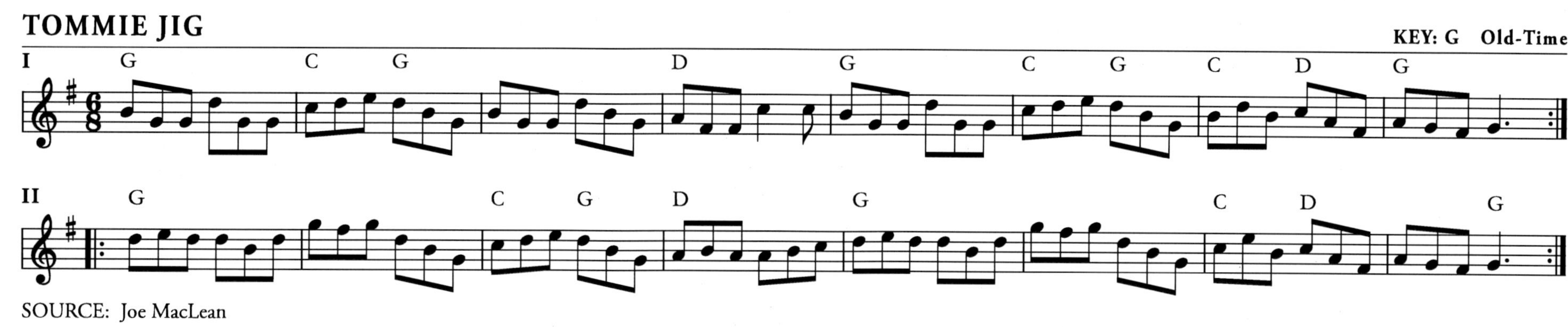

SOURCE: Joe MacLean

TONGS BY THE FIRE ❁ COME TO THE RAFFLE ❁ TONGUES OF FIRE

KEY: G Irish Jig

THE TOP OF CORK ROAD

KEY: Am Irish Jig

SOURCE: Johnny Cronin and Joe Burke

TOSS THE FEATHERS ❁ KILLIAN'S ❁ MARTIN ROACHFORD'S ❁ SHANK'S MARE ❁ TOSS THE FEATHERS Nº 1

KEY: Am Irish

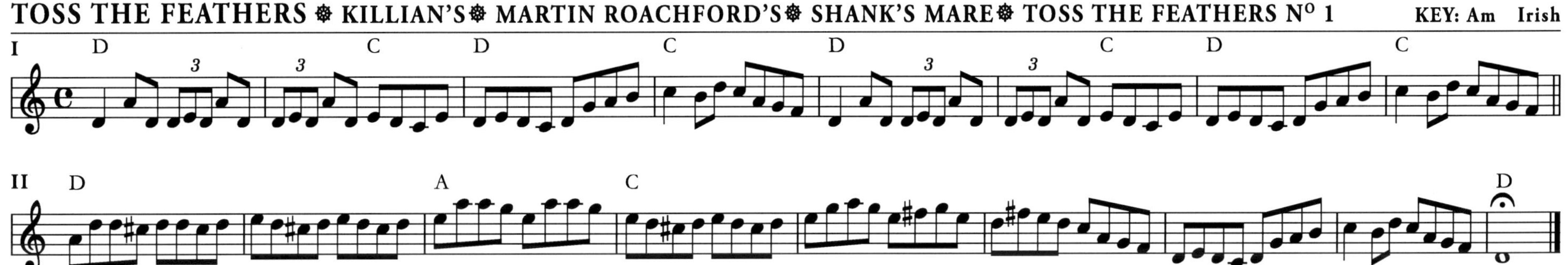

SOURCE: Johnny Cronin and Joe Burke

TO THE LADIES ❁ IRISHMAN'S HEART TO THE LADIES ❁ BUTTERMILK MARY ❁ COLEMAN'S FAVOURITE ❁ FOND OF THE LADIES ❁ THE FROLICSOME DAME ❁ LA GIGUE DES IRLANDAISES ❁ HALEY'S ❁ HEALTH TO THE LADIES ❁ IRISH MILLER ❁ THE IRISH ROVER ❁ AN IRISHMAN'S LOVE ❁ MOININ JIG ❁ THE MOUNTAIN ROAD ❁ THE MOUNTAINY BOY ❁ THE NIGHT OF THE WEDDING ❁ O'MAHONY'S ❁ O'MAHONEY'S JIG ❁ OVER THE CALLOWS ❁ PADDY CLANCY'S ❁ PAT BEIRNE'S FAVOURITE ❁ THE QUEENSTOWN JIG ❁ THE RUNNER ❁ SADDLE THE PONY ❁ SWEET BIDDY DALY ❁ AN IRISHMAN'S GIFT TO THE LADIES ❁ LITTLE BOY TED IN THE HAY

KEY: A Irish/Northern

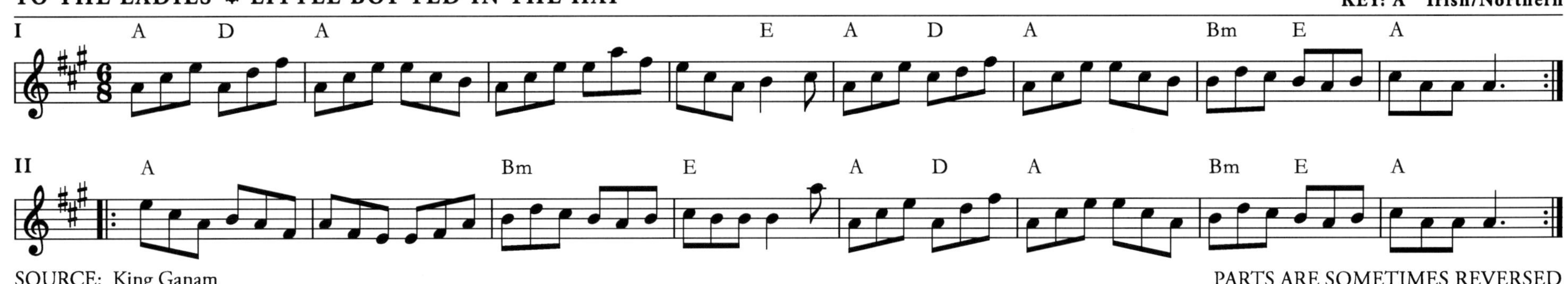

SOURCE: King Ganam

PARTS ARE SOMETIMES REVERSED

TRIPPING UP THE STAIRS ✵ TRIP IT UP THE STAIRS ✵ PADDY O'FLAHERTY ✵ THE PLAINS OF KILKORKERY ✵ THE PRIDE OF KILDARE ✵ ROSCABURY ✵ SACHO'S ✵ SACKO'S ✵ SACKOWS ✵ THE SYRACUSE ✵ TRIPPING UP STAIRS

KEY: D Irish Jig

I D G D A D A D G D A D

II Bm A Bm A D

TUGBOAT ✵ TUG BOAT

KEY: G Texas

SOURCE: Dick Barrett

TUNES FROM HOME ✵ KOMME LILLE MAKKE

KEY: G Scandinavian Schottische

TURKEY IN A PEA PATCH ❁ BUZZARD IN A PEA PATCH

KEY: D Southern

SOURCE: Buddy Thomas

TURKEY IN THE COTTONWOOD ❁ TURKEY IN THE COTTONWOODS

KEY: B♭/F Northern

SOURCE: Joe Pancerzewski

TURKEY IN THE STRAW ❁ THE JOLLY OLD MILLER ❁ THE MILLER BOY ❁ NATCHEZ UNDER THE HILL ❁ SUGAR IN THE GOURD ❁ TURKEYS IN THE STRAW ❁ MARIE CHAMBERLAND ❁ DO YOUR EARS HANG LOW

cf OLD ZIP COON *et al*

KEY: G Old-Time

TWINKLE LITTLE STAR ❁ TWINKLE STAR ❁ TWINKLE TWINKLE ❁ TWINKLE TWINKLE LITTLE STAR ❁ LITTLE STAR ❁ BRILHA ❁ BRILHA ESTRELINHA

KEY: G Bluegrass/Old-Time

I G C G A D

G C G D G

II G D

G C G D G

UNCLE HENRY'S REEL

KEY: A Northern

UNCLE JOE ❁ DID YOU EVER SEE THE DEVIL, UNCLE JOE ❁ DON'T MIND THE WEATHER SO THE WIND DON'T BLOW ❁ HOP HIGH LADIES ❁ HOP LIGHT LADIES ❁ HOP UP LADIES ❁ MAY DAY ❁ McCLEOD'S REEL ❁ McCLOUD'S REEL ❁ MISS MacCLEOD'S REEL ❁ MISS MacLEOD'S REEL ❁ MISS McCLOUD'S REEL ❁ MRS MacCLEOD'S REEL ❁ MRS MacLEOD'S REEL ❁ MRS McCLEOD'S REEL ❁ MRS McLEOD'S REEL ❁ CAKE'S ALL DOUGH ❁ GIGUE AMERICAINE ❁ MRS MacLEOD OF RAASAY ❁ GREEN MOUNTAIN ❁ WALK JAWBONE ❁ HOP HIGH LADIES THE CAKE'S ALL DOUGH ❁ BILLY BOY ❁ DID YOU EVER MEET THE DEVIL, UNCLE JOE

KEY: G Irish/Old-Time

VICTORY BREAKDOWN ❁ VICTORY

KEY: D Old-Time

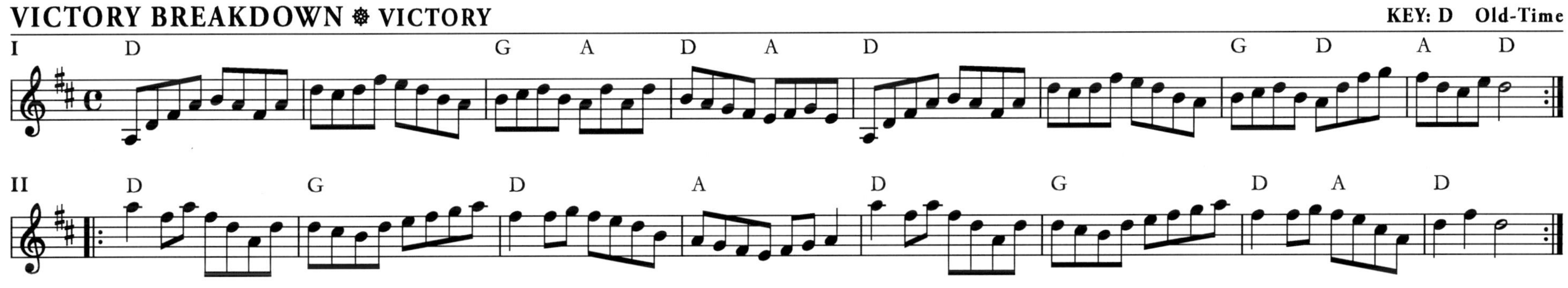

WADE HAMPTON'S HORNPIPE ❁ HAMPTON'S HORNPIPE—A

KEY: B♭ Old-Time

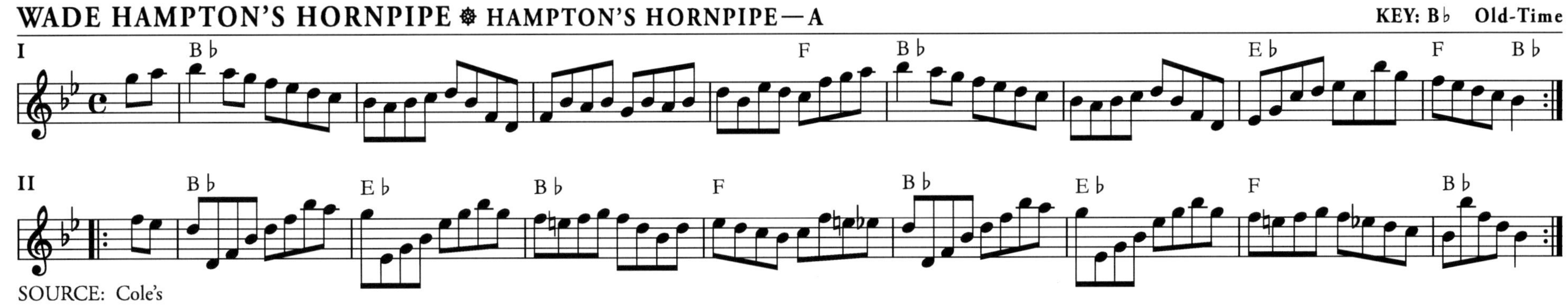

SOURCE: Cole's

WADE HAMPTON'S HORNPIPE ❁ HAMPTON'S HORNPIPE—A

KEY: A Old-Time

SOURCE: Cole's

WAGONER ❁ THE DRUNKEN WAGONEER ❁ GEORGIA WAGONER ❁ JOHNNY WAGONER ❁ JOLLY WAGONER REEL ❁ TENNESSEE WAGON ❁ TENNESSEE WAGONEER ❁ TENNESSEE WAGONER ❁ TEXAS WAGONER ❁ WAGNER ❁ FRENCH JIG ❁ THE HERO ❁ MISS BEROWN'S REEL ❁ NORTHEAST TEXAS ❁ OKLAHOMA WAGONER ❁ WAG'NER ❁ WILD WAGONER ❁ JOHNNY WALKER ❁ REEL MARIE

KEY: C Bluegrass/Southern

WALKER'S STREET REEL ❁ MADAME BOLDUC ❁ CARPENTER'S REEL ❁ GIGUE DES ARTISANS ❁ LABORER'S REEL ❁ REEL DES TRAVAILLEURS ❁ THE TRAVELLER ❁ TRAVELLER'S REEL

cf CARPENTER'S REEL *et al*

KEY: G Northern

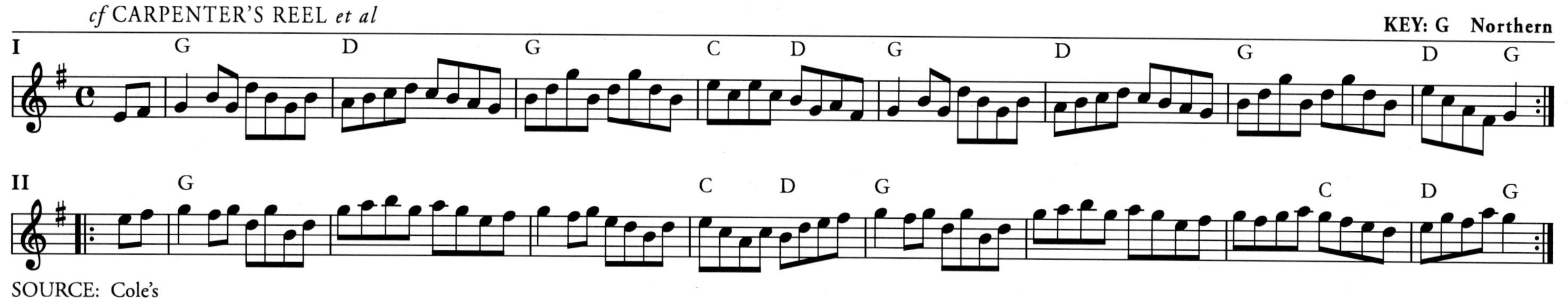

SOURCE: Cole's

WALKING IN MY SLEEP

KEY: G Bluegrass/Southern

SOURCE: Arthur Smith

WALKING IN THE PARLOR—LONG

cf WALKING IN THE PARLOR—SHORT

KEY: C Southern

SOURCE: Frank George

WALKING IN THE PARLOR—LONG

cf WALKING IN THE PARLOR—SHORT

KEY: D Southern

SOURCE: Frank George

WALKING IN THE PARLOR — Short

cf WALKING IN THE PARLOR — LONG

KEY: C Southern

SOURCE: Wilson Douglas

WALKING IN THE PARLOR — Short

cf WALKING IN THE PARLOR — LONG

KEY: D Southern

SOURCE: Wilson Douglas

THE WANDERING MINSTREL ❁ THE DANDY SCHOLAR ❁ THE EASY-GOING MUSICIAN ❁ MERRY MAIDEN ❁ CAPE BRETON JIG ❁ GUINESS IS GOOD FOR YOU ❁ DONLAND ROAD ❁ THE GALLANT BOYS OF TIPPERARY

KEY: D Irish Jig

SOURCE: Johnny Cronin and Joe Burke

WAXIES DARGLE

cf THE GIRL I LEFT BEHIND ME *et al*

KEY: D Irish

WEAVE AND WAY

KEY: G Bluegrass

WESTERN GALS ❁ BLUE-EYED GIRL ❁ FLY AROUND ❁ FLY AROUND MY PRETTY LITTLE MISS ❁ SHADY GROVE ❁ SUSANNA GAL ❁ WESTERN COUNTRY ❁ BLUE EYED GAL ❁ BLUE EYES RUN ME CRAZY ❁ FARE THEE WELL MY PRETTY LITTLE MISS ❁ PRETTY LITTLE PINK ❁ SUZANNA GAL

KEY: D Southern

WESTFORK GALS ❁ WESTFORT GALS

KEY: D Old-Time

WHEN JOHNNY COMES MARCHING HOME—Am ❁ JOHNNY I HARDLY KNEW YE ❁ GUNS AND DRUMS ❁ THE ANIMALS WENT IN TWO BY TWO

Old-Time Jig

WHEN JOHNNY COMES MARCHING HOME—G

cf KINGDOM COMING *et al* & THE YEAR OF JUBALO *et al*

Old-Time

SOURCE: Bill Reser

WHEN YOU GO HOME ✵ BORING THE LEATHER ✵ COME WITH ME NOW ✵ THE CONNAUGHTMAN ✵ DOWN THE BACK LANE ✵ HUMOURS OF AYLE HOUSE ✵ THE KILFINANE ✵ THE SHOEMAKER'S FANCY ✵ THE KILFINANE JIG KEY: D Irish Jig

WHISKEY AND BEER ✵ ANOTHER JIG WILL DO ✵ TIGHT BREECHES ✵ TIGHT BRITCHES ✵ WHISKY AND BEER KEY: D Irish Slip Jig

WHISKEY BEFORE BREAKFAST ✵ RILEY'S FAVORITE ✵ SPIRITS IN THE MORNING ✵ THE SCOTTSMAN ✵ WHISKEY 'FORE BREAKFAST ✵ WHISKEY FOR BREAKFAST KEY: D Irish/Bluegrass

WHISTLING RUFUS ❁ WAY DOWN SOUTH IN DIXIE ❁ RUFUS BLOSSOM

KEY: G Bluegrass/Old-Time

SOURCE: Kerry Mills

A WIFE OF MY OWN ❁ I'VE GOT A WIFE OF MY AIN ❁ BEAUTEOUS FAIR MOLLY ❁ BLESS MY SOUL WHY SHOULDN'T I? ❁ BORING WITH A GIMLET ❁ BORING WITH THE GIMBLET ❁ JACK WON'T SELL HIS FIDDLE ❁ RAGGED LADY ❁ SPATTER THE MUD ❁ NAEBODY ❁ MY LOVE'S WEDDING

KEY: Em/G Irish Slip Jig

I Em D Em D Em D Em D

II G D G Em D G D G D G D G Em D G D G D

III G D G D G D G D Em

SOURCE: Dudley Laufman

WILD HORSES ❁ BUCK CREEK GALS ❁ CHICKEN STAMPEDE ❁ COUNTRY DANCE ❁ CRIPPLE CREEK ❁ FIRST TUTTLE TAP ❁ GEORGE BROWN'S BON VIVANT ❁ HOP ALONG SALLY ❁ JIG COTILLION ❁ KELTON'S REEL ❁ McCARREN'S CELEBRATED REEL ❁ MY OLD DAD ❁ OLD DAD ❁ OLE DAD ❁ PIGTOWN FLING ❁ ROCKY MOUNTAIN ❁ ROCKY MOUNTAIN HORNPIPE ❁ ROCKY POINT JIG ❁ SOFT SOAP ❁ STONEY POINT ❁ STONY POINT ❁ WAKE UP JACOB ❁ WALK ALONG JOHN ❁ WALK ALONG JOHNNY ❁ WARM STUFF ❁ WILD HORSE ❁ WILD HORSES AT STONY POINT ❁ GOIN' UP CANEY ❁ PAPPY LOONEY'S ❁ PIG TOWN ❁ THE PIGTOWN HIGHLAND FLING ❁ THE PILLTOWN

KEY: G Old-Time

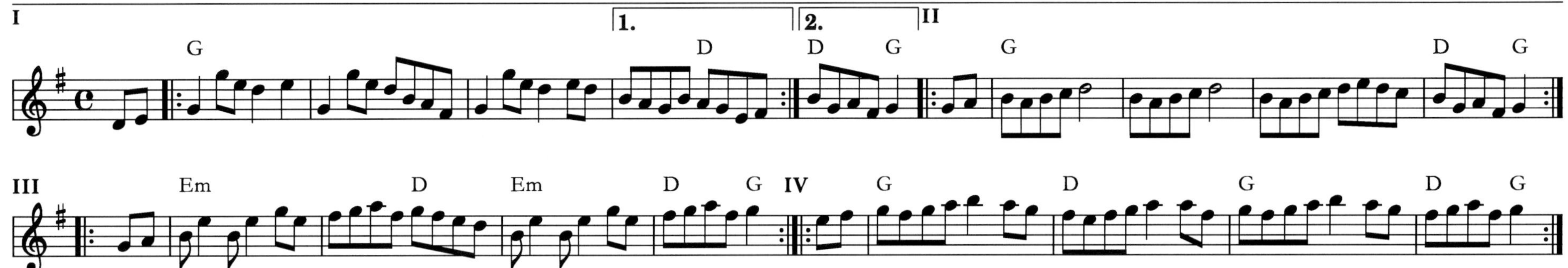

SECOND PART IS OPTIONAL. IF LEFT OUT, REPEAT FIRST PART IN ITS PLACE

WILLIAMSON'S HORNPIPE

KEY: A Bluegrass

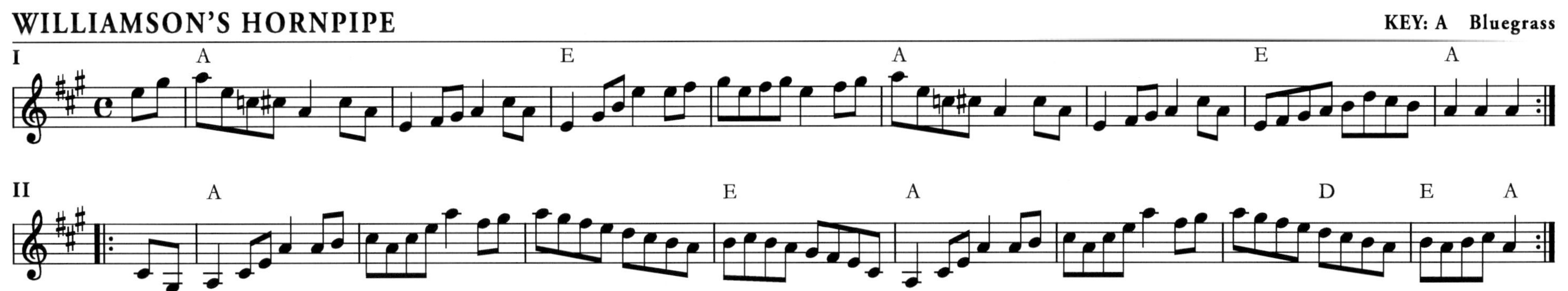

WIND THAT SHAKES THE BARLEY ❁ I SAT IN THE VALLEY GREEN ❁ THE KERRY LASSES ❁ THE WIND THAT BLOETH THE BARLEY ❁ DA WIND DAT SHAKES DA BARLEY ❁ FIELDS YE FANCY ❁ THE LITTLE PACK OF TAILORS ❁ THE PACK OF TAILORS ❁ THE WIND THAT BLOWS THE BARLEY DOWN

KEY: D Irish/Old-Time

WINNIPEG REEL

KEY: G Northern

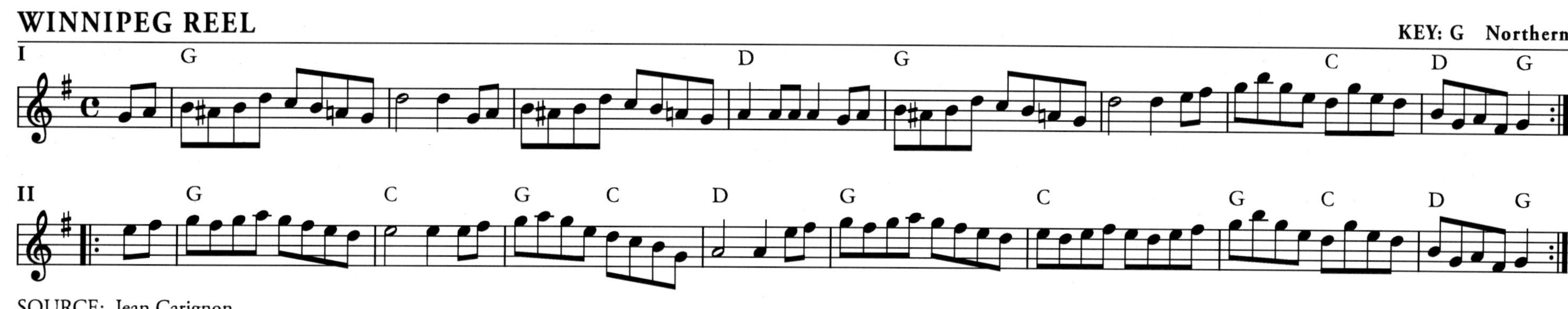

SOURCE: Jean Carignon

WOMAN OF THE HOUSE ❁ THE LADY OF THE HOUSE ❁ THE MISTRESS OF THE HOUSE ❁ THE OLD WOMAN OF THE HOUSE

KEY: G Irish Reel

SOURCE: Kathleen Collins

WOODCHOPPER'S BREAKDOWN ❁ **THE PEA SOUP REEL** ❁ **THE WOODCHOPPERS** ❁ **WOODCHOPPER'S REEL** ❁ **WOODCUTTER'S BREAKDOWN** ❁ **WOODCUTTER'S REEL** ❁ **WOODCHOPPER'S HORNPIPE** ❁ **PEA SOUP** ❁ **THE WOODCHOPPER** ❁ **LUMBERJACK'S REEL** ❁ **REEL DES BUCHERONS** ❁ **WOOD CHOPPER'S BREAKDOWN** ❁ **LE PETIT BUCHEUX** ❁ **REEL LE B** ❁ **WOODCHOPPER'S BALL**

KEY: D Northern/Old-Time

SOURCE: Cyril Stinnett

PARTS ARE OFTEN REVERSED

YEARLING ❁ **HELL AMONGST THE YEARLINGS** ❁ **HELL AMONG THE YEARLINGS** ❁ **TROUBLE AMONG THE YEARLINGS** ❁ **HELL AFTER THE YEARLINGS** ❁ **DEVIL AMONG THE YEARLINGS** ❁ **ROUND UP THE YEARLINGS**

cf CRICKET ON THE HEARTH *et al* & MARMADUKE'S HORNPIPE *et al*

KEY: D Old-Time

THE YEAR OF JUBALO ☸ JUBALO ☸ JUBILLER ☸ THE LAND OF JUBALO ☸ DOODLETOWN FIFER ☸ JUBILO ☸ LINCOLN'S GUNBOATS ☸ YEAR OF THE JUBILO

cf KINGDOM COMING *et al* & WHEN JOHNNY COMES MARCHING HOME—(G)

KEY: G Old-Time

YELLOW BARBER ☸ ARTHUR BERRY

KEY: D Southern

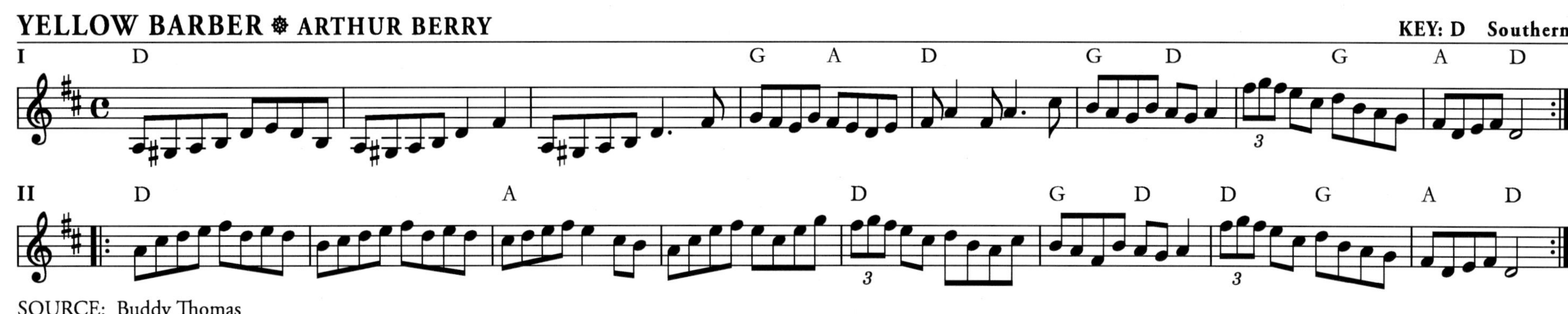

SOURCE: Buddy Thomas

YELLOW GAL

KEY: A Southern

☸ ☸ ☸

INDEX

of

TUNE TITLES

☸ ☸ ☸

There are 2500 titles in this index.

Included are all of the titles listed for all of the tunes in this book.

INDEX OF TUNES

LIST OF RECORDINGS

www.melbay.com/31104MEB

1 Ace of Spades
2 Acrobat's Hornpipe
3 Adrian's Reel
4 Alfie's Hornpipe
5 Amateur Hornpipe
6 Anderson's Reel
7 Angeline the Baker
8 Anne-Marie Reel
9 Ariel Hornpipe
10 Arkansas Traveler
11 As I Went out upon the Ice
12 Bachelor Jig
13 Ball and Chain Hornpipe
14 Bally Desmond
15 Banish Misfortune
16 The Banjo Old-Time Polka
17 Banjo Tramp
18 Bantry Bay
19 Barlow Knife
20 The Barmaid
21 La Bastringue
22 The Battering Ram
23 Bay of Fundy
24 Bee's Wing
25 Beet Pie
26 Belfast
27 Belfast Jig
28 Belle of Lexington
29 Bessie Brown
30 Big Indian Hornpipe
31 Big John MacNeil's
32 Bill Cheatham
33 Billy in the Lowground
34 Billy Wilson's Clog
35 Bitter Creek
36 Blackberry Blossom G
37 Blackberry Rag
38 Black Cat in the Briar Patch
39 Black Mountain Rag
40 The Black Nag
41 The Blackthorn Stick
42 The Blarney Pilgrim
43 Blue Eagle Hornpipe
44 Blue Goose
45 Blue Mountain Hornpipe
46 Blue Mule
47 Bobby Shafto
48 Bonaparte's Retreat
49 Bonnie Dundee
50 Boston Boy
51 Boston Boys
52 Bottle Bank
53 The Boys of Blue Hill
54 Briar Picker Brown
55 Brilliancy
56 Brown Button Shoes
57 Brushy Run
58 Buffalo Gals
59 Bull at the Wagon
60 The Bunratty Boys
61 Burnt Potato Jig
62 Butterfly Slip-Jig
63 Byrne's Favorite Hornpipe
64 Byrne's Hornpipe
65 Campbell's Farewell to Red Gap
66 Carmody's Jig
67 Carpenter's Reel
68 Carrick Jig
69 The Cat Rambles to the Child's Sauce Pan
70 Cattle in the Cane
71 Charming Molly Branigan
72 The Chateauquay Reel
73 Cheat Mountain
74 Cherokee Shuffle
75 Childgrove
76 Chippewa Breakfast
77 Cincinnati Hornpipe
78 Cindy
79 Citaco
80 Cock of the North
81 Cold Frosty Morning
82 Coleman's Cross
83 Coleraine
84 Colonial Breakdown
85 Colored Aristocracy
86 Coming Down from Denver
87 Constitution Hornpipe

369 The Rakes of Kildare
370 Rambler's Horpipe
371 Reavy's Reel
372 Red Apple Rag
373 Redbird
374 Reddigan's
375 Red-Haired Boy
376 Red Line Hornpipe
377 Redwing
378 Reefer's Hornpipe
379 La Reel du Cultivateur
380 Reuben
381 Ricker's Hornpipe
382 Rickett's Hornpipe
383 The Rights of Man
384 Rippling Waters Jig
385 Roaring Mary
386 Robinson County
387 Rock the Cradle Joe
388 Rocky Pallet
389 The Rocky Road to Dublin Old-Time
390 The Rocky Road to Dublin Irish
391 Rory O'Moore
392 Rosemary Lane
393 The Rose Tree
394 The Route
395 Run Boy Run
396 Rushes and Peppers
397 Rutland's Reel
398 Rye Straw
399 Sail away Ladies Old-Time
400 Sail away Ladies Bluegrass
401 Sailor's Hornpipe C
402 Sailor's Hornpipe F
403 Sailor's Hornpipe G
404 St Adelle's Reel
405 St Anne's Reel
406 Sally Goodin
407 Sally Johnson
408 Salt Creek
409 Salty River Reel
410 Sandy River Belle
411 Sandy Road
412 Saratoga Hornpipe
413 Say Old Man
414 The Scholar
415 Scotland the Brave
416 Sean Ryan's Hornpipe
417 Sean Ryan's Jig
418 Sergeant Early's Dream
419 Seth's Reel
420 Sheep and Hogs Walking through the Pasture
421 Shelbourne Reel
422 Ships Are Sailing
423 Shoemaker's Reel
424 Shootin' Creek
425 Shoot the Turkey Buzzard
426 Silver Spear
427 Silver Star Hornpipe
428 Sinking Creek
429 Six Penny Money
430 Sleepy-Eyed Joe
431 The Small Hills of Offlay
432 Smash the Windows
433 Snoring Mrs Gobeil
434 Snow Deer
435 Snowflake Breakdown
436 Snowflake Hornpipe
437 Soldier's Joy
438 Soppin' the Gravy
439 Sorenson's Rhinelander
440 Sourwood Mountain
441 Spanish Jig
442 Speed the Plough Irish
443 Speed the Plough Old-Time
444 Spotted Pony
445 Star of Munster
446 Staten Island Hornpipe
447 Success to the Fleet
448 Sugar in the Gourd A
449 Sugar in the Gourd Am
450 The Sunshine Hornpipe
451 Swallowtail Jig
452 Swamplake Breakdown
453 Swedish Walking Tune
454 Swinging on the Gate
455 Teetotaler
456 Teetotal Jig
457 Telegraph Hornpipe
458 Telephone Hornpipe
459 Tennessee Fiddler
460 The Ten-Penny Bit
461 Texas
462 Texas Gales
463 Texas Two-Step
464 The Tin Wedding
465 Tom Billy's Jig
466 Tommie Jig
467 Tongs by the Fire
468 The Top of Cork Road
469 Toss the Feathers
470 To the Ladies
471 Tripping up the Stairs
472 Tugboat
473 Tunes from Home
474 Turkey in a Pea Patch
475 Turkey in the Cottonwood
476 Turkey in the Straw
477 Twinkle Little Star
478 Uncle Henry's Reel
479 Uncle Joe
480 Victory Breakdown
481 Wade Hampton's Hornpipe
482 Wagoner
483 Walker's Street Reel
484 Walking in My Sleep
485 Walking in the Parlor Long
486 Walking in the Parlor Short
487 The Wandering Minstrel
488 Waxie's Dargle
489 Weave and Way
490 Western Gals
491 Westfork Gals
492 When Johnny Comes Marching Home Am
493 When Johnny Comes Marching Home G
494 When You Go Home
495 Whiskey and Beer
496 Whiskey before Breakfast
497 Whistling Rufus
498 A Wife of My Own
499 Wild Horses
500 Williamson's Hornpipe
501 Wind That Shakes the Barley
502 Winnipeg Reel
503 Woman of the House
504 Woodchopper's Breakdown
505 Yearling
506 The Year of Jubilo
507 Yellow Barber
508 Yellow Gal

Other Mel Bay Tunebooks

WWW.MELBAY.COM